By the same author

Adam's Farm: My Life on the Land

Like Farmer, Like Son

A MEMOIR

Adam Henson

with Ian Gittins

BOOKS

1 3 5 7 9 10 8 6 4 2

BBC Books, an imprint of Ebury Publishing
20 Vauxhall Bridge Road,
London SW1V 2SA

BBC Books is part of the Penguin Random House group of companies whose
addresses can be found at global.penguinrandomhouse.com

Penguin
Random House
UK

First published by BBC Books in 2016
This paperback edition published 2017

www.penguin.co.uk

A CIP catalogue record for this book is available from the British Library

ISBN 9781785940729

Printed and bound in Great Britain by Clays Ltd, St Ives PLC

To my darling mum, Gillie Henson. Without her constant love and support, neither Dad nor I would have been able to achieve what we have today.

Contents

INTRODUCTION

A Rare Breed

I t is in the nature of memoirs that they traditionally begin with a birth. In my case, I feel as though the only way to open is with a death.

When my father, Joe Henson, passed away in October of last year, I was touched by the warmth and passion of the many tributes that he received. He had always been at the centre of my family's life, but it was moving to realize that he had meant so much to so many other people, too.

Dad's death was a news event. Broadsheet newspapers ran lengthy obituaries, praising his lifelong devotion to farming and his ground-breaking work as the conservationist who opened the Cotswold Farm Park on our farm in 1971 and who was founder chairman of the Rare Breeds Survival Trust two years later.

Were it not for Dad, many species of British domestic rare breeds would be long gone.

Countryfile, the BBC's weekly rural affairs and agriculture show that I have worked on for 15 years, put together a great tribute to him. It ranged far and wide through his life, and his own years of TV work, before my colleague and friend, John Craven, delivered the perfect eulogy: 'Joe Henson was himself a rare breed, a true gentleman who believed passionately in the animals and breeds he preserved for the nation.'

It was moving to appreciate the depth of the public feeling for my father – yet my grief, obviously, was primarily a personal one.

It's devastating for anybody to lose a parent, I know, but my relationship with Dad was particularly close and intimate. Right from my first days, he was my rock; my mentor; my hero. It is no exaggeration to say that he taught me virtually all I know about both farming and television. Without him, I would not be doing what I am today.

My life has mirrored my father's to a quite uncanny degree. Today I run Bemborough Farm, the farm where I grew up and that Dad nurtured for nearly 40 years before passing it on to me in 1999. Its centrepiece remains the Cotswold Farm Park, his pride and joy and his life's defining passion.

I have also been lucky enough to follow Dad onto television. Thirty years before my nervous BBC debut, he was blazing a trail on TV shows like *Animal Magic* and *In the Country*, discussing farming with passion and eloquence. He made presenting look so easy – and as I now know, after years of first-hand experience, it really isn't!

Dad was no ordinary farmer, and no ordinary man, and his natural patience and calm were all the more remarkable as his own early life was not easy. As a kid, I always knew that he came from a showbiz family: his father, Leslie Henson, was a West End comedy actor who hosted *Sunday Night at the London Palladium* and was a huge pre- and post-war British celebrity.

I knew that. What I didn't know was just how unorthodox, difficult and challenging my father's early life was. It was a secret that he and my mum kept incredibly well: only three years before his death did Dad write my three sisters and me a letter telling us his full, amazing story.

People say 'Like father, like son', and the story of my life, which I am about to tell in this book, is so intimately entwined with the story of Joe Henson. It is a tale that begins 50 years ago, with me in short trousers by his side in the place I still call home: Bemborough Farm.

CHAPTER 1

Farm Boy

I am sure that there must be a downside to growing up on a country farm, surrounded by animals, with acres of fields and woods to hand to run and roam and play in. There must be minus points – but try as I might, I can't remember what they were.

When I cast my mind back to my childhood on Bemborough Farm, in the heart of the Cotswolds, my memories are of fun, adventure and, most of all, freedom. To a curious, wide-eyed nipper, it was like growing up in a giant playground. It felt as though every day brought some new distraction to investigate and explore.

In fact, you know the eternal argument about whether kids' personalities are shaped by nature or nurture? I guess I got the best of both worlds: I was nurtured by nature.

I was born on 8 January 1966 and christened Adam John Lincoln Henson. As with most things in my family, there was a story behind that. My father was Joseph Leslie Henson, after his own father, Leslie, and for five generations Henson children had been given a middle name beginning with the letter 'L'.

My parents had already applied that principle to the three elder sisters who had come before me. Their first daughter had been christened Elizabeth Lesley, the second was Mary Louise, and the youngest was Rebecca Lucinda.

There again, you can give children names but there is no guarantee that they will use them. Elizabeth has always been known as Libby. Mary never liked her first name and so has always been Louise or, as we call her, Lolo. And Rebecca shortened her name to Becca.

In true pedigree livestock breeding tradition, all our names had a meaning. My three sisters were all named after our grandparents or great-grandparents, while my two middle names came from my mum's dad and my dad's granddad respectively.

I guess it's fair to say that we are a family that values tradition!

The three girls and I had arrived at roughly two-year intervals, so my mum and dad already had Libby and Louise when they took over Bemborough Farm in 1962. It can't have been easy for them with a toddler and a baby in arms, but my mum and dad have always been nothing if not resourceful.

They had met at a wedding at the parish church in Cirencester in 1956, when my mum was still called Gillian Richards. They were both seeing other people at the time, and Dad had even gone to the wedding with his partner. Then he spotted this beautiful woman with long red hair standing in the church . . .

At the reception after the ceremony, Joe Henson introduced himself to Gillian Richards and asked if she would like a drink. She asked for a BabyCham, and he returned from the bar with a bottle of Champagne.

That was the end of their existing partners.

The funny thing was that neither Mum nor Dad came from farming stock. Mum was originally from Coventry but during the war, after one particular air raid, they'd returned from the shelter to find that their neighbour's house had been completely destroyed. Nana and my mum then went to stay with some relatives in Wales, leaving her dad working nights at a local factory. The very next day he came home from work on his motorbike to find that their own house had been demolished overnight, so decided to carry on riding and join the family in Wales.

Mum went to school in the Rhondda Valley and then trained as a teacher. She was working in a primary school in Cheltenham when she met Dad.

Dad had grown up in London. His family situation had been complicated, to say the least, but he was raised primarily by his mother, who was a music-hall dancer and actress. She had been born Harriet Collins, but everybody knew her by her stage name: Billie Dell.

Despite his parents' theatrical backgrounds, Dad had no thespian leanings. Instead, from an early age, he was totally obsessed with animals. His mum gave him an old sixpence in pocket money every Saturday and he would spend it on a new lead farm animal for the model farm in his bedroom that was his pride and joy.

He got to see the real things when he was four years old. In 1936, his mum and he were living in Northwood, in west London, where a farm called Park Farm lay just up the road. It was the kind of farm where the hens were free-range, the pigs lived in stys, the cows were hand-milked and horses and ponies delivered the milk. Dad loved it. He spent so much time there that, when he left school at sixteen, Park Farm gave him a job. From that moment on, there was no doubt what he would do with his life.

Showbiz stood no chance: as Dad was always fond of joking, he ran away from the theatre to become a farmer.

After agricultural college and a couple more farming jobs, Dad met and married Mum, started their family and, with an old school friend named John Neave, began searching for a farm to take over. Bemborough Farm then measured 400 acres and was owned by Corpus Christi College, Oxford, and Dad and John applied for the tenancy.

The farm had two traditional farmhouses, as well as cottages to house agricultural workers and three large barns: Lott's Barn, Taylor's Barn and Oxford Buildings. At 800 feet above sea level, it had wonderful views across the rolling Cotswold Hills, but got seriously chilly and windy in the winter. It still does.

The main farmhouse on the property was dilapidated and in a pretty sorry state, but my parents were so keen on the farm that they didn't raise any objections. When the college told them they wouldn't spend any money on the house, my mum told them, 'Oh well – we'll just have to make the best of it.'

That clinched the deal. The college liked the fact Dad was a proper local farmer and my parents were clearly motivated by a love of the land, so they gave them a three-generation tenancy on Bemborough Farm. That is incredibly rare – you would never get anything like that nowadays.

In fact, the college were so pleased with their new tenants that they did then spend money doing up the farmhouse. Not that I could have cared less what the house was like when I came along four years later. For me, right from the start, it was all about the great outdoors.

The great thing about being a kid growing up on a farm is that every day is an adventure. Right from being a toddler I would be running around outside, playing games with my sisters or with my favourite farm Labrador, Gemima. As well as the farm we had woods next to our land, so we would be off building dens in there.

We would make up our own crazy games to play. One was called Kick the Bucket, which sounds a bit ghoulish, but was an adapted version of Tag. We would put a bucket in the woods and all run off to hide. You had to kick the bucket before the searcher found you. Yep, it was sophisticated stuff!

Another of our improvised games was Snakes. The girls and I would tie together pieces of baler twine, used to hold hay bales together, then dangle them out the back of the Land Rover as Dad drove round the farm through all the puddles and down muddy tracks. We loved it, although I am not sure what Health and Safety would make of it today.

Growing up with three older sisters, I got a bit spoiled and mollycoddled. It was a little like having four mums – but it also had its spiky moments. Like all siblings do, the girls would wind me up something rotten, and I would lash out and make one of them cry.

Then I would be for it. Mum would come to investigate the noise, tell me 'You mustn't hit girls!' and smack me on the legs.

She was brilliant at hitting me on the back of the thigh, just below my shorts, where it really stings.

Yet on the very rare occasions she smacked me, I had always deserved it. I know you can't hit kids nowadays, it has to be all about the naughty step, but 50 years on, I think those occasional bouts of corporal punishment from my mum did me no harm whatsoever.

It was always Mum dishing out discipline like that; Dad never would. Mum ran the household, kept us clean, fed and organized us, Dad included. She laid down the law and took no messing, but also showed us heaps of love and gave out plenty of cuddles.

In contrast, Dad hardly changed a nappy or pushed a pram, and I never heard him raise his voice once at any of us. Typical of his generation, he was all about work, the farm and earning money to look after the family.

Mum was fantastic at being a farmer's wife, especially given that it was not a lifestyle she had been born into. She was still teaching when she and Dad took over the farm, and in fact had taught both Libby and Louise at the local primary school.

As long as I live, I will never forget the wonderful roasts and pies that Mum used to make on Sundays. As for the spreads she would lay on for our birthday parties – they were truly spectacular.

For me, though, the thrill about growing up on Bemborough was always going out on the farm with Dad. From as soon as I could walk, I would be out by his side as often and as long as I could. The poor chap must have thought he had grown an extra shadow as he trudged along with Gemima and me in tow.

Not that he minded. In fact, he seemed to love having me there, even though I usually made the jobs twice as long for him. From as young as two or three, I would be helping him feed the chickens and rabbits and move the animals around – well, as much help as a toddler can be!

Dad loved talking to me about the animals. He was a great communicator and taught me so much, even at that raw age. I suppose he saw in me the same keen, excited young boy that he had been 30 years earlier on Park Farm.

We had a few escapades out in the fields, of course. Now and then, Dad would take us children to help move the livestock and so we would be trying to herd sheep along rutted tracks or country lanes.

Sometimes these tracks would have holes in the walls or the hedges, or gateways without a gate, so Dad would position us kids in those gaps to stop the sheep getting away through them. One day I was doing exactly that as Dad herded 300 ewes down the lane.

Sheep are impulsive creatures, and the whole flock decided as one that they were coming through my gap. I can vividly remember the sight, the noise and the smell as the sheep ran up to me, knocked me down and trampled me into the mud.

Dad was always a brilliant storyteller, and for years would retell the tale of how I jumped up from the ground, spitting dirt from my mouth and crying my eyes out, to apologize to him: 'I'm so sorry, Dad, I just couldn't stop them!' I wasn't worried about being battered and bruised by stampeding sheep, just upset that I had let him down.

Another day, Dad heard me screaming just outside the

farmhouse door. We used to keep geese in a paddock there and a particularly vicious gander had jumped at me, knocked me down and was pecking lumps out of me. To this day I'm still wary of hissing ganders.

Mum used to help out on the farm as well, not just doing the books but also on the land. Before I was born, she had driven tractors at harvest time, patiently crisscrossing the fields with Libby and Lolo sitting beneath her in the tractor's footwell. After I came along, she worked the grain dryer.

From as young as I can remember, Dad was teaching all of us children the wonders and beauty of the land. Every season is different on a farm, but for impressionable, excited kids, there is something to love about each of them.

Spring was all about the fresh green leaves on the trees, snowdrops in the garden and the first daffodils and crocuses. Dad would point all of them out to me and explain what they were. His enthusiasm was incredibly infectious.

When I was a little older, he would take me out with him as he walked the dogs on crisp spring mornings, listening to a cacophony of birds singing the dawn chorus. After the grey depths of winter, it was like somebody had turned a light on. It was wonderful seeing the grass starting to grow in the fields, and newborn lambs tottering after their mothers.

Even before I was old enough to help him, I would watch Dad turn the cattle out when spring came. They had spent the long winter months housed undercover to stop them churning up the wet ground and make it easier to feed them with silage.

People always smile at lambs skipping and jumping around, but it was even more amazing as a boy to see cows with calves at their feet do the same thing when they were let out of their sheds and into the fields. The cows would stick their tails in the air and half a tonne of beast would jump for joy at the scent of spring in the air. Believe me, it is a wonderful sight – as any farmer who keeps cattle will tell you.

Dad would also point out the brown hares. During spring, groups of males would chase the females around, waiting for them to come into season. The females would literally box them off until they were ready. I guess it was one way for Dad to teach me about the birds and the bees!

As hares live above ground, rather than in warrens like rabbits, Dad and I would sometimes be walking across a field and see one lying perfectly still in its scrape, hoping not to be spotted. My heart would be beating fast as we got incredibly close before the hare bolted and bounced away. On occasion, we would find a leveret – a very young hare – but Dad made it clear to me that we should leave it well alone. The poor thing looked abandoned, but its mother would return to feed it a couple of times per day.

We have always been lucky enough to have deer on the farm, and Dad would point out the differences between muntjac, roe and fallow deer. For many years the fallow herd had a majestic white stag, who to my young eyes looked the most beautiful creature on earth.

As spring led into summer, the birds would begin to nest, the rooks would be busy in the rookery and wildflowers would start to appear in the meadows. Dad was keen to point out wildlife to us, and it felt like the most important and valuable education we could ever receive.

Buzzards are quite common in the Cotswolds nowadays, but when I was growing up they were rare. They would climb to great heights in the thermals or perform acrobatic acts as their youngsters played. We would hear their distinctive mews and scan the skies to spot them.

They weren't the only birds to catch our attention. Hovering kestrels would balance on the wind to spot their prey in the long grass, or sparrow hawks would fly low along the edges of dry stone walls and hedges, ready to surprise their unsuspecting victims. Excited, my sisters and I would compete to point them out to each other.

We would see green woodpeckers, with their distinctive undulating flight, or hear great spotted woodpeckers as they hammered away to search for bugs in dead, standing trees. Dad would always be on hand to answer my questions – it seemed to me like there was nothing that he didn't know.

At dusk we would see barn owls. When I was little we had a project on the farm to reintroduce breeding pairs and Dad fed them dead chicks every day until their brood had hatched and they were sure to stay. I suppose it was one of the very early ways I learned about the food chain.

Occasionally we would find owl pellets – the regurgitated remnants of the food that they have consumed. We would take them home and soak them in warm water to find the little teeth, jawbones and fur from the voles and field mice that had been eaten.

In fact, whenever we found skulls, bones or fur, Dad would test us to identify which creature they had come from. I took it all for a great game at the time but, thinking back, it was an amazing education in nature.

It was always exciting to spot bats, which were prolific around the farm. They would roost in the loft of our farmhouse (in fact, they still do) and take advantage of the many insects that were attracted to the lights in our yard.

During the summer, one of the year's highlights as a boy was haymaking. I thought the smell of the long grass when it was freshly cut was so special. It would then be left to dry in the summer sunshine for three to four days before being baled.

Even as a tiny, pre-school-age boy I was desperate to join in. The whole family and whichever friends were around would all help out and stack the hay in the Dutch barn. It was hard, sweaty work for them, but I remember a lot of laughter.

As a child, I grew to learn that harvest meant that the long summer nights would soon end and autumn was just around the corner. The look of the landscape would change dramatically, from yellow crops blowing in the wind to the stubble that is left behind that had to be quickly cultivated to create a seedbed for the following crop.

I'll never forget how happy I was every autumn as we picked blackberries on the farm. I always knew the end result would be one of Mum's delicious blackberry-and-apple pies. Nearly 50 years on my mouth still waters thinking about them.

Winter would mean flocks of fieldfares and redwings feeding off the sloes on the blackthorns and rosehips as they moved south. It was the time of morning frosts, ices on troughs, crystals on the leaves and eagerly scouring the snow on the ground for animals' footprints.

Dad would show us the signs of where an owl had swooped down and grabbed a mouse, with marks where its wings had scraped on the snow, and a hole where its feet had plunged down to seize its prey. He was great at teaching us precisely which animals left which kinds of prints, so we could follow a fox's pawprints around the yard to see where it had gone.

We had some ferocious winters on Bemborough when I was a very young boy. Mum would stack the giant chest freezer with enough food to feed an army for months and we would all huddle around the log fire. It must have been a pain for my parents but it thrilled my sisters and me. The snow would stack up and block the drive and I would race around outside making snowmen and igloos.

One year when I was really young we were completely snowed in. Dad stacked all the animal feed on to an old car bonnet and roped it to a shire horse. We all sat on the bonnet as if it were a sledge and the horse pulled us over the enormous snowdrifts to feed the livestock. What an adventure!

From as early as I can remember, Dad's business partner, John Neave, who ran the arable side of the farm, was always around with a friendly word. He was a calm, gentle man, a lot heftier and stronger than Dad, who did all of the practical repairs around the farm. My sisters and I called him Uncle John, and that was exactly what he was like: a kindly uncle.

Spring was – and remains – one of my favourite seasons due to lambing. The girls and I had been pottering around lambing pens since we were in nappies, and when the season came around, Dad would straw down the yard outside our kitchen door and it would become the centre of our world for six weeks.

Dad would help the ewes to give birth and then us kids would lead the new mums and their lambs into individual pens that he had rigged up with wooden hurdles in the stables around the yard. One of my jobs was to feed them hay and sheep nuts from a little bucket. It was so much fun.

From a very young age I was learning about animal husbandry and how to spot problems with the ewes and lambs. Dad taught me how important it was to get every lamb up on to their feet, even if they were asleep. Once it was up, if the lamb took a big stretch and looked bright, it was a sign that it was healthy and fit. If it stood hunched up, as if it was balanced on a sixpence, then it needed attention and extra sustenance.

Dad's bedroom overlooked the paddock, and at nights during the season he'd set his alarm for every two hours, so he could get up and look out of the window to see if any ewes were about to lamb and needed help. This went on for more than a month, so the lambing season maybe wasn't quite so much fun for him as it was for me, but he never moaned about it.

Naturally, I became really fond of some of the animals. We had a lovely old longhorn bull called Patrick and a shire horse called Kitty, and I grew particularly attached to a pet sheep called Friendly Fred.

Friendly Fred only had one ear and was quite a character. As a lamb he had lived for a while at the local hunt kennels, and when he came to us he seemed genuinely to think that he was a dog. He would run around the other ewes and lambs as if he were a sheepdog.

Dad was having problems with foxes taking his lambs and, ever ingenious, he fastened a bell to Friendly Fred. Each time that Fred saw a fox creep into the field, he would set off after it with his bell pealing – 'Ding, ding!' – and the fox would get scared and run off. Fred was very effective. I don't think it was because he thought he was a foxhound, just that he thought the fox was a dog and he loved dogs.

Even so, from my very earliest years I was aware of the animals' ultimate fate. I always knew that our livestock would eventually go off to slaughter and I knew that was how it had to be. It was the same whenever a little lamb got hypothermia, and Dad brought it into the kitchen so we could bottle-feed it by the Aga. Mum had the patience of a saint caring for these weak lambs, but I knew I could wake up in the morning and find it either skipping around – or dead. It was upsetting, but such was farm life. We got used to it from a very early age.

I used to love seeing my grandparents on my mum's side. Jack and Betty Richards – or, as I called them, Grampy and Nana – were lovely. They would come to visit us on the farm or, far more excitingly, we would go to stay with them near Swindon, where they ran a grocer's shop.

This was brilliant because there was a sweet shop within the grocer's, where the girls and I spent an awful lot of time – so much so that the sweetshop was named the Totty Shop, after Libby's childhood nickname. Not that I cared about that: I was too busy maximizing my own sweet intake.

My dad's parents were a different matter. His famous dad, Leslie – or Lally, as Dad always called him – had died nearly ten years before I was born, so I never got to meet him. That is a regret for me: when I was a kid, Dad spoke very fondly of him, and he sounded quite a character.

His mum, Billie Dell, was still alive but not in good health. In fact, my one vivid memory of her was her coming to us to die.

Billie had throat cancer from a lifetime of smoking, and was moved into an upstairs bedroom in the farmhouse in 1970 so that Mum could nurse her through her last few weeks. I can still recall her arriving and Mum helping her up the stairs.

I was too young to really know what was going on, but I remember that she hugged and kissed me a lot – a bit too much, I thought at the time. Her neck was covered with lumps and bumps, which looked horrible to me.

It says a lot about Mum that she was so caring for Billie at the end, as I was to learn in later life that they'd had a prickly relationship. Billie was a formidable woman who had doted on Dad and when Mum started dating him, she had given her quite a hard time.

There again, Mum has always been able to look after herself.

Far more regular, and more fun, visitors to the farm were my Uncle Nicky and Aunty Una – better known to the wider world as the actors Nicky Henson and Una Stubbs.

My dad's brother Nicky was 13 years younger than him and had clearly inherited far more of their parents' theatrical genes. He was in his mid-twenties then and had already been to RADA and appeared in a load of films. Obviously, this meant nothing to me whatsoever – I just thought he was a great laugh.

Aunty Una was very caring and loving, a little bit twee and giggly and sort of ditzy; a lot like her TV persona, I suppose. She was famous by then for appearing in the BBC comedy *Till Death Us Do Part* as Alf Garnett's daughter (not that I was a regular viewer; it was hardly an age-appropriate show for a five-year-old).

Una had been married before, to another actor called Peter Gilmore, who starred in *The Onedin Line*. They had adopted a son, Jason, who now lived with Nicky and Una, and came to visit us with them. Jason was my age and it was nice to have another boy to play with for a change.

Nicky and Una had another two boys, Christian and Joe, but they were just babies, so were far too boring for me to be bothered about. After all, how can a baby build a den?

Aunty Una used to bring us Harrods' chocolates at Easter and amazing Christmas presents. When it rained or at Christmas, we would all sit around and play board games and charades. She was particularly good at those. Maybe she was using us as a practice run for *Give Us A Clue*, years later?

I used to love their visits. Nicky was as good a storyteller as my dad, and they would swap hilarious stories of their beloved late dad, Lally, and his adventures and escapades. I was not to learn until years later that not all of the Lally tales were quite so cheery.

Yet any family politics obviously went right over my head in those days. All I wanted to do was play on the farm. There was always something going on. We had chickens and cross-breed hens running around the yard just because Dad liked them. We would collect the eggs if we saw them, but really they were just glorified pets.

They drove my mum nuts. She kept beautiful flowerbeds and the chickens would wander around the garden and scratch them to pieces. Dad would just smile and say that a lovely hen in a garden is just as nice to look at as a rose bush.

At the time, I agreed with Dad wholeheartedly on that point. Mum never looked as if she remotely did.

Kids can always immerse themselves in something they love 100 per cent and I was totally steeped in the day-to-day life of the farm. Dad could see this in me and encouraged it, inviting me to join him on various farm-related outings. In particular, I will never forget the first time he took me off to the market. He strapped me into the child's car seat and off we went, to what seemed to me the most exotic and thrilling place in the world. (Actually, it was Andoversford market.) Dad knew everyone there and watching those big, gruff farmers bidding for bulls and rams excited me.

Yes, it's hard to think how I could have been any happier in those early, blissful years. But into even the most contented life, a little rain must fall.

I had to start school.

I hated my first day at Temple Guiting Primary School. It seemed a terrifying place to me, and my mum had to drag me in through the school gates, screaming and shouting and crying (to be honest, that incident pretty much sums up my entire academic career!).

Aged five, I just didn't see the point of school. I didn't like it, I didn't want to leave the farm every day and I didn't want to go there. It was a small school, 40 or 50 children, but I only knew one girl, who was the neighbouring farmer's slightly older daughter, Joanna Hickman.

Joanna agreed to look after me and help me to settle in, but school still felt like an alien environment. It was weeks before I reluctantly accepted that I had to keep going.

There again, some of the teachers weren't too welcoming. I found the headmistress, Mrs Kennedy, very scary. One of my friends at school, Nigel Butler, used to play her up, and she would lock him in the sports cupboard in the dark.

I'm not sure what OFSTED would make of that today.

One day Nigel, his cousin Neil and I were chasing a little girl called Anna Clark around the schoolyard with sticks (I have no idea why – we were just playing). Mrs Kennedy saw us and made us stand in front of the whole school assembly.

She was going to cane us, and told the three of us to hold our hands out, palms up. As she swished the cane down hard, we all flinched and reflexively pulled our hands back. The cane hit the ground so hard that it broke into three pieces and the other kids all burst out laughing.

Thankfully, Mrs Kennedy didn't have another cane, so that was the end of that – a lucky break to say the least!

I grew to tolerate Temple Guiting but I never really liked it. I was rubbish at learning to read and write and not very good academically. All that I wanted was to be at home, on the farm.

But luckily for me, life at home was about to get even more exciting than it already was – because Bemborough Farm was about to make history.

CHAPTER 2

'Nobody Will Pay to See Farm Animals!'

It was always about the animals for Dad. Ever since he had been a little boy saving his pennies each week to buy a new lead sheep or cow for his bedroom farmyard, he'd adored them. He was, he freely admitted, an 'animal anorak'.

When he had first taken over Bemborough with John Neave in 1962 they had been short of money and had to devise a low-capital farming system. They started out just growing barley, with a few commercial sheep thrown in.

This was hugely frustrating for Dad, whose passion for farming was all about breeding pedigree livestock. Mainly as a hobby, he bought two Gloucester cows and two Gloucester Old Spot sows from local farmers.

When my eldest sister Libby fell off her pony, damaging her back, and subsequently sold it, she asked Dad to buy some Cotswold sheep with the money. Libby still owns those sheep's descendants even today.

Dad's love for rare breeds might have remained a low-level hobby had he not been invited in 1969 to join a working party set up jointly by the Royal Agricultural Society and the Zoological Society of London. Its purpose was to find a home for a collection of rare-breed farm animals from Whipsnade Zoo.

The zoo had decided to jettison these unglamorous creatures for more exotic animals, and to make way for the first breeding herd of white rhinos. The farm animals got moved to Reading University while their fate was decided. Dad went to Reading, looked at the rare indigenous sheep and cattle and was hooked.

He had always loved zoos, and an idea began to gnaw away at him – if people were willing to pay to look at gorillas and tigers, why wouldn't they do the same to see a wonderful collection of unusual farm animals? When he came back to Bemborough, he talked over his idea with John Neave, who agreed.

Dad convened a meeting of the working party on his farm in 1970 and said that he and John would buy the majority of the discarded Whipsnade animals in order to use them as the basis of a farm park at Bemborough. They would charge the public admission and look to educate them in rare-breeds' survival and conservation.

It was to be the first rare-breed farm park of its kind in Britain – and, as far as anyone knew, the world.

So it was that in 1971, when I was five, the farm received an influx of Highland, Longhorn, White Park, Belted Galloway and Dexter cattle, plus Jacobs, Soays and Portland sheep and a single Norfolk ram. They were the first inhabitants of a new, visionary and very risky venture: the Cotswold Farm Park.

Dad's landlords, his bank, John Neave and Mum were all behind him, but there was no guarantee the farm park would work. Would it be a (forgive the pun) cash cow, or an expensive, self-indulgent hobby and drain on resources that could drag the farm down?

The farm park hit problems before it even opened. A lot of Dad's mates thought he had gone mad: 'Nobody will pay to see farm animals! You see one sheep, you've seen 'em all!' was the general reaction.

Some of the more reactionary locals were also furious, fearing it would attract thousands of unwanted tourists to Gloucestershire to clog up the country lanes. They started a petition to try to stop the place opening.

Dad came into his own. He was always great at defending his ideas, and he set off on a local charm offensive, explaining to his opponents what the farm park would be all about and how it could benefit the area. Slowly, one by one, the locals came around to the plan.

Of course, I didn't know about any of this until years later. At the time, I just loved the thought of a load of new animals on the farm and enjoyed mucking about on the swings that Uncle John had installed at the farm park for visiting kids to play on.

Well, somebody had to try them out, right?

Day-to-day life on the farm was always busy, but as the big opening day neared the activity levels went crazy. Uncle John did all the building, fencing and laying water pipes as it all took shape.

Mum was a miracle worker. Dad might have been great at buying livestock but the finer details of finance were not his forte, and Mum now took on running the books for the farm park, as she already did for the farm.

The farm park was going to have a shop and a café, and the night before the opening my mum, Nana and a lovely lady called Janet Goode (who still works for us, 45 years on) were busy making mountains of sandwiches and baking cakes. I can still picture the fruits of their labours piled up on our big old sideboard.

We had an abandoned caravan on the farm that was converted into an impromptu snack bar. Mum set herself up in there and got busy brewing tea and coffee and had ice cream at the ready to sell to the farm park visitors.

But how many would there be? The farm park was obviously a gamble, and now that I'm older I realize just how nervous Mum and Dad must have been about their audacious new business venture.

They didn't need to be. It was a success from the start.

Even the locals who had been opposed to the Cotswold Farm Park were curious and came down to have a look. The word spread, and soon it was getting visitors from right across Britain, and even further afield.

In its very first year, 20,000 people flocked to Bemborough Farm and the farm park. The entrance fee was just 10p for adults and 5p for children but at the time, with the investment Dad and John had made, every penny helped.

As a kid you are totally flexible and love new things, so this massive influx of people onto our land didn't bother me at all. It seemed fantastic to me that all these people wanted to look at our animals.

Dad also talked to my sisters and me so we understood just what the rationale behind the farm park was. He would tell us about things like the poignant position of Gloucestershire Old Spot pigs, which at one time were a mainstay of Cotswolds farming, but now had fallen badly out of favour.

The Old Spots were big docile pigs with floppy ears: lovely creatures. However, intensive farming was all the rage in the early 1970s and most farmers wanted lean, fast-growing, commercial sows. They were starting to see the poor Old Spots as outmoded and just a silly relic of the past, almost a laughing stock. To draw a parallel, I think at that point turning up at market with Old Spots was a bit like pulling up to a sports-car rally in a battered Morris Minor. The breed was irrelevant and even threatened with extinction – which was where the farm park came in.

Dad also did a very clever thing to keep my sisters and me interested in the farm park – he gave us a vested interest in it. He gifted each of us kids a rare breed from the park and told us that we were responsible for looking after them. Libby got Cotswold sheep, Lolo had Shetland sheep, Becca had Southdown sheep and I was given the Exmoor ponies.

There was quite a nice story behind the ponies' arrival in the park. A local landowner, Roddy Fleming, was one of the people who thought Dad was bonkers to open the farm park. He didn't understand about rare-breed conservation at all and was very sceptical about the whole thing. However, when the park took off he came down to have a look and totally changed his mind. He told Dad, 'I've got Exmoor ponies on Exmoor and they are really rare. Would you help preserve them?' He gave Dad a couple for the farm park.

To be honest, at five years old I would have preferred to be given sheep and was slightly jealous of my sisters, but I threw myself into looking after the ponies. Dad told us that we had to maintain the breed, and buy and sell the stock.

Whenever we sold an animal, half of the money would go into our piggy banks. It was a brilliant idea, because it helped us to learn about rare-breed conservation while also teaching us that the farm park was actually a business.

So we would go off to markets and farms with him to choose and buy our new stock of rams and ponies. It all felt very exciting and responsible and grown-up, although obviously Dad was nudging us in the right direction and giving us lots of gentle advice on which rams and ponies to choose.

I took the whole thing extremely seriously, although the big drawback from my point of view was that the farm park only had three Exmoor foals, so there wasn't that much wheeling and dealing for me to do. Perhaps that was a good thing – I was only five years old!

There again, although Exmoor ponies didn't really float my boat, a horse seemed totally essential to my intended career path at that age. I used to love Western movies on TV, and decided that I wanted to be a cowboy.

I used to bang on about this so much that when I was six my dad bought me a pony. He was a sweet-looking little Appaloosa horse that was white with black spots all over his body and so we called him Domino. And my parents indulged my cowboy fantasy to such a degree that I even had a Western saddle, split reins and a little Stetson for when I took myself out for a li'l old mosey around the wide-open spaces of our fields. It was great – or, rather, it would have been, had Domino not been pathologically naughty.

Every time I took him out, we would get half a mile from the stable and Domino would buck me off, before trotting away happily on his own. I always ended up walking home, bruised and battered, which put me off the idea of being a Cotswold John Wayne.

Every childhood day on the farm brought fresh adventures. One such involved our two rare-breed Dexter cows, a miniature strain of the Irish Kerry breed, who were called Marmite and Marmalade. In the winter we used to keep them in a field called Big Larches, a rough grassland field with thorn and scrub.

One day, Dad decided that Marmite looked close to calving and put her in a loose box by the farmhouse. He checked her every day, and when she had still not calved after a week, he got worried and called in the vet.

The vet had a good look at Marmite and said that she had calved already. This was bad news, and Dad told us that she had probably calved prematurely with a stillbirth.

Libby persuaded Dad to go and look for the dead calf and the two of them headed off into the scrub. As they searched high and low, they could not believe it when a tiny calf suddenly reared her head above the bracken, gave them a frightened stare and crashed off through the bushes. They gave chase, catching her when she got tangled in some briars.

The baby calf had somehow survived on her own in the woods for nine days. We knew some deer lived there, and Dad wondered if one of them had lost her fawn and 'adopted' the tiny heifer calf as a replacement. That might have explained why she was so wild and skittish!

The amazing thing was that when Dad put the calf with her mother, Marmite accepted her, even though she had not seen her for nine days. The whole thing seemed quite miraculous, so that was what we called the calf: Bemborough Miracle. She became a popular attraction in the park.

The farm park made Dad even more evangelical about conserving rare breeds, if that were possible. I remember him being on the phone for hours trying to buy animals, as well as heading off to local Women's Institute meetings to talk about them. They were everything to him.

This passion was cemented in 1973 when he helped to found the Rare Breeds Survival Trust (RBST), a charity to protect and conserve the kind of endangered indigenous breeds that we kept in our farm park. As its most driven member, Dad was promptly made the body's chairman.

The appointment was a fantastic recognition of all the great work that he had done to date, and Dad always said he was incredibly honoured by it. Aged seven, I didn't really comprehend all of the extra work it must have been for him, but I could see how proud he was.

In truth, however, I was far more impressed by a much more exciting development that happened around the same time. Dad started going on the telly.

The opening of the Cotswold Farm Park had been big news and a load of newspaper and television journalists had come to cover it. The one I was the most excited about by far was Johnny Morris from the BBC children's TV show *Animal Magic*.

I didn't watch that much TV as a kid – well, apart from John Wayne films, obviously – because I always preferred running around the farm, but I adored *Animal Magic*. It was a must for any kid who loved animals, and Johnny Morris's funny voiceovers for the elephants and monkeys cracked me up.

Johnny came down with a film crew and interviewed my dad in the farm park. I think they even talked about Bemborough Miracle, the heifer calf. Dad was a natural on camera – you can't keep those show-business genes down! – and his love for the subject came across really well.

The footage caught the eye of one of the series' producers in *Animal Magic*'s Bristol offices and he phoned up and asked if Dad would like to be an occasional presenter. It was always my dad's instinct to say 'Yes' rather than 'No', so he said he would give it a go.

Wow! My dad was going to be on *Animal Magic* with Johnny Morris! It seemed such a big deal to me. It was even more impressive because Dad suffered from an affliction that was hardly an asset for working on TV: he had a stammer.

Apparently his stammer had been really bad as a boy, when he often couldn't get his words out at all. He once told me that it had used to really annoy his actor dad, who would yell at him about it. I thought, *Wow, his dad did that? How horrible!*

His stammer had got a lot better as he had grown up but it still wasn't completely cured. I would occasionally notice Dad stumble over his words if he got too excited or nervous about something – and as I now know, being in front of a television camera can be hugely nerve-wracking.

Yet when he started the presenting work he hid it and coped brilliantly. With his thespian London background I suppose

31

he had a 'BBC voice' anyway, and before long he was jokingly referring to himself as *Animal Magic*'s 'tame farmer'.

It all seemed pretty amazing to me. We kids were so proud of him, and I particularly remember watching a show where Dad used traditional methods to train a team of oxen to pull him in a wooden sleigh. It was great children's TV, but as ever with *Animal Magic* – and with Dad – it also had an educational purpose: to show kids just how important oxen had once been in agriculture.

Watching Dad on *Animal Magic* was fantastic. Going to see him film the show was even better. Once or twice he shot programmes during my school holidays, and let me go down to the studios in Bristol with him.

It was exciting, especially if we were taking some of our rare-breed animals down with us to appear on the show, but I was never totally overawed by it. There again, I suppose that, having hung out with Nicky Henson and Una Stubbs since birth, I was quite blasé about celebrities by then!

Even so, it was a thrill to talk to Johnny Morris, who was lovely. I'm not sure, but I think I asked him for his autograph.

So I was now seven years old, having the time of my life on the farm with my sisters and our dog Gemima, loving the farm park and even mingling with TV stars. Life was pretty grand, but my blue sky did have one troubling and very persistent cloud.

I really wasn't doing well at school. Temple Guiting Primary and I had never got on, and with the exception of a star turn in the school production of *Oliver!*, the teachers' reports on me were getting worse and worse.

Let's be frank here: I have never been gifted academically. However, rather than knuckling down and trying to work harder at primary school, I went the other way. I would be naughty and act the class clown to get attention, and that approach was getting me into trouble.

My sisters had all done pretty well at school so I was bucking the family trend – and not in a good way. My parents were concerned and decided to see if a venerable private school might help me to up my game.

Mum and Dad therefore pulled me out of Temple Guiting and put me into the junior school for boys at Cheltenham College. This should not have been a problem logistically: Libby, Lolo and Becca were already all studying in the convent in Cheltenham. However, there was to be a major difference between their circumstances and mine.

The junior school's headmaster, a Mr Davies, decided that as I would probably want to join the after-school sports clubs, the 20-minute drive to Bemborough Farm was too long for me to be a day student. I would have to become a boarder.

So that was that. Suddenly, out of the blue, I was off to boarding school.

CHAPTER 3

Tears in the Dorm

Bemborough Farm was the centre of my world. It was all I had ever known, or wanted, and for a carefree, animal-loving eight-year-old boy, I suppose that it was pretty close to being my personal heaven on earth.

Now, I was about to be dragged away from this paradise to a place that, initially at least, seemed suspiciously like hell.

I don't think my parents were particularly happy about me going to boarding school. It hadn't been their idea in the first place, but they wanted the best for me and my education, so when the headmaster at Cheltenham informed them that I would have to be a boarder, they went along with it.

Before I went away, we had an unusually glamorous family holiday. We usually went to places like Bournemouth, but in 1974 we holidayed in Tenerife where we walked up the local volcano, Mount Teide, and I was mesmerized by the stinky clouds of sulphur belching out of the ground around us.

I celebrated my eighth birthday out there. The day after we came back, I started at Cheltenham.

I still vividly remember that night we came back from Spain and I had to pack for boarding school. The school had sent over a huge trunk with a list of all the things we needed to put in it: jumpers, jackets, trousers, socks, pants. Mum sewed my name into all of them and I was allowed to choose a few of my favourite teddy bears to take with me.

It all didn't seem real, somehow. I couldn't believe it was happening. There had been a mistake, right?

The next morning, I stroked Gemima goodbye – wait, was I *really* going to leave her? – then we got into our red Volvo and Mum and Dad drove me over to Cheltenham. We pulled up in front of a huge, imposing red-brick building with a tarmac playground in front of it.

If I had been intimidated on my first day at Temple Guiting, this was something else again.

The car park was full of boys and parents pulling trunks out of the boots, and teachers welcoming the new arrivals. Someone showed Mum, Dad and me to the dormitory that was to be my home, we unpacked my trunk, and then I went back outside with my parents and waved goodbye as they drove off.

More than 40 years later, I can still recall the hollow feeling inside of me as I watched them leave.

Public school life and being away from your family is a massive shock at such a tender age. Over the next few days and weeks, I tried to get used to a whole new, totally alien routine and a bewildering number of rules and regulations.

I shared a dorm with ten or eleven other boys who were all the same age as me. A prefect, who was an older boy named Henry, slept in the dorm with us. He could report us to the teachers or discipline us himself if there was any tomfoolery or mucking about. Thankfully, Henry was the son of a local agricultural auctioneer, Mr Drury, who knew my dad well, so he looked out for me.

Initially, there were a lot of tears. The school had a rule that new pupils could not have any contact with their parents for three weeks after arriving. The idea was it would help you to acclimatize to your new environment and stop you pining for home too much.

It didn't work.

I missed everything about home – not just Mum and Dad, and my sisters and Gemima, but everyday life on the farm, from waking up to the cockcrow to hearing the noises from the farmyard as I fell asleep at night. My childhood had very few unhappy days, but those first few weeks at junior school were easily the worst.

Most nights I cried into my pillow after lights out, hoping it would muffle the noise so that nobody would hear me. I'm pretty sure it didn't work – because around the dorm I could hear plenty of other boys doing the same thing.

Of course, I had to toughen up very quickly and put on a hard veneer, as if I didn't really care. The boys were all in the same boat and missing our homes and families like mad, but we never talked about it. The most that you might say, if someone asked you, was that you felt 'a bit homesick'.

This was an understatement, to say the least.

Luckily, I made friends quite quickly with a few other boys in the dorm and in my classes. I guess we bonded because we were all in this horrible, strange situation together. It made our friendships deep and lasting ones: I still see some of them even today.

The first three weeks at school before I was allowed to go home for a weekend were torture. Every morning, as soon as

I woke up, I was counting down the days, and my heart leapt when – *at last!* – Mum swung the car through the school gates.

As soon as we got back to Bemborough I wanted to play outside and follow Dad around the farm and muck about with my sisters as if nothing had happened and Cheltenham was just a bad dream. I felt as if I was eight years old and on prison leave.

After a few blissful but bittersweet hours, it was time to go back. I sobbed in the car all the way to Cheltenham and it set my mum off crying as well. We pulled up outside my dorm building and I wiped my eyes, hugged her, gave her a goodbye kiss and trudged slowly back in.

In fact, that sad routine was repeated at the end of all my first few visits home. Mum must have dreaded it as much as I did.

I missed my sisters terribly, particularly Becca. She and I were the closest in age, we played together a lot, and we were always known in the family as 'the little ones' as compared to Libby and Lolo, who were 'the big ones'. My going to Cheltenham was a wrench for Becca as well as me: she lost her playmate.

Once, during my early weeks at Cheltenham, Mum called in unannounced to visit me with my sisters. She just picked them up from their school and drove over. I was in the playground and ran delightedly to the Volvo, thinking she had come to take me home.

When she told me it was only a flying visit, I was devastated and burst into tears: 'I want to come home! Why can't I?'

'I'm sorry, Adam, I just thought we would pop over and say hello,' said Mum, who looked as upset as me.

I was inconsolable and sobbing uncontrollably. Mr Davies, the headmaster, was patrolling the playground and spotted me. He was a huge man – he had used to play rugby for the British Lions – and he simply picked me up and marched off.

He was carrying me under his arm like a parcel and I was crying, kicking my legs and thrashing my arms, trying to hit him. He took me to his office and made me sit on a bench for two hours until I calmed down.

That evening, the headmaster phoned my mum. 'Don't *ever* do that again,' he ordered her. 'It's far too disruptive for the boy.'

Now and then some of the more daring – or desperate – Cheltenham boys tried to escape. It was our version of trying to dig a tunnel out of Colditz. The pupils never got very far before they were caught and disciplined.

I was involved in one breakout plot. Two or three boys and I stashed a load of sweets and cans of soft drinks and made a plan to sneak out of the dorm after lights out and go down the fire escape, across the playing fields and up the hill to freedom.

When the big moment came, I bottled out of it and didn't go, but a couple of my friends went ahead. It took the school the whole of the next day to find them and their poor parents must have been terrified. Mum and Dad made me promise that I would never do that and, reluctantly, I did.

Yet slowly, gradually, I began to get used to my new life at Cheltenham. Going to public school at least had one desired effect: it improved my academic performance.

I was never going to be top of the class, that was for sure, but returning after classes every day to the dorm, rather than to the distractions of the farm, gave me no excuse not to knuckle down and, at least, study a lot harder.

There was not a single day that I didn't want to be on the farm, but I did begin to enjoy a few things about junior school. There was a little lake in the grounds, and I could ride my bike around it and sail my little model boat across it.

We were allowed pets, and I had a hamster called Hammy (how original!). Dad also gave me a lop-eared rabbit to keep at school. I called him Mushy Peas, for reasons that escape me now. He'd race around the cricket field and if I called him – 'Here, Mushy Peas!' – he'd run over and jump on me, which was weird for a rabbit.

Yet the main thing I got into at junior school was sport. The school year was divided into three terms – winter, spring and summer – when we played rugby, hockey and cricket respectively. Mr Hunt, the games teacher and rugby coach, was by far my favourite teacher in the school.

I might not have been much cop in the classroom but I was decent at sport and ended up in the first team for each discipline, as well as representing the school in athletics. I suppose all those early years running around the farm all day long stood me in good stead.

Even so, I have a very short attention span, so I found cricket utterly frustrating. If you are not batting or bowling, you end up just being stood out in the field all day, which I found totally boring.

Rugby was far more like it. I loved the game from the first time we played it. I was too small for the scrum but was quick and could tackle well, so playing in the backs at inside centre suited me. I liked the fact that the backs were the guys who got all the glory when they scored the tries.

Before too long I was the captain of the junior school rugby team. It was the start of a love affair that has lasted all my life, and through my adult years I played rugby for various teams right up until a few years ago when my creaky old body couldn't take it any more.

You had to stay in line at Cheltenham because if you played up, the discipline could be ferocious. Every day we started the morning with assembly, and some days a teacher would reel off a list of names of pupils who had to report to Mr Davies's office for a caning.

One day they read my name out: 'Henson!' (It seemed that no boys had first names at Cheltenham.) I had no idea what I was supposed to have done wrong, and was given no explanation, but I had to shuffle off and wait outside the headmaster's door nonetheless.

Mr Davies wasn't just intimidating because he was physically domineering (we all nicknamed him 'Beefy' because he was so huge) but because he administered canings to us boys with a sandal that he had nailed a piece of wood to. It sounds positively sadistic now, and I guess it was – it was borderline child abuse, really.

That morning, he gave me such a whack on the back of the leg that I was aching for days. Afterwards, I had to sit on the windowsill in his office for ten minutes and think about what I had done. This was difficult for me, as I had no idea what my misdemeanour had been in the first place.

Lesser transgressions would result in a particularly banal

punishment. If you cheeked the dorm prefect, or your bed or cupboard was untidy, he would order you to report to the housemaster – in your sports kit. The housemaster would then send you back to the dorm, where you had to change back into your school uniform, then back into your sports kit to see the master again. You normally had to repeat this bizarre ritual four times.

It was so ridiculous that we boys tried to introduce short cuts to speed things up. We would keep our rugby shorts on under our trousers, knowing that we'd have to change back into them in five minutes anyway. If you got caught doing that, it would be back off to Beefy and his caning sandal.

You could be arbitrarily disciplined for anything in school – right down to, and including, your shoes not being polished enough. My favourite punishment by far was being sent outside to run around the sports field; I actively *liked* that one.

We were allowed weekend visits home every fortnight or every three weeks, depending on the length of the term. There again, 'weekend visit' is a rather misleading term for the miserly leave we were granted.

We had classes six days per week. On Saturdays, we had lessons in the morning then sport in the afternoon. That was great, as my parents would often come to watch me play rugby or hockey.

On Sundays we had compulsory church in the morning. If it was a visit weekend, I would sit on the hard pew until 11 o'clock, bitterly resenting being there and itching for the sermon and the hymns to end so I could get out of there. Then we had to be back in school by 6 p.m. It didn't leave me a lot of time on the farm, which made my short visits both precious and painful.

The end-of-term holidays were blissful, of course, and Mum

and Dad tried to make them fun for me, probably because they knew just how much I disliked being at Cheltenham. Those holidays were all special, but I will never forget the year that Dad took me to the Orkney Islands.

The Rare Breeds Survival Trust was worried that the last surviving flock of 287 North Ronaldsay sheep – a breed that dates back to the Stone Age – were all living behind a sea wall on the Scottish island of the same name. They had developed a taste for seaweed, so it would only take an oil slick or a bout of foot-and-mouth disease in the flock to wipe the entire breed out.

As RBST chairman, in 1974 Dad deputed himself to travel up to the Orkneys and buy one of the smaller islands, Midgarth, also known as Linga Holm, for the Trust. Shortly afterwards he took me, aged eight, back with him to help him transport the sheep from North Ronaldsay to their new home.

It was such a treat and I could not have been more excited. Dad drove us to Scotland and then we caught a little propeller plane over to Orkney. I loved sitting close behind the pilot, gazing through the cockpit window.

Looking back, Dad probably persuaded Mum to let him take me as it would be a proper father/son bonding experience. How right he was. That night we shared a room in a B&B, and I remember feeling proud that Dad and I were going to go and do real men's work together.

The next morning we caught a very cold, choppy ferry out to North Ronaldsay and set about capturing the sheep. It is a very small, nippy breed and I was slipping and sliding all over the desolate island's very wet rocks as we tried to help the crofters usher the scampering animals into their pens.

That was the easy bit. The crofters helped us to get them into crates and then on to a steamer, which chugged across the rough, grey seas to nearby Linga Holm. Then Dad and I had to pass the sheep one by one from the steamer to men who were waiting on a barge, ready to transport them to the island.

It was like trying to juggle jelly. I was stumbling around the steamer, which was rocking and rolling on the waves, trying to grab the elusive, slippery little creatures to throw them to the locals on the barge. Somehow, during a long, adrenaline-fuelled day, we managed to transport more than 100 sheep.

Dad had loads of paperwork to do for the local authorities and the Trust, but I was desperate to go lobster potting and so he took me the next morning. We didn't even have life jackets, but off we went anyway onto the freezing cold North Sea with our lobster pots.

Some people might have found it hellish. I felt as if I had died and gone to heaven.

Another 100 of the North Ronaldsays came south and were divided into groups to found flocks on the mainland. Ten of them, inevitably, made their way to Bemborough.

There are still only around 500 of the breed surviving in the UK today, and the fact they take so long to mature and yield such small carcasses means that they are never likely to be commercially viable. But at least they are not threatened with extinction as they were before Dad and the RBST got involved.

Just as Dad had always been able to do, he made that trip educational as well as amazing fun – and I continued to reap the benefits of it back at Cheltenham. I was never particularly good at English at school – in fact it was one of my weakest subjects – but my trip to the Orkneys made for one 'What I did in my holidays' essay that I actually *did* enjoy writing.

Between terms at junior school my parents took us on some great holidays. The best was a trip we made over Christmas and New Year in 1975. As a young man Dad had studied at Cirencester Agricultural College, and one of his former classmates and oldest friends, a farmer called John Hutson, now grew sugarcane on a farm in Barbados. John invited Dad and our whole family out for Christmas and we had the most amazing time.

The sun beats down in the Caribbean even in December, and we soon raced off to the beach and rented a motorboat to go water-skiing. Off I went: bouncing over the waves and through the wind and the water with no T-shirt on. This really wasn't the wisest move for a pale-skinned little ginger boy, and I ended up with huge sheet blisters across my entire back.

I had to sleep on my stomach, and it didn't help when the friendly Bajan women who had never seen a little red-haired white boy before took to coming up and slapping my back as they greeted me! Polite and British as ever, I kept smiling through the pain, and it was a fantastic trip.

Back home on Bemborough, Uncle Nicky was sometimes around when I went home for weekends from Cheltenham. Sadly, he and Aunty Una had split up by then. Nicky was a bit of a Jack the Lad, and I think the truth was that he just couldn't cope with the responsibility of having two young kids. He preferred the crazy 1960s anything-goes life that he had been living very enthusiastically.

Uncle Nicky was a very well-known actor and quite the celebrity by then, and the newspapers obviously took an interest when he and Una divorced. He started using the farm as a bit of a bolt-hole where he could just relax, play his guitar and hang out with us.

Nicky is a real larger-than-life character and I used to look forward to his visits. He also took to bringing his actress girl-friends down with him to enjoy some time away from the prying paparazzi. Susan Hampshire came down once.

When I was a very young boy, I always dreamed of taking over the farm from Dad when I grew up. While I was away from Bemborough during those long, seemingly never-ending terms in Cheltenham, that desire didn't fade – it grew stronger.

I ached to be there, and when I was at home over weekends and during the holidays, I threw myself into farm life more than ever. I wanted to know how everything worked and to be part of it. This delighted Dad, who was never too busy to educate me.

He would take me with him to the markets and other farms to help buy livestock. I was so excited when he trusted me to buy my first ewes when I was about nine, and took me to see Mr Briggs near Warwick. Mr Briggs was renowned as the best breeder of Oxford Downs with his famous Gorse Flock. He used to trim their fleeces beautifully.

We had a rough old sheepdog on the farm called Carlo who was a bit of a maverick. He used to bite the postman and the tyres of any visiting cars, and for some reason never liked Mum, but he loved me and let me play with him.

Carlo was a long-coated dog and his coat used to get all mangled and matted: Dad used to call these bits the 'diggy-daggies'. When I was home from school, one of my regular jobs used to be getting the sheep shears and coaxing Carlo into letting me cut off his diggy-daggies.

I also learned how to herd sheep. It was one of the very few jobs around the farm that Dad was not too good at. He just used to shout and yell at Carlo and the other dogs. He never lost his temper with us kids, but he often lost his rag with the mutts.

So he mostly left the herding to our stockmen, good local countrymen like Bob Brunt and Roger Brown. I would go out to the fields with them and watch them working in perfect harmony with the dogs, calling out 'By!' for them to go left and 'Away!' for right.

Around that time I got a dog that I loved even more than Gemima or Carlo. It was Christmas, and Mum and Dad told us that they had got us a special present each. My sisters all eagerly opened theirs. One of them got a bicycle; another got a saxophone.

I didn't get anything and thought I had been missed out until my dad said, 'Oh, and there's yours, Adam.' In the corner of the room was an old tea chest with some Christmas wrapping paper on top of it. I ran to the chest and looked in to see a liver-and-white springer spaniel puppy.

She was a tiny little thing and I adored her the second I set eyes on her. Dad had a much-loved aunty called Benita and he had named his own spaniel Ben in her honour, and so I completed the tribute and called my puppy Nita.

Nita and I quickly became inseparable whenever I was home from Cheltenham. Mum had a strict rule in the house that the dogs were not allowed upstairs but she made an exception for Nita, who used to sleep on my bed with me. Whenever I was running around the farm from then on, she was normally by my side.

Nita was such a big part of my childhood – and beyond. She lived right through my teens and into my twenties and was so special. From the day I got her, I don't think I have ever been without a dog. I would never want to be.

On another, rather less happy school holiday at home from Cheltenham, however, Nita and I were almost parted for good when I very nearly came to a sticky end.

Dad had always told my sisters and me never to go in with the farm bulls on our own. If we had to, we should always carry a stick, and if the bull went for us, we should stand our ground, wave the stick and shout at it. We should never run away.

When I was about ten, I was out in a field with one of our stockmen helping to move some cattle. There was a White Park bull amongst the herd that was quite aggressive, and he suddenly turned and charged at us. It was terrifying.

The stockman took one look at the bull, turned on his heel and fled, leaving me on my own. It felt totally counter-intuitive but I managed to do what Dad had told me and stand my ground. Luckily, the bull stopped charging and sloped away and I managed to escape out of the field.

I seem to recall that this particular stockman was let go from our employment very soon afterwards. This may very well not have been a coincidence.

CHAPTER 4

Dad Goes International

As one term gave way to another in Cheltenham, I came to tolerate life at boarding school. It would be a stretch to say that I grew to love it but at least I no longer actively despised it, while working harder at my studies meant that I managed to improve my academic performance from poor to average.

I was still living for the weekends and holidays when I could escape and get back to the farm and my family – but there was a spell in the mid-seventies when my dad was away as often as he was there.

After his successful appearance on *Animal Magic* led to him becoming their 'tame farmer', Dad was offered quite a lot of work as a freelance television presenter for BBC countryside shows. He was getting as used to boom mikes and film crews as he was to cowsheds and pigsties.

Having largely conquered his stammer, Dad liked doing TV. Although he told me that he hated doing pieces to camera, as he was apprehensive that his voice would let him down, if you gave him an animal to talk about he was in his element. He was great at engaging the audience.

The TV work also provided a useful supplementary income to the farm. This must have come in handy in 1976, when the atypically long, hot summer meant that the crops all failed and even the grass in the farm park died.

That same year, Dad presented a one-off BBC documentary called *Barnyard Safari*. It was a show that traced the natural history of farm animals and examined how their behaviour had changed since the days when their ancestors ran wild.

We were very rarely allowed to watch television at boarding school and this was still years before the invention of video recorders, but I loved the few times that I managed actually to watch Dad on TV. I felt proud of how good he was and how clearly he explained the country life that he felt so passionately about.

Then, during that blazing summer of '76, the BBC upped the ante somewhat when Dad's TV career went international.

They asked him to host a series called *Great Alliance*, which was to comb the world to find stories of wild species of animals that had been trained to work cooperatively with humans. It would mean him being away from Bemborough for weeks at a time.

Most wives would have baulked at being left alone to look after four kids for such long stretches, but in her typical no-nonsense style, Mum told Dad that of course he had to do it. It was a great opportunity for him, and she knew it would bring in much-needed income for the farm.

John Neave assured Dad that he could look after the farm while he was away, so off he vanished on his grand globetrotting adventure. That summer he dotted himself around the world like Phileas Fogg. It seemed every time I went home, Mum would tell me he was in an even more exotic locale.

Dad went to France to learn how the locals had tamed and domesticated once-feral Camargue horses. In Sri Lanka, he watched men putting elephants to work. He journeyed on to Australia to film domesticated camels, and even found himself behind the Iron Curtain in Hungary, as well as in the Sudan, where he discovered how camels were being farmed for their meat and their milk yields, and used for racing, too. This was all a long way from Gloucester cattle market.

While he was in Australia, Dad visited some Tamworth pig farms as the bloodlines in the UK were becoming thin on the ground. Once back in the UK, on behalf of the RBST he arranged for two boars to be imported to improve the breed's genetic diversity here.

His adventures weren't all about the animals, however. Dad told me a brilliant story about his trip to Sudan. The sound-man, Keith Rogerson, had incredibly heavy bags but he soldiered on with them valiantly, insisting that they contained essential equipment.

During their journey, the TV team's cortege broke down and they ended up in a Bedouin village where the food was particularly primitive. Much to everyone's delight, Keith then popped open his mega-cases to reveal tins of peaches and Ambrosia cream rice. The TV team lived off this for the next two days before they could set off again on their travels.

Because I was at boarding school I probably didn't feel Dad's absence as keenly as I would have if I was still living at home, and his trips seemed amazing to me. The mobile phone had yet to be invented and there were not many phone boxes in the Sudan desert so, barring the odd postcard, Dad simply vanished for weeks.

When he came back between shoots, he brought me some fantastic presents. I went through a spell of collecting masks and he got me some great ones from Africa. He brought me a boomerang from Australia, and I spent hours spinning it around the farmyard.

One strange side effect of Dad's increased telly work was that it made him a little bit of a celebrity. I would be walking around the farm park with him during school holidays, and visitors would come running up to him and ask him for his autograph.

It always seemed quite funny to me – *Why did these people want Dad to write his name for them?* – but Dad loved it and took to it really well. He always had time to chat to his new fans about the farm or the TV shows. Now that the identical thing happens to me, 40 years on, I try to do the same.

Despite some of his friends' doom-laden predictions, the farm park was doing well and Dad was delighted – not to mention relieved – to see his vision validated. My sisters and I began to be drafted in to help him give demonstrations to the visitors.

Dad had taught all of us from a very early age how to lamb a ewe. When we were kids, our small, nimble hands made us especially useful. It is a fascinating process, and even today I haven't lost the sense of wonder at seeing a life being born.

The trick is that a lamb has to come out with its two front feet and nose first. If it has a leg back or its head back, you need to put your hand inside the ewe and manipulate the lamb into the correct position. It is particularly hard to do with rare-breed sheep, which often have very small pelvises.

We would put a little gel or soap on our hands to make them slippery and gently ease the lamb out of the mother. It was not always easy. Sometimes in a problematic birth the lamb would be positioned the wrong way round, or the poor little thing's legs would be trapped behind it.

Dad or one of our stockmen would generally take over then, donning rubber gloves and gently manoeuvring the creature into place inside its mother's womb. Sometimes they would have to fasten a noose made of string around the lamb's head, behind the ears and into the mouth to avoid crushing the windpipe and strangling it. Once it was born, getting the lamb to breathe involved massaging its chest, tickling its nose with straw and, if that didn't work, gently swinging it by its back legs.

That is a skilled, delicate operation, although thankfully it normally seemed to work. Yet not every lamb makes it. Even today, when they get the best and most skilled midwife care possible, around 7 per cent of lambs – and 2 per cent of the ewes – don't survive the birth.

Though we were only young children, all this for us was part of life's rich tapestry and we quickly learnt about life and death. Many children are sheltered from such things, but I believe it is an important part of education in the ways of nature.

Under Dad's sympathetic tutelage, all four of us kids became competent lambers, with Libby and I the most enthusiastic. We graduated to doing it in front of the farm park crowds, with Dad providing the running commentary, and after some initial nerves, I really enjoyed doing those shows.

That was interesting. I never had any youthful desire to be the centre of attention, and certainly not to be famous, but there again, I loved being in the drama productions at Cheltenham. I guess maybe there always was a show-off in there.

Another of my farming rites of passage came when Dad and one of his stockmen, Robert Boodle, taught me how to milk a cow.

This had been Dad's favourite job as a boy when he used to hang out at Park Farm in Middlesex. He often spoke about it eloquently and poetically, sharing his memories of leaning into the warmth of the cow and coaxing the milk from the udders.

We didn't ever have a dairy herd on the farm and the rare-breed cows reared their own calves so we only really had to milk them if they had mastitis and needed milking out to remove the pressure and infected milk, or sometimes at calving time, when they initially had too much milk for the newborn calf. For our milking demonstrations at the farm park we would use a Gloucester cow to hand-milk.

I loved doing it. The important thing to realize is that a cow has four teats, and in the udder each teat has its own bag of milk. The art is to trap the milk in the teat with your thumb and your forefinger by squeezing the teat, so that the milk can't go back up into the udder.

With your other fingers, you then have to squeeze carefully downwards so that the milk is forced out of the orifice at the end of the teat, which is actually quite tiny. It's a gentle and subtle process, and the only way to get really good at it is by repeated practice.

If you handle it too roughly and the milk retreats back up, it can cause discomfort for the cow and she is likely to try and knock you away with a sharp kick. Thankfully, our house cow for the demonstrations was fairly placid.

One tip that Dad gave me was that as you sit on the milking stool at the side of the cow, you must lean forward and put the top of your head into the flank of the cow, just in front of her thighbone. It means if she decides to lift her leg to move you away, you can feel the kick coming and move back with the bucket in your hand to avoid the strike.

When a cow kicks its back legs they swing out sideways, so the safest place to milk an unwilling cow, particularly if she is in a cattle crush, is right behind her. However, this puts you in another kind of danger zone as the cow's udder is very near to her back end.

When cows are on spring grass, their dung comes out like slurry. They also tend to relieve themselves if they are in an unfamiliar situation or around strangers – i.e. in a handling system or a milking parlour.

Let's just say that being covered in poo is an occupational hazard for a modern dairy farmer. Maybe it's just as well that Bemborough has never had a dairy herd.

As I headed towards my teens, in some ways I was leading a strange life of contrasts. I loved the freedom and closeness of life on the land, but was still spending my weekdays among the restrictions and rigid formality of boarding school.

I would tell my closest friends at Cheltenham about the farm and a few times some of them came to spend the weekend or visited in the school holidays. They loved it and I guess it helped them to understand why I was banging on about it all the time.

Once, Dad spoke to Mr Davies and the headmaster gave permission for a school trip to Bemborough. Everybody piled on to a coach and Dad gave them a guided tour of the farm park. That was probably my favourite day in all of my time at Cheltenham.

Even after my chastening experience with Domino all those years earlier, I had never totally shaken off my desire to be a Cotswold cowboy. I still loved Western films and liked the idea of having a gun, and when I was about thirteen, Mum and Dad got me an air rifle. It proved to be only the start.

Dad used to go on local pheasant shoots and could see how keen I was to join him, so in time he got me a shotgun and paid for me to have shooting lessons. After that, whenever I was home and he had some time, he would take me out with Nita and we'd go out shooting rabbits and pigeons. I cherished this time with Dad.

He was still making occasional TV cameos as the BBC's 'tame farmer', and at the end of the seventies he got asked to take on a new role. He became a regular presenter of a new rural affairs show, *In the Country*, alongside Angela Rippon and Phil Drabble.

Angela Rippon was a huge name at that point as she had spent years reading the BBC evening news as well as charming the nation with a surprise appearance as a high-kicking chorus girl on a *Morecambe & Wise Show* Christmas special. Yet she had no airs and graces: I met her when she filmed on the farm and although she was very correct and professional in her work, she was approachable off camera and seemed lovely.

Phil Drabble was also great and was a proper countryman who hosted the TV sheepdog trials show *One Man and His Dog*. I once visited his house, where he had literally hundreds of guinea pigs living in his garage, who ran out through little popholes to graze on his lawn.

Life at Cheltenham rolled on and when I was fourteen I transferred from the junior school to the senior school across the road. This was quite an eye-opener – and not in a good way.

Although I was never exactly a willing scholar, I suppose by then I was a bit of a big fish in the little pool of junior school. I was one of the oldest kids, doing OK in my classes, I was a prefect, and I was still the captain of the school rugby team.

This easy life came crashing to a halt when I graduated to the senior school. If going to boarding school at eight had shown me the loneliness that that institution can engender, the senior school demonstrated its capacity for arbitrary cruelty.

The age range in the school was fourteen to eighteen and I didn't like the look of some of the older boys at all. Were they really the kind of adults that the school was trying to churn out? They were arrogant, pompous and full of themselves, and there was a lot of *Lord of the Flies*-type bullying.

The prefects would dispense random punishments such as making you stand in a corner of the room with your arms out for hours until they ached, or whipping you with towels. It was painful and humiliating, and I wondered what on earth they were getting out of it.

I tried to keep my head down and didn't get the worst of the bullying, but now and again I got a bit of a kicking from some senior boy who decided he didn't like the look of me. I never went to the teachers, or even told my parents. I don't know why. It just seemed that the safest thing was not to make a fuss.

Things improved a little in the second year, when we all got individual rooms with at least a degree of privacy. It was nice at least to be able to spend some time in your own space.

Academically, I was still studying hard, largely because I had no choice, and so keeping my head above water. Biology and Geography were my best subjects. I wasn't great at Maths or languages, and I had to take extra English lessons because I was struggling a bit. To be honest, I think I have always been slightly dyslexic.

My favourite subject, oddly enough, was Art, and particularly pottery. I used to really like throwing pots on the school's electric wheel and got quite skilled at this. Some of my pots were works of art, if I do say so myself.

Yet sport was still my main passion. As well as continuing to play my first love, rugby, I became very good at hockey. The selectors for Gloucestershire County came to watch one of our games and selected three of us for trials, including myself. It was a thrill for me to go on to captain Gloucestershire Under-16s.

Obviously the early teens are when every boy suddenly gets interested in girls, and I was definitely no exception. I had brief liaisons with two girls from the girls' school called Jackie and Priscilla, then I dated Clara, whom I first met and started chatting to in the street in Cheltenham.

God knows what we talked about, because I have never been any good with chat-up lines. In any case, like most teenage relationships, none of them lasted very long.

When I was sixteen, it was time for my O levels and all of those hours of stultifying study in the dorm and the school library came off. I passed eleven. They weren't all great grades, or anything, but it was a very decent performance and I was really pleased, as were my parents.

The only exam I remember clearly is pottery. We had to make something that showed the conflict between convex and concave forms, and I threw loads of pots, cut them up and made this amazing sculpture inspired by the layers of an onion. I was so proud of it, and I even got a grade A – very rare for me – for pottery. For a while, I thought that maybe that would be my future career, but that idea didn't last long. I couldn't imagine there was much money in it.

In any case, Cheltenham and I were to go our separate ways before I began my A levels. I was tired of being away from the farm, I hated the bullying and the snobbery, and I just didn't think I could face two more years of the senior school.

I found an ally in my youngest sister, Becca, who at the time was going through a rebellious, anti-establishment punk phase. She didn't like me being unhappy there and told me that I shouldn't be in the bourgeois public school system and had to get out.

So I went to my parents and told them that I really wanted

to leave boarding school and come home. There was a lot about it that I didn't like, I wasn't enjoying it, and I wanted out.

Mum and Dad didn't really argue with me. I guess they just figured that I was sixteen years old, I knew my own mind and, in any case, I had knuckled down, done nine years – nine years! – at public school and passed my exams. They could hardly accuse me of not giving it a go.

I think in some ways it was also a relief to them. They had never been keen on sending me away in the first place, and the school fees had cost them an arm and a leg. The extra money for the farm would come in handy, and they simply decided if I didn't want to be there, what was the point?

So I said goodbye to the dorms, playing fields and quads of Cheltenham and moved back home, ready to begin A levels at the local state Westwood's Grammar School when summer was over. I left boarding school with a huge amount of relief but also some mixed feelings.

After those first weeks, I had never hated the school as such, and in fact nowadays I look back at those years with an odd fondness. I enjoyed the sport, and cycling around the playing grounds and catching minnows in the lake, and I made some great friends there.

If I had attended Cheltenham College as a day pupil, as half of the boys did, I would probably have loved it. What I had hated was being away from my home, and being wrenched away from the bosom of my family at such a young age.

My parents sent me to boarding school with the very best of intentions and with heavy hearts, and I don't have a sliver of resentment towards them for it. In many ways I am grateful, because it gave me an amazing education, and there was no way I would have passed so many exams without it.

Public school gave me a lot. I had opportunities in sport that I would never have got otherwise and it helped me to develop decent social skills and the ability to interact with people.

Even so, the pain of being apart from my family had just bitten too hard, and too deep, for too long. I have many good friends who send their kids away to study, and that is fair enough – it is entirely their decision.

But if I learnt one thing in my time at public school, it is that I would never, ever send my own children away to board.

CHAPTER 5

Lads Will Be Lads

They say that you should always be careful what you wish for, because it might just come true. When I left boarding school to move back to Bemborough Farm in 1982, aged sixteen, I felt as happy as if I had won the lottery (or in those days, I suppose, the football pools).

The only problem is that some people who win the lottery don't spend their winnings all that wisely.

When I moved back into my bedroom at home at the end of my last term at Cheltenham, it had been nine years since I'd lived there full-time. It was hard not to notice that a lot had changed in the atmosphere in the house.

My sisters had all left. Libby, Lolo and Becca had all gone to Cheltenham Tech at sixteen to take A levels and then headed off to university. Libby had gone to Oxford to study zoology, Lolo was in London studying anthropology and Becca had just joined her in the capital to do stage management.

I think during my absence they had all got a bit restless. Bemborough Farm is pretty remote, and I guess as they hit their teenage years they had all felt isolated and longed for life and adventure and to go out and see the world, as most adolescents do.

I was the opposite: I was just so delighted to be home! Nita was as happy as me that I was back. I quickly fell into my new routine of getting the bus to Westwood's Grammar School every morning, secure in the knowledge that I would be getting the same bus home every afternoon, rather than heading for a grim dorm.

I fitted into the new school at once. I got to know people and made friends right away. Once again my friend Jo Hickman was there, in the upper sixth, and she showed me round just like she had at primary school.

This time, however, although a little apprehensive – as anybody going to a new school would be – I was also excited. I registered to study A levels in Geography, Biology, Geology and something called General Studies and, totally demob-happy from Cheltenham, set about enjoying myself.

The facilities at my new school were nothing like those at the college. Where boarding school had vast sports fields with pristine turf, Westwood's had sloping pitches that led down to the neighbouring sewage works. Some of the classes took place in Portacabins.

This didn't bother me in the slightest. Westwood's Grammar suited me down to the ground.

The school played football and cricket and I managed to get into the first team for both. Unfortunately my hockey career was left behind, but I was determined not to lose rugby.

Together with a few mates in my year, we decided to join the local rugby team at Stow-on-the-Wold. I was introduced to the club by a great friend of Mum and Dad's, John Wright, the local builder and undertaker.

John was a wonderful man and larger than life in every way. He looked after us seventeen-year-olds like adopted sons, encouraged us to play hard on the pitch and then led the singing in the bar, whether we had won or lost.

To start with I was too small to play for the firsts – this was of course men's rugby now, with some monstrous blokes. I soon grew and filled out and made my way into the first team, and I was to play on and off for Stow-on-the-Wold for the next fifteen years.

Westwood's Grammar School had a lovely, friendly and relaxed atmosphere. The teachers were very good and not overly strict, although they expected the sixth-formers to show some initiative and self-discipline towards their studies.

Being a grammar, it was reserved for pupils who had passed their eleven-plus exams and therefore pitched at a fairly high academic level. I clearly needed to study very hard to do well there.

Unfortunately, having come from a school where there were firm timetables and very strict teachers, I hadn't learnt self-discipline and was easily distracted.

Leaving boarding school had felt like escaping prison and suddenly I had all this freedom. In its way, Cheltenham was as institutionalizing as the army: you had no choice but to study hard, polish your boots and iron your shirt. Discipline was drilled into you every day.

But now I was on civvy street – and I could do whatever I wanted. It was hard not to rebel a little, and so that was exactly what I did. I wanted to enjoy myself in the normal ways that you just couldn't at boarding school.

I went to my lessons and tried to concentrate, but when the girls' hockey was taking place just outside the window it was very difficult to pay attention to tectonic plate movement in Geology. Mr Kennedy, who was a brilliant teacher, told elaborate stories during his lessons to break the monotony of learning.

It was a great tactic, but it didn't always work. One day he noticed me struggling to concentrate and instead gazing out of the window watching the hockey. The girls were making a right mess of training because the PE teacher was off sick. The team captain was trying to control things, and failing badly.

Mr Kennedy was a keen sportsman and knew I had played hockey for the county. I think he had noticed the chaos so sent me off to get my sports kit and take the hockey lesson. This was heaven – released from class to coach sixteen-year-old girls at hockey!

My attitude to homework was pretty cavalier. I'd tell my mum that I was off to my bedroom to do some work, but would end up sneaking out to take Nita for a walk, do some shooting or help the shepherds on the farm.

It made sense to me. There are always important jobs to do on a farm, and in my eyes these took priority. I think my dad was pleased to have the extra pair of hands, too.

I suppose my easy-going, carefree attitude made me quite popular at Westwood's Grammar, which was useful because I was always on the lookout for a nice girlfriend. And one girl in particular had caught my eye.

Charlie Gilbert was a fun, very pretty blonde girl in the year below me whose dad was a local butcher. I first noticed her when I was asked to demonstrate some of my pottery skills to her class, which was a very welcome excuse to show off. The school had only recently got a potter's wheel and the art teacher, although brilliant with the brush, was no potter, so was glad of my help.

I thought Charlie was gorgeous and I definitely fancied her, but I can't pretend it was love at first sight like in the movies. We got on, though, and became good mates and part of the very lively sixth-form social scene that was going on then.

A whole gang of us would head off to the local café during school lunchtimes, go to each other's houses and, whenever we could, go to the pub in the evenings. We would have a few pints of the local Donnington BB bitter (with lemonade to take the horrible taste away) down the Farmers Arms, stick the jukebox on and play pool or skittles.

Having discovered girls and beer, this was probably the first time in my youth that my life did not revolve totally around the farm. Even so, I was still hugely happy helping Dad out or giving demonstrations at the farm park – and he and Mum had worked out a plan to keep me motivated.

When I moved back home at sixteen, they began paying me to help on the farm. It was definitely an added incentive. The money wasn't much but it was enough to buy some vaguely cool clothes and lots of Donnington BB to drink while I wore them.

So most evenings I would come home from school, change out of my uniform and work for a couple of hours. There was always plenty to do, and if the alternative was doing my boring homework, I was even happier to muck in.

Much like Dad, I have always been drawn to the animal side of farming rather than the arable. However, the crops were just as important at Bemborough, if not more so, so I would also help John Neave with that side of the business.

Uncle John had three tractor drivers who regarded their own machines as sacrosanct. Nevertheless, once I had left Cheltenham I was sometimes allowed to drive them. I had a little open-cab Dexta tractor to turn over any wet hay and straw, and graduated to the grain carts.

Yet I still gravitated naturally towards the livestock side of things, and I was delighted to be educated in the ancient and venerable art of sheep shearing by a local expert, Bob Burt, who went by the self-explanatory nickname of Bob the Cider Drinker.

Bob used to come to the farm to shear for Dad, and taught me how to use the electric shears (he could also use hand shears, like great big pairs of scissors, but that was a real skill and very hard work). Much like human hair-clippers, the electric shears had attachments for cutting and for combing that you had to change when they got blunt.

The modern technique for sheep shearing is to stretch the sheep's skin with one hand and move the shears up and down the flank with the other. Bob favoured an old-fashioned method of shearing around and around the body. My own technique was a bit Heath Robinson, but I was soon giving demonstrations in the farm park.

The first trick to shearing is holding the sheep still, which they don't tend to want you to do. First you set them down so they are comfortable, which means that they are resting on their thighs and not their backbone.

It's crucial to keep their feet in the air, because if one foot so much as touches the ground they will be scrambling to their feet and escaping. Then you move the sheep into about six or seven different positions as you basically pivot it around the electric machine.

Each movement of the shear is known as a blow, and you try to move it down the sheep's belly, around its back leg and up to the neck then down one side, before repeating the process on the other. The secret is to do it as quickly as possible to cause the least stress you can to the sheep – and to the shearer.

If you get the sheep's body in the wrong position, the skin wrinkles and the shears can cut it, which is not great for the sheep and looks unprofessional in a demonstration. So you need to keep the sheep in such a position that the skin is tight and the shears glide over the top of it.

As long as the sheep is being held in the correct position it shouldn't fight to get free. However, the rams of many of our rare-breed sheep, such as Jacob, Manx Loaghtan and Hebridean, have four very long horns that you have no choice but to tuck between your legs during the shearing process – a risky business indeed!

When I was a callow teenager, some of those sheep weighed more than I did and we would have epic tussles. I didn't win all of them. I would reel away from a lengthy sheep shearing session with big black bruises all over my legs, my tummy and even my chest.

Despite this, I loved it, and still do. Sheep shearing is almost like a sport, you get such a sweat on doing it, and of course there is always the personal challenge of seeing how many you can do in one day. I think my personal best to date is about 120, which is nowhere near the output of the professional shearers who use the Bowen method.

This was named after a New Zealand shearer called Godfrey Bowen, who was to transform shearing in the mid-twentieth century by honing a new technique based on the best of all the existing styles. In 1957, he broke the world record for a second time by shearing a scarcely believable 463 sheep in nine hours.

It may look a rudimentary skill to the untrained eye but at its best sheep shearing is a graceful art form. Consider what the *Guardian* newspaper once wrote about seeing the great Mr Bowen in his pomp:

> Godfrey Bowen's arms flow with the grace of a Nureyev shaping up to an arabesque, or a Barbirolli bringing in the cellos. Watching him shear is even more remarkable than seeing a finely tuned machine.

Working with sheep, and livestock in general, is certainly a good way to keep fit and strong. Sheep can be fleet of foot, especially if you are trying to get hold of them to de-maggot them or remove bramble from their wool. Often I would find myself sprinting full-pelt after an errant sheep and rugby-tackling it as if playing for Stow-on-the-Wold.

When I was a teenager, a lot of international rugby players were farmers by day, which makes sense. After I told my mates on the Stow team about my farm exertions, a couple of them came to help me out at Bemborough and viewed it as bonus training.

Another job you have to really put your back into is cleaning out the stables. Our stables were basically loose boxes in the yard, right next to the farmhouse, where we kept various animals from pigs to cattle.

We bedded the animals down with straw, adding a clean bed to the top so the muck was left underneath, where it became compacted. This is known as deep litter bedding but, of course, once it got too deep it needed to be cleaned out. The doors of the loose boxes were too small to get any kind of machine inside, so I would have to roll up my sleeves and go in with a fork.

As with everything in farming, there is an art to it. Because the straw is so layered, you don't want to dig it the way that you would dig a garden. Instead you scrape it with a muck fork, which is a four-pronged fork, rather than a normal pitchfork, which has two prongs. This means it is hard work, but not actually backbreaking.

There would normally be two of us in the stable, one scraping the muck and throwing it to the door of the box, and the other chucking it out into the bucket of a tractor in the yard. From there, it was loaded into a trailer, then carted to the muckheap. It was certainly handy having rugby mates along to take on some of the workload.

Now I was on the payroll part-time, I would do my fair share of work during the lambing season. During springtime I got the bus home from school, changed into my work clothes and went straight out to the yard and the sheep shed.

Some evenings I would be heading off to the pub for a drink, and Dad would say, 'Well, you check the sheep when you get back in because I am off to bed, and you are on the 11-till-2 shift.' So I'd have a couple of pints inside me, and get back to find it all kicking off in the lambing shed.

Sometimes a mate would come back with me to help me out and we would be busy until two in the morning, lambing ewes, feeding weak lambs and trying to keep on top of everything. I would crawl into bed in the early hours and have to be up at eight for school.

There again, what with farming, girls and my reliably active social life, school was a long way down my list of priorities by now. Charlie and I had started seeing each other, although we didn't go on one-to-one dates as much as we went around in a big gang with our mates.

We were still hanging out down the Farmers Arms, not to mention attending Young Farmers Society meetings and the Friday- and Saturday-night discos in local villages such as Guiting, Chedworth and Bourton-on-the-Water. We would all have a few drinks and then crash at somebody's house.

The Young Farmers Society meetings were good fun. The local branch in Shipston would hold talks and competitions and I'd find myself competing against other YFS branches at stock judging or dressing a chicken (I avoided the flower arranging, which wasn't my strongest suit).

The discos were slightly hairier. With the alcohol flowing they would often degenerate into fights, although thankfully I always steered clear of those. When the local biker gangs took to showing up for a scrap, well, that was the end of the discos.

While this was all going on, I was enduring that other teenage rite of passage of desperately trying to pass my driving test. It took me rather more attempts than it does most young drivers (or had taken any of my sisters).

To be specific, it took me four tests.

I took my first one just after I turned seventeen. I was so confident that I didn't even bother to have any lessons. I had been driving tractors and an old Land Rover Defender around the farm for years – how much harder could driving on a road be?

In fact, I thought it would be easier. There would be no gates to open, no cows in the way, I wouldn't have to whistle out of the window to move sheep along – what a doddle! I rolled up to my test in Cheltenham expecting it to be something of a formality.

How wrong I was. It had until then slipped my attention that there were other, rather important aspects of driving that had never concerned me as I tootled around our fields in the Land Rover. Stuff like mirror-signal-manoeuvre, for example. Or using your indicators.

I failed my first test for being over-cautious. Maybe I was driving at tractor speed? I was determined not to make the same mistake on my second test a few weeks later, but maybe I over-compensated as I was failed for pulling out at a junction too quickly.

My third test was a bit of a disaster. My mum was out so my dad promised that he would drive me to the test but he was in the fields working on some sheep and forgot all about it. I had to speed over to the field to fetch him, spattering the car with good old Bemborough mud as I went.

Covered in sheep muck, Dad jumped into the car and drove straight to the testing centre in his wellies. We must have looked a pretty rum pair in the waiting room: an old farmer stinking of sheep and his spotty, ginger-haired son.

From the look that the inspector gave us as he came in, I reckon I had failed before I even got in the car.

At this point, I started thinking that maybe the car was part of the problem. I had taken my first three tests in my sister Becca's battered old Morris Marina, which she had left on the farm when she went to London.

Becca's car was rather distinctive, in that after she bought it second-hand she had painted it a disturbingly bright red, for no reason other than she felt like it. As we had all been using it as an old banger to get around the farm for months, the Marina was also looking somewhat worse for wear.

Could it be that Cheltenham's driving-test examiners were predisposed against seventeen-year-old lads turning up for their test in flaking, old, bright-scarlet rust-buckets? I decided that they might be, and tried another tack.

I took my first-ever driving lessons and the instructor was actually quite impressed with my co-ordination and general driving skills. He helped to iron out a few of my more, shall we say, agricultural driving habits and I took my fourth test in his shiny, immaculate car. That time I sailed through it.

Yet passing my driving test was to prove a decidedly mixed blessing. It was only a matter of days later that I had my first crash.

I had borrowed another sister's car – Libby's Austin Maxi – to drive to a rugby match at Stow-on-the-Wold. After the game I went to the pub with a couple of teammates and probably had a pint or two more than I should. I'm not proud of it, but that sort of thing went on a lot in rural areas back then. Nobody really gave it a second thought.

As I pulled out of the car park, I saw a car coming towards me but knew I had time to get out before it reached me. That was before I saw the speeding car that was overtaking it. I swerved to avoid it and drove straight into a ditch.

We had to leave the car there and a mate drove me to his house. I phoned Dad and confessed what had happened, and my call to Bemborough was rapidly followed by another one – from the police.

Dad told the police I wasn't there and persuaded them not to speak to me until the morning, which was probably a good thing as I may well have been over the limit. The police came to my mate's house the next day and gave me a good ticking-off before going over to pull the Austin out of the ditch.

Libby was furious at what I had done to her car, largely because she was planning to sell it in the near future, and I had to pay the local garage to fix it up. It was also one of the very few times in my life that I ever saw Dad lose his rag and shout at me.

Dad never really liked drinking. If he ever went out he would have a pint and a half, but never any more than that. Like many things about him, the reason was only ever slowly to become clear to me as the years went by.

His own parents, it seemed, had both been quite enthusiastic drinkers. His father, Lally, was part of a fairly louche London showbiz set and certainly not averse to an after-show tipple or ten. His mum and dad loved him very much and showed him a huge amount of attention, but they both loved to party too.

They often had showbiz types and celebrities of the time back to the house. Dad would sit on the stairs and listen to the laughter and stories rising up from down below. This must have been an amazing experience for a young boy – but too much alcohol inevitably has its downsides.

Another time he told me that Lally and Billie had both been ferocious chain-smokers and he hated the smell of cigarette smoke. As a child, Dad suffered from travel sickness, which wasn't helped by his parents constantly smoking in the car.

Dad would often have to ask them to stop the car to be sick. That didn't stop them smoking: they would simply wind the windows down. It was just one of a drip-drip-drip of stories that made me wonder exactly what my dad's childhood had been like.

Parking Libby's Austin in a ditch certainly taught me my lesson on the drink-driving front and I never did it again. In any case, I had another, unavoidable-looking car crash looming on my horizon. My school exams were coming up.

Despite the best efforts of Westwood's Grammar, I had done hardly any work towards my A levels. I just had too much fun stuff going on to bother with studying. Mum could see I was slacking and would send me to my room to do my home-work but, well, you can lead a horse to water and all that ...

I knew my reckoning was coming and I went into denial. On the day of the first exam I really didn't want to go, and told Mum that I was sick. She saw straight through my pathetic story and told me, 'Go and do it. Go and face your demons.'

I was floundering in the exam halls as two years of dossing and ignoring my coursework caught up with me. Geography was my favourite subject and the teacher, Mr Kennedy, was great, but halfway through the paper I realized that I just couldn't do it.

Instead, I drew a picture of a pint of Guinness with a hand around it and waved to Mr Kennedy to gain his attention. When he came over to me, I passed the picture to him. He frowned at me, took it to a corner of the room and brought it back a minute later. In red, he had ticked it and marked it: 10/10.

Yet really it was no laughing matter. I was expecting the worst and it duly arrived. That summer, when the letter from the examining board arrived at Bemborough Farm, it contained no surprises at all:

BIOLOGY	FAIL
GENERAL STUDIES	FAIL
GEOGRAPHY	O LEVEL EQUIVALENT
GEOLOGY	O LEVEL EQUIVALENT

So I had taken four A levels and failed the lot. Clutching the piece of paper, I realized that here were my chickens coming home to roost.

It was pretty awful. My parents didn't give me too much of a hard time but they were really disappointed. I felt as if I had let them down, let my teachers down and, especially, I had let myself down. Being Jack the lad didn't feel quite so funny now.

It felt like a wake-up call, because it was. I was eighteen and I had completely wasted the last two years. What was I going to do next? In fact, what was I going to do with my life?

I considered my options. The idea of pottery came briefly to the fore again, but it always seemed unrealistic and my heart wasn't really in it. If I were honest, I couldn't really imagine spending my life sitting at a clay wheel.

How about acting? I had always enjoyed being in the school plays and had occasionally toyed with the idea of following it as a career. Again, however, when I looked at this notion in the cold light of day, it seemed pretty unlikely.

Was I even good enough? And, in any case, although I loved Uncle Nicky, I had observed his lifestyle for years and wasn't sure I fancied it. Acting seemed to be feast or famine. Nicky would get a starring part in a play or a big TV role, become over-excited and spend all the money, then be out of work and broke for months. That didn't appeal to me.

No, there was only really one option. I wanted to do the thing that I had longed to do ever since I was four years old, chasing chickens around the yard, helping Dad to herd sheep and following him around the farm like a pathologically eager shadow.

It was a no-brainer. I wanted to be a farmer, and I wanted to succeed the Bemborough Farm tenancy from Dad one day. So there was only one thing for it. I was going to have to take a deep breath and knuckle down.

I was going to have to try to get into agricultural college.

CHAPTER 6

'Anything Over 45 Per Cent Is Wasted Effort'

When they hit their teenage years, my sisters had all become frustrated by the remoteness of Bemborough Farm and longed for adventure and big-city life. I never suffered quite the same degree of *wanderlust*, but when it came to applying to agricultural college, I also decided to get away.

Cirencester Agricultural College was just down the road but it specialized in land management and attracted posh landed gentry, which put me off. However, I knew a lad from a local village who had studied at Seale-Hayne College in Newton Abbot, and he raved about the place.

It sounded interesting so Mum and Dad drove me down to Devon to have a look around. I liked the look of the college from the start and particularly liked the fact that they told me they would take me as long as I passed one A level. A lot of colleges were asking for three.

So, Seale-Hayne it was. Hopefully!

Back then, all agricultural colleges insisted on one particular condition before accepting students: you had to have spent a year working on a farm that was not the farm where you grew up. Well, sometimes in life it is not what you know but who you know, and at this point nepotism came firmly into play.

While filming *In the Country*, Dad had gone with Angela Rippon to shoot a report on the Chatsworth Estate in Derbyshire. He had hit it off with the owner, the Duchess of Devonshire, and the estate manager, and now contacted them to ask if they might consider taking me for a year's placement.

They were open to the idea, so I went for an interview with the estate manager, the farm manager and the Duchess of Devonshire herself. They grilled me on what I had learned at home: could I foot-trim or turn a sheep, had I worked with cattle, could I calve a cow, could I drive a tractor?

Dad had taught me well so my answer to almost everything was 'Yes' and it was fairly clear that I had all the skills they were looking for. Yet the interview was nerve-wracking and a bit scary: after all, I was a gawky eighteen-year-old trying to talk to a duchess.

In fact, she was more than 'just' a duchess. Deborah Vivienne Cavendish was originally born Deborah Vivienne Freeman-Mitford and was the youngest of the famous Mitford sisters, the six aristocratic siblings who were such major – and controversial – figures in British society in the 1930s and 1940s.

After my interview, she invited me for lunch in Chatsworth House and it was the whole silver-service *Downton Abbey* scene, with butlers and footmen waiting on us. It was terrifying, and when I mistakenly put my salad on my plate rather than in my salad bowl, I felt mortified.

I didn't need to. The Duchess, who was in her sixties, had sat me next to her and was very warm and charming. She asked me what I was interested in, and we talked about farming, shooting, fishing and country life as a whole.

After Dad had visited Chatsworth with Angela Rippon, he had helped the Duchess to open her own little rare breed farm park. When she had inherited Chatsworth House she had been faced with crippling inheritance tax bills, which meant that the estate was in financial difficulties.

The Duchess had sold off a lot of art, put the house into a trust and opened it to the public, and was casting around for other ways to fund her estate – hence the farm park. It was fascinating to realize that somebody who owned such a huge house and estate could be struggling.

In fact, her situation is not so unusual for the landed gentry. Families inherit vast piles that cost hundreds of thousands of pounds to maintain every year and they have no income to do so. It's why so many aristocratic homes become National Trust properties, and also why the Duchess years later agreed to the 2005 film *Pride & Prejudice* using Chatsworth House as Pemberley.

The Duchess and I got on well and she offered me the job on the spot. She would give me a contract for a year to work on the farm, with the gamekeepers and with the estate manager, to get a good overview of running a farm on an estate.

The Chatsworth estate was around 8,000 acres and included woodland, lakes and fishing on the river, plus deer, a dairy herd, sheep and cattle grazing on moorland and in lowland pastures, as well as the arable farm. Including me, there were around ten staff employed to run the farm.

Accommodation-wise, I was to share a house on the estate with three men – Tony, Jim and Mark – who were renting it and working at various non-farming jobs locally. They were all a few years older than me, but they took me under their wing and we rubbed along well.

Initially life at Chatsworth was exhausting, and certainly kept me fit. My house was a couple of fields away from the farm, so every morning I would be out of bed and running frantically over the land to begin work at 7.30.

My duties were all jobs that I was fairly used to. I would be driving tractors, feeding and bedding down the cows, and looking after the sheep: feeding, lambing, foot trimming, dipping and drenching them.

The downside to my job was that it was work experience and therefore unpaid until I had worked a 40-hour week. It meant that I had to work an eight-hour day before I even began to earn anything, so I was always keen as hell to work overtime. It made for some very long shifts.

In addition to the work experience, of course, I had to re-sit and pass one of my A levels to secure my place at Seale-Hayne. Once again, Dad helped me out. I enrolled at Chesterfield Tech to retake Geology A level and Dad paid a private tutor he knew there to give me one-to-one tuition.

So, every Tuesday, after I had finished work on the estate, I jumped into my car and drove across the Peak District for classes at Chesterfield Tech. On alternate weeks I saw Dad's friend for extra tuition. It was all a bit of a grind after doing a full day's slog on the estate, but I knew it would be worth it and therefore knuckled down.

The house we lived in at Chatsworth was freezing cold and the four of us would often spend the evenings huddled around the Aga or the open fire. That didn't stop us from turning it into quite the party house. We had a few very lively evenings there.

The place was exactly as messy as you would expect a house rented by four blokes to be. Tony, Jim and Mark got on my case for shirking my share of the housework, but I made up for this by doing most of the cooking. Well, that was my defence, anyway.

While I was at Chatsworth, Mum got seriously ill. She was diagnosed with breast cancer and apparently the initial prognosis from the specialists was not good at all. Over a few weeks she was to have no less than three operations.

I was naturally incredibly worried about her but didn't know exactly how serious the situation was, even when Libby moved back home to help out. Mum and Dad were very much of the stiff-upper-lip generation who play things down and don't want to make a fuss or unduly worry their kids.

They were always very good at keeping things to themselves – or very bad at sharing problems, whichever way you want to see it. In any case, Mum displayed her trademark grit and determination to beat the cancer and has happily remained clear ever since.

Charlie and I had stopped dating by then. We didn't have any big rows or bust-ups: we just vaguely drifted apart, in the way that most teenage relationships come to an end. She was still at Westwood's doing her A levels the year that I went to Chatsworth.

It had all been perfectly amicable – in fact, I went back home for her eighteenth birthday party – but it did also leave me free to meet somebody new. I met my next girlfriend at one of the parties that we threw in the house at Chatsworth. It was great to date a local girl who knew the area and had lots of friends in the district, which helped me to feel welcome and part of the social scene.

When I wasn't working on the estate, studying for my A level or seeing my girlfriend, I was playing rugby. After getting a few games for Bakewell, I got noticed and was selected to represent the Derbyshire county team, which was a big deal for me.

It was an even greater honour to be asked to play for the Three Counties, the team that represents Nottinghamshire, Lincolnshire and Derbyshire. This was the highest level of rugby I ever played and I loved it.

Rugby can be a pretty hard sport and I often came home from games with black eyes, or covered in bruises and stud marks. Thankfully, I managed to avoid any major breaks or concussions and when you are young you recover pretty quickly. Throughout the country rugby players are generally great people and Derbyshire was no exception.

I was working hard and enjoying life at Chatsworth and used to bump into the Duchess around the estate quite a bit. She liked shooting and was a good shot, and if I wasn't playing rugby on a Saturday I would join the other staff and locals being paid £10 each to beat the pheasants out of the woods for her and her friends.

The Duchess was always engaging and inclusive. A lot of her shoot guests wouldn't speak to the beaters and gamekeepers and probably considered us to be lowlife, but she would say hello and chat, which I was always very impressed by.

Her manner and way with people always stuck with me, and the Duchess reminded me of Dad in some ways, as he too always had time to stop and talk to people no matter what their background.

Once she spotted me among the beaters, called me over and introduced me to a man she described as 'somebody who farms in the Cotswolds – one of your local neighbours'. It was Lord Vestey from the Vestey Estate, who was like royalty around our way. We chatted for a while.

I was still trekking over to Chesterfield every Tuesday night to cram for my Geology retake and finding it hard going. To try to help myself, I would write my essays, read them into a tape recorder then play them back in the tractor as I was rolling the fields.

It was enough to send myself to sleep.

Still, all of this uncharacteristic academic endeavour paid off for me. When I re-sat the A-level exam in Chesterfield, I even managed to restrain myself from drawing a pint of Guinness. As my year at Chatsworth was drawing to a close, my result came through:

GEOLOGY   D

It wasn't exactly a stellar performance but it was, at least, a pass, and it meant that I would be able to take up my place at Seale-Hayne. I phoned the college admissions office to give them the good news.

'Oh,' said the voice at the other end of the phone. 'You didn't need to do that – we had given you a place anyway.'

So all those midweek drives across the Peaks, hours of study and tedious days on a tractor listening to myself drone on about soil classifications had been for nothing! I didn't know whether to laugh or cry.

Perhaps I deserved it: if I had buckled down and worked hard at school, I would never have been in that situation. When I talk to young people now who are considering a career in farming, I recommend they work hard at school to gain the qualifications they need to progress to agricultural college or university.

It makes sense to them. Agriculture today is more forward-thinking and technology-aware, and so having a farming qualification will open the door to a variety of rewarding careers.

It had been a fun year at Chatsworth and I really enjoyed being back at Bemborough in the summer of '85. My place at Seale-Hayne was nailed down, for once there was no exam fear or guilt hanging over me, and the Westwood's Grammar gang were around to pick up where we had left off (which was mostly down the Farmers Arms). My girlfriend and I had drifted apart by then, so I was young, free and single.

My Uncle Nicky was still down to visit fairly often and was reliably entertaining. By now he would come with the woman who was soon to become his second wife – the Royal Ballet senior principal ballerina, Marguerite Porter.

The first time I met Marguerite, I don't think I had ever seen anyone who looked less suited to being in a farmyard. She was so delicate and dainty, slim and beautiful and looked as if she were made out of porcelain.

Marguerite had to tread carefully across our rough fields because she couldn't afford to twist her ankle and be forced to cancel major ballet productions. Yet for all this she was a lovely person when I properly got to know her, and still is.

September rolled around and it was time to head off to Devon. Academia was not my friend and I didn't imagine my HND in agriculture would be easy but if I wanted to become a farmer – and I wanted nothing else – it had to be done.

In any case, I went down to Newton Abbot in positive mood. At least I loved the subject and knew a lot about it, and I was excited about moving to a new part of the country and the prospect of the whole college experience.

For many students, going to university at eighteen or nineteen is their first time living away from home, so they feel safest moving into halls of residence. I didn't want to do that. I could cook and look after myself and I had my year in Derbyshire under my belt. I fancied a little more freedom and independence.

So I moved into an all-male self-catering house about three miles from the college. There were around 20 guys, all with our own rooms, and shared kitchens and bathrooms. There was a similar-sized all-female house next door, which didn't strike me as bad news at all.

The HND course was a mixture of lectures and practical work. Seale-Hayne had its own farm, where they taught us how to deal with and tend to various animals, as well as educating us on the day-to-day running and minutiae of farm life.

I knew a lot of it already, of course, but I still picked up some useful tips.

The lectures and academic presentations covered topics such as animal husbandry, animal biology, cropping, and financial management. Basically, it was a comprehensive, all-round course in everything you needed to be a modern farmer.

The course was hugely interesting and useful, although I found some parts of it quite difficult, particularly the hard-core scientific stuff. I was keen to learn and determined not to repeat the mistakes of Westwood's Grammar so I dutifully turned up for the lectures.

Well, most of them, anyway.

I managed to up my academic game – but not that much. I was never going to be a distinction student, but I worked reasonably hard and my marks were solid if not spectacular. After the A-level debacle, fear of failing was certainly a spur.

Yet I was also keen to do lots of partying. The pass mark for the course was 45 per cent, and my fellow students and I invented a mantra: 'Anything over 45 per cent is wasted effort.' We wanted to leave plenty of time to enjoy ourselves.

I loved Devon from the off. It was great having Plymouth and Exeter just down the road, and some lads and I would often take off for weekends messing about on the beach. I also picked up my rugby career and started playing for the college, who had a very good side.

In Devon I began dating a really nice girl who lived in the all-female house next door. However, at this stage of my life, I think I was just too much of a lad for her and after a few months she dumped me for another student.

My grandfather Leslie Henson with co-stars Fred Astaire and his sister Adele in a production of *Funny Face* at the Princess Theatre, London. (Getty Images)

Leslie and Billie off to the races.

Leslie, Billie, Nicky and Dad in the garden at Northwood, 1954.

Mum and Dad
getting married, 1957.

The Cotswolds – there's
no place like home.

Early days at the Cotswold farm park.

Leslie's sister, Great Auntie Benita, my godfather, Martin Grieves and godmother Janet Anstee with Lolo, Libby and me at my christening.

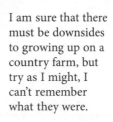

I am sure that there must be downsides to growing up on a country farm, but try as I might, I can't remember what they were.

Family time – Christmas at Bemborough.

A wannabe cowboy on naughty Domino.

Us four kids with
Uncle Nicky and
Nana Billie.

Libby, Becca, Lolo and me
helping out at Moreton Show.

Loved a feather.

Dad spreading
the word about
rare breed
conservation,
with longhorn
oxen.

Dad presenting *In
the Country* with
Angela Rippon.

Dad with his business
partner, John Neave.

First XI hockey photo at Cheltenham Junior School (I'm sat in the middle row, second from left).

'No dogs upstairs!'

Celebrating after winning the Gloucester/ Somerset league.

Exploring Ayres Rock with Duncan, 1988.

The Ford Falcon XB that we travelled around Australia in.

Dad and Libby filming for a period drama.

Mum's birthday, 26th April.

I was quite upset, but I wasn't about to fight him over her – he was huge, as well as a really good bloke. *Plenty more fish in the sea*, I thought – and in any case, they're married now, so she obviously made the right choice.

My HND was a sandwich course, so in the second year all of the students dispersed to different parts of the country to live and study on working farms.

I went to work at Home Farm in Great Wilbraham, near Cambridge. This was a deliberate decision on my part as it was an arable farm. I've always loved livestock and I felt I knew that side of things pretty well but there were definitely sizeable holes in my knowledge of growing crops and operating machinery.

If I am honest, I found the crop side of things a bit boring compared to dealing with cows and sheep, but Uncle John helped Dad to run a large arable operation at Bemborough Farm. I knew that this was an important part of the business back home, so it was important to improve my skills in this area.

My time in Cambridge was pleasant enough if a little dull. There were just three of us working on the farm: Chris, the farm manager, and Colin, the tractor driver, whom I liked but didn't have a lot in common with.

Chris was a great guy. He taught me how to drive a combine harvester and how to maintain it, from refuelling it to servicing the engine and greasing it up. I also learnt how to use the drills and the sprayers.

In the early weeks, we did a lot of spraying and a bit of fertilizing. For the spraying, I had to don protective clothing and mix up all the chemicals that tackle weeds, insects and fungi insects to eliminate any diseases that might attack the crops.

It wasn't exactly scintillating but I stuck at it and picked up knowledge that was to stand me in good stead for decades to come. I have to admit that, like most students, I managed to bend and break my fair share of equipment, but Chris and Colin were incredibly patient.

Chris was also a rugby player and invited me to go with him to play for Huntingdon Stags. I enjoyed it, as ever, but it was half an hour's drive from the farm and I didn't get to mix with the rest of the team socially over a few pints after the games, which is half the fun.

After the spraying and fertilizing, there was a lull on the farm as we waited for the harvest and I found myself doing stuff like polishing the combine, trimming the grass and painting gateposts to fill the long hours of the day. It was a bit of a yawn.

That all changed when the harvest season rolled around.

We would gather at 7.30 in the morning and spend the first two hours getting the combine ready for the day's work. By 9.30 the dew would have dried and the crop would be ready for cutting, so we would jump on and get to work.

The harvest season only lasts about eight weeks so we would be on the combine literally all day, right until the dew came in at night. Some days we would go on until midnight, making the most of the day's harvesting potential for as long as the weather permitted.

There's a real knack to combine harvesting. On the front of the combine is what is called a header, which has a reel that knocks the crop onto a knife with a great long cutter bar. This cuts the crop at the base of the stalks before the auger feeds it into the guts of the machine.

The trick is to keep the header nice and full so that you maximize the input. You have to go at the right speed so that the combine can thrash the crop efficiently. The fan blows the chaff and dust off and the wheat is filtered through into a grain pan.

If you drive too fast, it doesn't give the combine enough time to thrash all of the grain out of the straw. It can't run through the sieves quickly enough and ends up falling out of the back of the combine and being wasted.

If that happens, there are sensors that tell you that you are losing crop and you have to alter your speed and reset the sieves. You also can't try to combine when it is too wet, as it will clog up the header and you'll get nowhere.

I had never been allowed to drive the combine harvester on Bemborough before I went away to college and now I could certainly see why. It is a hugely complex and responsible job and there is so much that can go wrong. Yet the next time I was home at harvest, I couldn't wait to jump on it.

They were long and punishing days harvesting in Cambridge and I would fall into bed exhausted at the end of them. It felt as if no time had passed before my alarm would be going off and I'd be trudging into the sunrise to do it all again.

The slog was alleviated somewhat when a mate of mine from Seale-Hayne, Nick Wall, arrived to help. We needed an extra pair of hands and Nick arrived like the cavalry, which lifted my flagging spirits considerably. It always helps to have a new friendly face around.

In truth, apart from the eight weeks of harvesting, my nine months in Cambridge went quite slowly. A tutor from the college came over to visit once, I suppose to check that everything was OK and I wasn't going mad and wrecking the farm. Luckily, Chris seemed pleased with how things were going and had nice things to say about me.

Even so, it was a relief to return to Newton Abbot and to throw myself back into studying and the social whirl. It was also good to see some girls again after my monastic stint in the depths of Cambridgeshire. I met a lovely girl who was in the year below me at Seale-Hayne, and we soon started going out. This relationship was to last a couple of years.

Back in Devon, I also became friendly with a guy on my course who was to exert a vast influence on my life for the next 30 years – and rising. His name was Duncan Andrews.

Duncan was in the same year and on the same course as me at Seale-Hayne, but I hardly knew him for the first half of my time there. He had spent his first year in a hall of residence and I naturally tended to socialize mostly with the lads that I was sharing the house with (and the girls next door).

After I came back from Cambridge, however, our paths crossed a little more often. We both played rugby and we bumped into each other around the college and at parties and got on well.

Unlike me, Duncan was not from a farming background. His dad worked for a farming company, but he did their books as an agricultural accountant. Duncan had grown up on the Isles of Scilly before his family relocated to Winchester.

He was clearly a good guy, very kind and decent as well as being great fun, and we always had a really good laugh together. I also admired the fact that he was very driven and organized when it came to coursework. I was probably a little jealous and wished I had some of his dedication. We became best mates and for the final year at Seale-Hayne we decided to share a house together.

College was a brilliant place to meet like-minded people and there was a whole gang of us who got on incredibly well. Because of its location we could enjoy walking on Dartmoor, visiting lovely country pubs on Haytor and we were also close to the sea and some great beaches.

Coming from the Scillies, Duncan knew all about boats. He bought a little speedboat, which meant that we could spend the weekends at the coast water-skiing.

Yet it was as the final exams loomed that Duncan came into his own. I realized that he was the exact opposite to me when it came to studying. He had an attention span, for a start, and self-discipline, and these qualities were to prove as invaluable to me as they were to him as we crammed for the finals.

When we revised together, he laid down the ground rules and the parameters and stuck to them rigidly. 'Right, we will work for two hours and then we'll go to the pub,' he would declare, and that would be exactly what we did.

Normally I would have closed my books and been propping up the bar after 20 minutes but his work ethic and tenacity rubbed off on me and I was so glad that they did. It also made the post-revision pints taste all the sweeter, knowing that they had been earned.

It worked, as well. The exams were difficult but, thanks to my intensive cramming, not impossible, and when the list of HND agriculture passes was published, my name was on it. I even got a distinction for my arable project in Cambridge, which meant a lot to me.

After my – shall we say – rather uneven academic record in the past, my parents were delighted by this success, and I was totally over the moon. Duncan and I had worked so well together that we decided to take on another, very different joint project.

We had been talking for a few months before the exams about maybe going travelling for a year. It's a popular option for agriculture students because you can easily fund your travels by working on farms in English-speaking countries such as Australia, New Zealand or America.

The timing also felt totally right. It had been a gruelling last few months at Seale-Hayne, enduring Duncan's rigorous revision regime and then surviving the exams, and now we were through it I wanted to cast off the shackles, celebrate ... and relax.

My long-term plan was to return home and work full-time for Dad on Bemborough Farm, and I was looking forward to that, but before then I fancied a great, once-in-a-lifetime travelling adventure. After all, all work and no play can make Jack a dull boy!

Mum and Dad liked the idea and were totally supportive.

Maybe in a funny way it might even have reminded Dad of his own globetrotting adventures filming *Great Alliance*.

So, what was stopping us? Nothing at all! It was time for Duncan and me to head for a land Down Under.

CHAPTER 7

The World Is My Oyster

A lot of people are – quite understandably – cynical about students vanishing off on gap years (or 'gap yahs' as they are often mockingly called). They see them as being no more than entitled posh kids hopping from exotic beach to beach, financing the whole jolly from their well-stocked trust funds.

Well, I am sure that a lot of gap years *are* like that. But I can't think of a less accurate description of what Duncan Andrews and I did in 1988–89.

As we planned the trip, Duncan's formidable discipline and organizational skills once again came into play. Firstly we contacted ex-Seale-Hayne students from the years above us who had done similar jaunts and pumped them for info.

They were happy to oblige and in no time we had an address book full of names and contact numbers of the farmers in Australia and New Zealand who had put them up and given them work. We began to put together a hopeful itinerary.

Without the benefit of well-stocked trust funds, we knew our adventure would be expensive even if we managed to work everywhere we went, so we both did a harvest before we left in order to stash some cash. I returned to Bemborough and impressed Dad and John Neave with my newfound combine-harvester skills.

During that summer Duncan and I were talking most days as we tried to plan the trip. Duncan sorted out our flight tickets to Australia, and the pair of us went up to London together to arrange our work visas.

The harvest was over and the trees were beginning to turn autumnal as I packed my rucksack and Mum and Dad drove me down to Duncan's parents in Hampshire. After a fond farewell consisting of me promising postcards and phone calls, and them telling me just to enjoy myself, they headed off home and Duncan's folks took us to the airport.

We were bound for Perth but before that we had planned a few days stopover in South-East Asia. The 12-hour flight to Singapore seemed to last forever but the pair of us had more than enough adrenaline and excited anticipation to keep us going.

We did a little bit of tourist sightseeing in pristine, spotless Singapore then got a coach to Kuala Lumpur. It all seemed alien, exciting and incredibly overwhelming. Singapore and Malaysia were easily the two most exotic places that I had ever seen.

There again, that probably isn't saying much: Duncan and I were still both distinctly green and wet behind the ears.

In Kuala Lumpur we visited a coffee plantation, explored the local street markets and dossed down in basic backpackers' hostels. This was all new and fresh to us but in no time at all it was time to move on to the first serious part of our trip: Australia.

Before we left the UK, a rugby mate of mine had put us in touch with his friend in Perth, who said he would look after us while we found our feet. He met us at the airport, took us to his house and put us up for a couple of days.

As we shook off our jetlag, I was simultaneously excited and daunted by the thought that Duncan and I were now on our own, travelling for a year, with everything we needed on our backs, and on the other side of the world from everyone that we knew and loved. It was such an amazing buzz.

Perth seemed a pretty primitive, rough-edged city in those days but we weren't intending to hang around there. We had our first paid work waiting for us on a farm about two hours south of the city in a little town called Boyup Brook.

Although Duncan and I were basically travelling for the fun and adventure, I also intended to learn as we went along. I really wanted to experience farming elsewhere in the world, and was particularly interested to see sheep production in Australia and New Zealand first hand.

Before we'd set off on this trip of a lifetime, I had got in touch with a guy named Colin McGregor, who had worked as a shepherd at Bemborough when he was a student. He had since moved to Australia, married a New Zealand woman, and was now running a sheep-shearing gang near Perth. Colin was happy for Duncan and me to join it.

Some farms around Boyup Brook had flocks of Merino sheep, which produced some of the most valuable wool in the world. The wethers (castrated males) of the flock were kept just for their wool and never sent to market for their meat.

Colin was in charge of a gang of six shearers who were all a few years older than us. They were quite something to watch. Working in a shearing shed, they would each grab a sheep, expertly shear all its wool off in 90 seconds flat, and go on to the next sheep with a minimum of fuss. Even Godfrey Bowen would have been impressed by some of these guys.

Duncan and I didn't actually do any shearing there. We were roustabouting, which meant that we were moving up and down the line of shearers, picking up all the wool from around them.

We then had to do the skirting, which is throwing the fleece onto a table so that it lands flat, outside up, which was quite a hard skill to acquire. We then picked all the dirty bits out of the fleece.

There was a professional grader working with the team, and he would look at the fineness of the wool and grade it on the spot. Duncan and I then had to roll it up and chuck the fleece into the appropriate bin and get back to our roustabouting. The bins of fleece were pressed and packed into huge hessian bales, ready to be transported for export all over the world.

Running around behind six professional shearers, we were working absolutely flat out. The gang did eight-hour days, only stopping for short morning and afternoon breaks and for lunch, and by the end of it we'd be absolutely exhausted.

We spent six weeks with Colin's gang, travelling from farm to farm to shear their flocks. Some evenings, Duncan and I could do no more than grab a bite of food then collapse in our cheap-and-not-all-that-cheerful hostel.

On other nights we would go to the local pub with the rest of the gang. They were rowdy evenings. The lads had the true Australian work-hard, play-hard mentality and usually spent all they had just earned that day – and more – on the night's drinking and gambling. For my part, I got a taste for the local Bundaberg rum.

Australia is such a massive country and Duncan and I were trying to work out how we were going to get around. One night with the shearing gang, we met a guy who was about to go off travelling himself and wanted to sell his car.

It was an old brown Ford Falcon XB, which is a big six-cylinder motor that looked like a giant Cortina and had only ever been made by Ford Australia. It was about 15 years old and the guy wanted A$500 for it. Deal!

Colin knew a farmer in a town called Katanning, two hours from Perth, who was looking for casual workers, so Duncan and I took turns to pilot the Falcon XB through Western Australia down the Great Southern Highway. To my eyes, the rolling hills and grasslands looked a lot like the Cotswolds.

When we arrived in Katanning the farmer, Mr Dewar, asked us whether we preferred livestock or machines. Duncan chose machines and I opted for livestock, which I was soon to find was a major error on my part.

Mr Dewar asked Duncan to drive the combine harvester, which meant he spent some very pleasant working days in an air-conditioned cab driving a state-of-the-art, cutting-edge Deutz Gleaner harvester imported from America.

I drew a different, much shorter straw, as my task was to drench his Merino sheep. All 16,000 of them.

I knew all about sheep drenching. I had been doing it on the farm at home since I was about fifteen. It is a process whereby you squirt a chemical down a sheep's throat and into its gut to kill the stomach worms that can affect its performance.

These worms are pretty unpleasant things. They live in the sheep's gut and lay eggs that are then expelled in its dung. These eggs then attach themselves to blades of grass, and when the sheep graze the grass, the cycle begins again.

Adult sheep build up a natural immunity to gut worms but young lambs are very susceptible to them so at Bemborough Farm we always used to blanket-treat all of our lambs every four weeks. It was a long and tiring process but very much worth it.

Eventually, the gut worms built up their own resistance to the chemicals that farmers were firing down their sheep's throats and so agricultural scientists had to refine their approach. They developed other chemicals, to which the worms also eventually became immune, and the battle went on.

Nowadays, the science of drenching is so sophisticated that we do something called faecal egg counting. You stand in the field literally waiting for your sheep to poo – ah, the joys of farming! – and mix the sample in a solution and view it under a microscope.

A photo is taken which is emailed to an expert who tells you how bad the infestation is and recommends a specific chemical from the four we now have to choose from. It means we are drenching our sheep far less regularly and far more efficiently.

But that is today. Back in Australia in 1988, things were far less sophisticated – and way more rudimentary.

Mr Dewar's son, Pete, gave me a huge pick-up truck (or Ute, as they call them; short for utility vehicle), an Australian kelpie sheepdog called Bob and a handling-pen system. After showing me where all the 16,000 sheep were grazing, scattered around the farm, he left me to it.

The Australian environment was something I had never seen before. The ground was hard and dry with such brittle grass that I was amazed the sheep could live off it. Rather than the rooks and pigeons that we had back home there were sulphur-crested cockatoos and galah parrots making a din. Occasionally, as Bob and I gathered the sheep, a group of kangaroos would bounce into sight and leap over the fences, disappearing into the bush.

Bob and I had to round up the sheep and get them into the holding-pen system, which was no easy task in itself. Then the *real* fun began. The pen is basically a funnel that feeds the animals into a sheep race, which is a narrow, waist-high alleyway.

The sheep would then be trapped in this corridor and it was my job to work my way along the sheep race of strong Merino sheep, get hold of each one under the chin and squirt the liquid down their throats. I then had to let the sheep out into a separate pen, get the next lot in and do it all again. Talk about a Herculean task!

This was where Bob came into his own. It was the first time that I had heard of the Australian kelpie, let alone seen one, but within a few minutes of working with Bob I completely understood why some farmers consider them to be the best sheepdogs in the world.

The origins of the kelpie are disputed. Some say that it is a relation of the Australian dingo, while other breeders hold that it is a descendant of the English North Country collie. Either way, they are efficient, well-oiled sheep-herding machines, incredibly strong and with limitless energy.

Bob the kelpie was invaluable in Katanning. He was amazing in so many ways. Not only would he bark on command; he even jumped onto the sheep's backs when I was pushing them into the sheep race to get them nice and tight, so that it was totally full.

I fell in love with the kelpie there and then and I knew, as soon as I got the chance, I would try and buy one to have on the farm at home.

Once Bob had helped me fill the race with his running up and down and barking, he would retreat to the shade under the Ute and leave me in the blazing sunshine to my work. The classic Akubra brimmed hat that you see so many Aussies wear was one of my first purchases, and it was money well spent.

It took me a month and a half to drench those 16,000 sheep and in truth at times it was a horrendous experience. It was 35 degrees in the shade, there were dust and flies everywhere, and I bitterly envied Duncan blithely tootling around the arable fields in his luxury combine.

Still, I got a real buzz of pride and relief when I squirted the drench down the throat of the very last sheep. What an experience (if not one that I would ever care to repeat)!

After three months of roustabouting and drenching, Duncan and I figured we had earned ourselves a bit of R&R and set off to have a look at Australia. We hopped into the Falcon XB and drove across the Nullarbor Plain.

This was truly amazing. The plain is a former seabed but now is basically arid desert. We would drive for miles down never-ending, totally straight roads, seeing no signs of life on the barren landscape except for the occasional kangaroo.

There was little other traffic except for huge lorries pulling two trailers behind them that were known as road trains. These vast vehicles were transporting livestock and other goods, travelling hundreds of miles at a time.

The truckers would often drive all night and had huge bull bars on the front of their cabs to protect the radiator from whatever they hit. On our travels it was evident that they hit plenty, as we passed the stinking carcasses of kangaroos, sheep and even the odd cow.

The temperature veered between 35 degrees and a near unbearable 40 degrees and while our plucky Falcon XB had a lot of things going for it, air conditioning wasn't one of them. Whenever Duncan or I were not driving we would be lying on the back seat, the windows open, trying and failing to cool down.

We were on the road for days. Our diet deteriorated as we were stopping at garages to buy food and the only thing they tended to have were the kind of rubbish meat pies that only get sold in garages.

We made up for that by doing our own cooking at night. We had picked up a tent and a few pots and pans along the way by now, so we stayed in campsites, knocking up rudimentary meals of meat, rice and veg.

If you're in London you have to see the Tower, and if you're travelling across Australia you have to see Ayers Rock. We drove all the way to this famous landmark in the heart of the country but, to be honest, it was a bit of a disappointment.

I don't want to be the kind of philistine who says, 'You see one rock, you've seen them all', but really it was just this big lump of red sandstone rock that you climbed up, only to gaze over a featureless flat landscape. It hardly seemed worth having spent days sweltering in our oven-on-wheels to get there.

Uluru, which is what the main rock is called, is sacred to the Aborigine people. Duncan and I walked a tourist trail with hired interpreters and saw a few Aborigines who played their traditional musical instruments and danced for us. Despite Ayers Rock itself not living up to my expectations, hearing the history of these fascinating, resourceful native Australians who had adapted over thousands of years in this harsh environment was a real treat.

On the whole on our trip, the Aussies were really friendly and welcoming. There was a lot of the expected banter about us being whinging Poms and all that, but that didn't bother us: we were no shrinking violets and could hold our own.

However, some of the attitudes towards the Aborigines made us very uncomfortable.

Working on remote rural Australian farms, a lot of the young guys we met had never been out of their home area and were very narrow-minded. They weren't nasty guys, but we would find ourselves wincing inwardly at their casual racism and sexism.

They had no time for the Aborigines, or Abos as they called them, and regarded them as little more than animals. They had horrible nicknames for them like 'Boongs', which they joked was 'the noise they make as they bounce off our cars'.

In towns like Alice Springs, we saw Aborigines come into the town drunk and cause trouble and we could understand why the local community didn't want that. But they are an amazing race with an extraordinary history and culture, and the disrespect and animosity towards them was shocking.

Duncan and I posted lots of letters to our parents as well as phoning home every couple of weeks. Yet we were having too much fun to be truly homesick until Christmas came around.

The Dewars, the family who owned the sheep-drenching farm, also had a place on the West Coast and invited us there for Christmas. There were lakes nearby and we got a chance to catch up on our water-skiing.

We spent Christmas Day on the beach surfing (well, there were hardly any waves, so I just posed around with a surfboard under my arm). It was fun but I couldn't help thinking of my family sitting down to Christmas dinner on the other side of the world, without me.

By now it was also time to jump back into the Falcon and earn some more money, and luckily we had something lined up. The father of a friend from Seale-Hayne owned a tea plantation up in the Atherton Tablelands near Cairns and he'd agreed to take us on.

Duncan and I did some utterly horrible jobs on this trip but this one was without question the worst. Within an hour of beginning it, I was pining for the halcyon days of drenching 16,000 sheep.

We were working in fields where the tea bushes had already been planted. The mature bushes had been harvested, but some of them had failed. Duncan and I were given the job of inter-row planting to replace the dead bushes.

There was a guy going along on a little tractor with an auger on the back, digging the holes. Another worker dropped off the new plants by the holes and we had to shove the plant in the hole, fill in the soil and stamp it in to make sure that it was firm and held in place.

It was incredibly hard to mould the red, sticky soil, which hardly had any give. To make matters worse, you can only really plant tea when it is raining. The Atherton Tablelands is one of the wettest places in Australia, so we were usually working in a downpour.

We would be labouring away in shorts, waterproof coats and boots, but often our feet got so soaked and uncomfortable that we ended up working barefoot. The spiders, toads and snakes that inhabit that part of Australia were never far from our minds.

The fields were horribly stony, and on the very few days that it wasn't raining so we couldn't plant the tea bushes, Duncan and I had to spend the day picking up rocks so they wouldn't get in the way of the planting. It felt like slave labour.

This impression was reinforced by the plantation foreman, a brusque and charmless South African in a cape and a huge wide-brimmed hat. He strode along the rows behind us, and if he ever caught any of us workers having a laugh or so much as exchanging a word, he would bark at us: 'Shut up! Keep working!' Had he been allowed to, I'm sure he would have carried a whip.

Every night Duncan and I retired sore and aching to the caravan park we were crashing out in. We only did three weeks on the tea plantation, and I wouldn't have lasted more than two days had we not had a fantastic incentive to stick it out – our next destination.

For every soul-sapping low on the Australian trip such as the tea planting, there was at least one breathtaking high. When we escaped our slave plantation, we drove straight to Cairns to go deep-sea diving on the Great Barrier Reef.

The contrast could not have been more pronounced. For a start, in Cairns we were staying in a fantastic backpackers' place right by the sea, with its own swimming pool. It had lots of young people and a great nightlife.

My sister Lolo had done a lot of diving before, and when she showed me her photos it always looked fascinating. When I saw it was an option as Duncan and I were first planning our trip, I was really keen to do it.

It didn't disappoint. After doing a two-day open-water diving course, we headed out in a boat that slept twelve people, to spend three days on the reef. Once there we donned our diving suits, snorkels, flippers and oxygen tanks and plunged into the deep blue ocean. We had bread to attract the fish to come to us.

It was a stupendous experience. The angelfish and clownfish were such vivid, vibrant colours that you felt like laughing out loud at their sheer beauty. The grouper fish that came up close for bread were so massive that it was a little bit scary.

There are fish called triggerfish whose teeth are incredibly sharp because they survive by eating coral. They make nests in the sand and when I unwittingly swam over one, the fish darted out and bit my leg. The nasty purple bruise took a few days to disappear.

The highlight of the Barrier Reef was a night dive, which was pretty mind-blowing. The water was pitch-black: even with a torch you could hardly see more than a foot into the depths of the ocean around you.

The instructors warned us that white-tip reef sharks were down there but said they 'weren't necessarily' aggressive and we'd be OK if we stayed calm and breathed slowly. I didn't see one, but I can't deny that the theme from *Jaws* was playing in my head.

My girlfriend and I had been talking on the phone now and then and she flew out for a few weeks. It was great to see her. She had a job lined up on a farm in New South Wales, but hooked up with us for a week or so before we went our separate ways.

The manager on her farm then told her that he needed a couple of students for a month's shearing work, so we drove over and worked with her for a while, sharing our tin-shack accommodation with an army of Huntsman spiders. They can move terrifyingly fast and are also known as Giant Crab spiders because of their size and pretty scary appearance. Their bite is relatively harmless but as I am allergic to any insect bite, I didn't want to find out how I might react if one of these monsters sunk his jaws into me.

Then, after more than eight months in the country, it was time for Duncan and me to say goodbye to Australia.

It was also time to bid farewell to the Falcon XB, which felt like an old friend by then. It had been a great buy, and we even recouped most of our money when we flogged it to a mate from Seale-Hayne who was also on the travellers' trail.

Give or take the odd dodgy meat pie, sadistic foreman and

triggerfish nip, Australia had been an incredible adventure and we only hoped that New Zealand would be half as good. However, this leg of our trip didn't get off to the best start.

Duncan and I flew into Auckland and tried to hitchhike out of the city but, for some reason, commuters into New Zealand's capital didn't seem too inclined to stop for two hulking blokes and their massive backpacks. After a fruitless hour we gave up and decided to switch to plan B.

Hoping to replicate the fun we'd had driving around Oz, we found a dodgy old car lot and bought ourselves a second-hand motor. However, this grey Austin Morris Maxi was to prove a bit of a comedown after the mighty Falcon.

For a start, it leaked oil like a sieve, as we found out on the drive from Auckland to Te Puke. We headed that way purely because we had the phone number of a friend of a friend who lived there, a dairy farmer called John Cameron.

At which point our luck truly changed. John had never heard of us before, but when we called him from a phone box, he said, 'Yeah, I know exactly where you guys are,' drove out to meet us and then took us to his farm, 20 minutes away.

He and his wife, Sylvia, gave us lunch and we chatted about our trip, farming, rugby and life in general. John had no work going on his dairy farm, but he phoned up a local mate who owned a kiwi plantation, then told us, 'Well, I've found you a month's work pruning kiwi vines.'

Duncan and I thanked him and asked if he could recommend any cheap backpacker places for us to stay in Te Puke. John shook his head: 'Nah, you two seem like good blokes. We've got a couple of spare rooms – why don't you stay here?'

It was an amazingly kind offer and we stayed with John and his family for the next month, as well as playing for his local rugby team, the Te Puke Pirates, with him. Maybe that was why he had invited us! We became firm friends, and are still in touch 25 years on.

The kiwi plantation work wasn't remotely as horrific as the tea plantation had been. It was just pretty dull. We were pruning the vines, which entailed walking along miles and miles of supported vines, trimming back the deadwood and tying down the new growth.

We were working with a couple of Maoris who seemed decent guys, although one of them had just got out of prison. I didn't like to ask what for. He took a shine to us, and on our last day there asked us, 'Why don't you blokes come to the pub with me? You can meet some of my mates.'

Well, who could resist? Duncan and I told him we had to go to the bank first to cash our month's worth of paycheques but we would see him in there. Arguably, this was not our wisest move.

We walked into the pub and into the famous scene from *An American Werewolf in London*. The bar was rammed with Maori members of New Zealand's infamous Mongrel Mob biker gang. Duncan and I were the only white blokes in there.

So we were sitting with a guy who had just got out of the nick, who knew we had hundreds of New Zealand dollars in our back pockets, and whose social circle seemed to be entirely composed of violent bikers. What could possibly go wrong?

We were getting suspicious looks from some seriously unhinged-looking Mongrel Mobsters, and these increased in intensity when our friend went outside for a smoke. It was certainly an experience, and we were relieved to get out of there and back into the leaky Maxi in one piece.

The kiwi plantation was the only work that Duncan and I did in New Zealand. We spent the rest of our three months there travelling and not a day of it was less than sensational.

Native New Zealanders call their land 'God's own country' and I could certainly see why. I fell in love with it from the off. Within a few days I knew that if I were ever to emigrate from Britain, here is where I would go.

Everywhere that we looked, the views were staggering. The dramatic forests, mountains, beaches and fields were all so beautiful they were beyond stunning. For someone who loves the countryside as much as I do, here was heaven.

There were probably a few questionable attitudes towards the Maoris that mirrored the prejudices against Aborigines in Australia, but everybody we met was unconditionally and incredibly friendly towards us, and invariably invited us in for a cup of tea or to stay with them. The place still occupies a very special place in my heart.

We drove our leaky old tub down through the North Island and got the ferry across to the South Island. We stayed with an old rugby-playing friend in Hamilton for a week, as well as travelling right to the bottom of Milford Sound.

When Duncan and I got the boat back to the North Island, we had to push the Morris Maxi off the ferry because it had a flat battery. Its brakes had also stopped working and we had to just use the handbrake, which was fairly terrifying.

After we got it patched up, we drove it to Auckland to get our next flight. We went to a local car auction to try to flog it but we felt like we had the worst vehicle there, and weren't surprised when nobody showed the slightest interest in our old banger.

Duncan and I were just packing up from the auction and hatching a plan to drive the Maxi to Auckland Airport, get our rucksacks out and leave it with its engine running, when a guy wandered up and offered us a derisory sum for it.

We bit his hand off. I felt as if we should be paying him.

We had earned money in Australia and a little bit in New Zealand but even so our funds were now running low, and I was beginning to eat into my savings a little as we embarked on the penultimate leg of our round-the-world odyssey: America.

After a nine-hour flight to Hawaii, Duncan and I hired a car when we landed in Honolulu. We could only afford it as we had hatched a cunning plan – we were going to live out of it.

So every day for a couple of weeks we parked the car next to a nice hotel, went and lay by their pool, used their luxury facilities and pretended to be guests. At night, we drove to a secluded spot of beach and slept on the sand.

This worked well until the hotel twigged that the two young English guys soaking up the rays on their beach loungers did not actually appear to have a room. After they confronted us and we came clean (it wasn't like we had a choice) they kicked us out.

I guess we had fondly imagined Hawaii being full of beautiful pouting women in grass skirts. In reality, it all seemed very touristy and oddly the women, grass skirts or otherwise, didn't seem overly interested in a pair of stinky, penniless limeys who slept on the beach.

There were also far more burger joints, industrial estates and trailer parks than we had anticipated from sultry Hawaii. The surfing scene was cool and we got up into the forested mountains for a day or two, but when it came time to move on, we didn't mind too much.

Having returned the slightly misused hire car to the rental company, Duncan and I flew on to Los Angeles. This was our first taste of the real America and it was pretty exciting.

Just being in a proper US city with its high-rise buildings was a thrill – although we had heard stories about downtown LA and were wary of venturing there. Instead, we played it safe and went to Disneyland, where I screamed my way around the rollercoasters like a big kid.

Duncan and I decided we could just about afford one last car hire, and drove along the Californian coast to San Diego with the top down. We wanted to go to SeaWorld but I was in two minds about it, for the animal cruelty aspects of it worried me. I was by no means sure that it was right to trap killer whales in swimming pools.

Nonetheless, we decided to go and take a look. Having worked with domestic animals all my life it was certainly impressive to see the trainers of these huge wild sea mammals perform daring tricks, swimming with them and being lifted out of the water on their noses, but it also made me feel uneasy.

Entertaining as all of that very American showbiz was, it was hard to believe that the animals didn't suffer all kinds of trauma. It was certainly a million miles away from the ethos of the Cotswold Farm Park.

Of course, since then, it has been widely recognized that killer whales are hugely intelligent, with highly sophisticated social groups, and that keeping them in isolation away from their family pods in badly cramped conditions is extremely cruel. My reservations at the time, sadly, were well founded.

A few days after that unsettling experience, we had a welcome meet-up with some familiar faces. John Cameron and the Te Puke Pirates were on tour in the US, and Duncan and I made the long drive to Arizona and had a couple of games of rugby and a few fun nights in Tucson.

En route back to LA, we stopped off at the Grand Canyon. It was an extraordinary sight, but we decided that we couldn't afford the helicopter ride over it and satisfied ourselves with a walking tour around the edge.

That may be my one regret about our travelling jaunt – that Duncan and I frequently erred on the side of caution when it came to money. I had always saved money from working on the farm at home so I wasn't in debt even by the end of the trip.

There are a few things that we didn't do to save cash back then, such as the helicopter trip or ballooning, which I now look back on as missed opportunities. However, that spurs me on to return one day and travel in slightly better style with my family.

There again, this prudence at least made us resourceful. The last leg of our trip was a flight from Seattle to Vancouver, and we came up with an ingenious way to get to the US Northwest.

We had heard of a scheme whereby American car owners paid people to drive their autos from A to B. We found an LA company that specialized in that and volunteered to take an old Pontiac to Seattle.

The Pontiac Trans Am had been in an accident so it was a bit smashed up but, without coming over all *Top Gear* here, it was a great car to drive. The owner insured it, we paid for the petrol (sorry: gas) and we drove up the West Coast to Seattle.

We stopped off in San Francisco and got the boat over to Alcatraz, the notorious high-security federal prison that operated from 1934 to 1969. I found the island fascinating, and I thought that the audio tour of the deserted prison cells and canteen really brought the place to life.

In fact, I was so inspired by it that when I got back home, I persuaded Dad to put an audio tour into the farm park. It didn't really work. There was quite enough life there already and we didn't need it.

America is such a vast, overwhelming country and Duncan and I felt as if we had hardly scratched the surface of a fraction of it as we flew out to Canada. Yet the initial view that I formed of it remains the one that I hold a quarter of a century on: it's an amazing place, but I wouldn't like to live there.

I can't for the life of me remember what had made us decide to end our adventure in Vancouver, but I am so glad that we did. In our brief stay we met some lovely Canadians, who seemed that bit friendlier and more genuine than had a lot of Americans.

Duncan and I did some good partying in Vancouver as we saw off the last of our dwindling cash in seriously bottom-of-the-range youth hostels. Yet the highlight for me by far was going to see the Canadian national sport: ice hockey.

It was like a cross between my two favourite sports, rugby and hockey, but it was far more violent than either of them, with fighting and skirmishes going on all over the rink. I just loved it and longed to be out there playing. Exactly what that says about me, I hate to think.

It had not been a typical gap yah, but our great adventure had been everything we had hoped for, and more. As Duncan and I boarded the plane from Vancouver to Heathrow, we knew we had memories that would never leave us until the day we died.

It was amazing how well we had got on. The two of us had never had a cross word, which was quite an achievement for two young blokes who had hardly left each other's sides for a year. I guess it is a sign of a very special friendship.

At the same time, I think we were probably both ready for a break from each other, and I was very ready to come home. Seeing the world had been wonderful but now it felt very much time for the next thing.

In those days, I didn't really have any meticulous life plan or strategy. I suppose I was fairly carefree and took each day and week as it came. Yet the ultimate goal that I knew I was working towards had never wavered.

I wanted to come back to Bemborough Farm, work for Dad and one day take over the farm tenancy. It was where my heart was, and always had been, and I knew there was nowhere else that I wanted to live and, eventually, hopefully to raise my own family.

There was a lot of hard work ahead and I still had a lot to learn about farming, but that didn't deter me at all. In fact, I couldn't wait to start.

Bring it on.

CHAPTER 8

My Life in the Squat

I t's understandable that most young people are highly loath to move back in with their parents after college. No matter how much you love your mum and dad, it is hard to find yourself back in your childhood bedroom after enjoying years of hedonistic freedom and independence.

It should have been particularly hard for me, who in autumn 1990 was moving back to Bemborough Farm at the ripe old age of twenty-four. So it is hugely to Mum and Dad's credit that for me it didn't feel like any kind of ordeal or imposition whatsoever.

It just felt like coming home.

There again, it probably helped that I wasn't actually back in my childhood bedroom. Mum and Dad realized that after five years away studying and travelling, I would need my own space. Come to think of it, I'm sure that they did, too.

Luckily, my return home coincided with the farm's livestock manager giving his notice. He had been living on the farm in a bungalow a few hundred yards from the farmhouse, so Mum and Dad moved me into there. Perfect!

I didn't just get his house: I also got his job. Dad was keen to formalize my role on the farm, and so appointed me as his new livestock manager, on the standard Agricultural Wages Board pay.

Dad was still overseeing the business and in charge of the livestock while John Neave ran the arable side. My new role would see me very involved in the livestock, shearing sheep and doing demonstrations in the farm park as well as driving tractors and combines and helping Uncle John with the arable work.

I was in charge of two stockmen, Jonathan Crump and Geoff Wiggins, who also lived in cottages on the farm. They knew their stuff, they were both really good guys about the same age as me, and we worked side by side really well.

The bungalow behind the farm buildings was empty when I first moved into it, but it didn't stay that way for long.

I've always been a gregarious sort so I was delighted when two mates moved in to keep me company. James Collett – or Jam, as I call him – was an old friend from school that I'd kept in touch with, who now ran the family garage in Bourton-on-the-Water.

Tim Lanfear was the son of the local NFU representative who had gone off to join the RAF. Tim had now moved back locally and was working as a fireman in Cheltenham. The three of us soon settled into a cool living arrangement.

It helped that Jam's girlfriend Caroline was also around a lot. We three lads took it in turns to do the cooking, but if Caroline was there she took over the majority of it and also mothered us in general. None of us had any objection to that.

When Caroline wasn't around, Jam, Tim and I exhibited exactly the levels of interest in interior décor, cleaning and tidying that you would expect from three fun-loving young blokes sharing a house. It wasn't long before we started to call the place 'the squat'. This was because the mice in the roof sounded like they had clogs on, so when people came to stay and asked us what the noise was, we told them that we had squatters.

It was just a real party house. Some might say den of iniquity (but I couldn't possibly comment). There were always loads of people hanging out, passing through or crashing out, and I have no idea how many lodgers ended up dossing down there (which was another good reason to call it the squat).

Two very good friends of ours were Steve Brinkworth and Paul Jennings, who came to party with us and ended up crashing out most weekends, as did many others who regularly enjoyed our hospitality. It was probably a good job that we didn't have neighbours to annoy.

In Katanning, Duncan and I had got on well with Pete, the farmer's son. I had airily told him what travellers always say: 'If you are ever over in England, give us a shout.'

One morning the Bemborough Farm phone rang. 'G'day, Adam, it's Pete Dewar,' said the voice on the other end. 'I'm at Moreton-on-Marsh station. Can I come to stay?'

I remembered the way that John Cameron had welcomed us in New Zealand and shot straight off to the station to pick him up. I imagined that Pete would probably be around for a week or two. He stayed for six months.

Pete did various jobs locally, including one he absolutely hated, which was picking sprouts in the winter months. He got paid piece rate, i.e. money for every bag he managed to fill. He was so bad at it that he filled very few bags and got paid very little, so in the end he gave it up as a bad job.

Yet when summer came on Bemborough Farm, he came into his own, helping out with shearing and sorting the wool. In the UK our wool is much coarser than the beautiful wool produced by the Merinos in Australia, but from Pete's dedication you wouldn't have known there was any difference. He would tirelessly sort through our fleeces and keep the shearing shed immaculate, just as he did back home.

I still try to maintain that attitude today. I foresee the value of wool coming back into its own in the future: after all, it was our native Cotswold breed that brought so much wealth to this area from its wool. We now have a flock of Romney sheep that were selected not only for their quality lamb production but also their wool.

Much like an Australian myself, I was firmly into work-hard, play-hard mode back then. It was hectic on the farm all week, then I would work Saturday mornings before playing rugby for Stow-on-the-Wold in the afternoon. Saturday night was always a party, either in a local pub or, more usually, the squat.

This meant I was turning up for work on Sunday mornings with a hangover more weeks than not, but Dad was totally relaxed about this. Although he didn't care for drinking himself, he was fine with whatever I did as long as I got to work on time and did what needed doing.

In any case, he knew that I was still taking work on the farm intensely seriously. I had gone to Australia and New Zealand partly to study how livestock production worked over there and had returned with some evangelical ideas about how we could improve our own operation.

I raved to Dad about the kelpie sheepdogs and how superbly effective they were. There weren't many of them in the UK at the time – in fact, there still aren't – but Dad gave me the green light to get one and see how it did.

Kelpies come in various different colours: red, black, red-and-tan and black-and-tan. I tracked down a red bitch, who I named Bundy after the Bundaberg rum I had enjoyed so much in Oz.

Bundy was a big success with the sheep. She was great in the pens with her barking, but not so good to cast out around the fields to gather a flock. However, Dad was impressed and I thought it would be a good idea to breed from her. We could work some of the dogs and sell others. I contacted a kelpie dealer in Australia, who said he would fly over some sperm for us to artificially inseminate her.

Well, the best-laid plans often go astray. Dogs with the scent of a bitch on heat will do anything to get to her, and while we were waiting for the Antipodean sperm to arrive, a Border collie managed to bite through our fairly flimsy farmhouse door and mate with Bundy.

She had a litter of 12 pups, which we mostly gave away. Her second litter was just one puppy but it was a pure kelpie red, so I gave that to Duncan as a working souvenir of our Down Under odyssey. He was named Red and was a wonderful character.

Bundy's third litter was via artificial insemination and was again 12 pups. They were a mixture of colours. Some of them were yellow, which I had never seen before, so I phoned a mate in Australia to ask him if yellow kelpies existed; I was concerned they had yellow Labrador or something in them.

My friend said yellow kelpies do come along but people in Oz tend not to keep them as they have pink noses and pads to their feet that can be very sensitive to dry soil, sand and sunburn. Yet I kept one yellow kelpie called Ronnie, whom I worked with for years and grew to love.

Twelve is really quite a huge litter, and although Bundy had coped with it once before, a vet advised me that to give her a chance we should really get rid of four or five of them. With only eight teats to go round twelve puppies, some would get pushed out and there was a risk they would starve.

The vet's instruction was easier said than done. I put all of the newborn puppies on the kitchen table, along with two washing baskets. *Right*. I would put the dogs I was keeping in one basket, and the ones I was getting rid of in the other.

'Now, you are a lovely big bitch, you are definitely a keeper – in you go!' I would put a puppy into the 'saved' basket.

'No, you are a tiny little dog, probably best if you go,' I'd say to the next one, putting it into the other basket. After I had worked my way through, there were four or five of them in that category. They wriggled around helplessly, squeaking, eyes still shut, searching for their mum.

'Actually, no, you are probably OK. You can go in the keeping basket. And you as well ...'

Soon, somehow, all 12 puppies ended up in the keeping basket. There was no way I was going to put any of them down, so I put them all back in the bed with Bundy and decided to let nature take its course.

I woke up the next morning to find that Bundy had separated the puppies into two groups of six. One lot was asleep and she was feeding the other six. When she had finished, she let them sleep, woke the other lot up, and fed them.

As soon as the pups were old enough, I began feeding them with a tiny pipette and some artificial milk that I got from the vet. For weeks, the kitchen was a mess of 12 constantly weeing, pooing puppies. Somehow, they all survived.

The kelpies weren't my only Australia-inspired innovation to try to get more from our sheep flocks. We had a good flock at the time but I thought we could improve their value at market, so I suggested we start to use a professional grader.

You decide when a lamb is ready for market by putting your hand on its loin and shoulder. It's quite a skill to be able to decide when it is not too skinny and not too fat but is just right.

Every market has its own graders who feel each lamb that is brought in. If it is too skinny or too fat, they mark its fleece to show the buyers it hasn't reached the grade, and then it is impossible for it to reach the premium price. When Dad and I brought a grader in to Bemborough to help us before the lambs reached the market, it definitely made a difference.

There were more ideas; I had plenty of them. The staff were still mostly using our battered old Land Rover to get around the farm, and I thought I had found a far better plan.

On the Australian farms, the workers had tended to zip around on quad bikes. They were faster and more mobile than Land Rovers and they used low ground-pressure tyres that didn't churn up the ground, unlike big 4x4s, which tended to chew up the tracks.

(They were also a lot more fun – it was a bit like riding go-karts – but that was by the by. I just thought they would be more efficient.)

Farmers and farm workers can be a conservative bunch and a couple of the stockmen were not very keen on this change, largely because they missed the comfort and warmth of the Land Rover on wet days. But as I told them, they had to get out to open the gates and work with the sheep anyway!

In addition, wearing suitable waterproofs to ride the quad meant they could stay warm and dry throughout their work, whereas they currently got soaked every time they left the Land Rover in jeans and a jacket. I understood their reticence, though, as it was an innovation: quad bikes weren't being used a lot back in the early nineties, although nowadays most farmers will have one.

It also made sense to me for us to get some mobile handling pens of the kind that Duncan and I had worked with in Oz. Dad had just one handling system in the paddock near to the farmhouse, which meant that if we wanted to do a treatment on a flock, we had to drive them half a mile or so across the farm.

I suggested that we took the mountain to Mohammed and buy a mobile handling system that would allow us to set up a pen in the field where the sheep were. It would put far less stress on the sheep and save us valuable working hours.

Investments such as quad bikes and mobile handling pens did not come cheap but Dad was extremely open-minded towards them. He was always naturally entrepreneurial and innovative, as well as very receptive to a good idea.

He would listen hard, and tell me, 'That sounds like it might work – let's give it a go.' Or, sometimes, 'I can see what you mean, but John and I tried it once and it didn't really come off.' Either way, he was always receptive and interested.

Unlike many farmers, Dad didn't want to carry on doing things the same old way forever. He liked that I had returned from my travels fired up with new plans and armed with a can-do attitude. Ever since setting up the farm park in 1971, he had been all about progression.

With my encouragement, we moved away from our old agronomist (the person who advises on how to manage our crops) and took on a more dynamic local company. We started to grow new crops such as linseed, providing the farm with a different income stream.

Adding to our passion for conservation and wildlife, I took the chance to enter the farm into an environmental steward-ship scheme. This meant that we were being paid by the government to care for and protect the wildlife on the farm.

Seale-Hayne College was very academic but had left me shy of some practical qualifications. Dad and John Neave therefore arranged for me to go on a string of short training courses with the Agricultural Training Board. I did a quad-bike course and chainsaw courses and I learned welding, spraying and how to drive a front-end loader. I even did a first-aid course.

I also got further schooling in the intricate art of sheepdog training from a farm manager called Dick Roper on his farm in Northleach. I had always been able to muddle by at sheep herding but Dick taught me so much more.

When it came to controlling a sheepdog, Dick was a virtuoso: in fact he was a member of the English sheepdog trialling team. Working a dog is a real art and, when you think about it, it is quite unusual to be controlling one animal and ordering it to control another.

I knew there were four basic commands in sheep herding for 'right', 'left', 'stop' and 'go', but Dick could take these basic tools and make them look so easy with a symphony of whistles. Bundy and I were a long way short of the expertise of Dick and his dogs, but his lessons were to stand me in good stead for many years to come.

I'd always used 'away' for right and 'come by' for left, which is standard across the UK, but Dick taught me that the only important factor is that the words were short, sharp and very different from each other. They could be Chinese or Tagalog as long as they were distinctive.

This was very different from my dad's approach.

Exasperated with his dog, Dad was prone to shouting, 'Will you jolly well lie down!' which meant nothing to the dog and was utterly ineffective. As I said, it was one of the very few farming processes of which Dad wasn't a total master.

If your dog is more than about 15 yards away – and so out of shouting distance – you have to transfer your commands to a whistle. Again, you have to develop a repertoire of separate and very different whistles that the dog will recognize instantly.

Dick explained to me that if you have a cold or a dry mouth, or even have been eating a load of chocolate, the dog will not be able to understand you. Even so, dogs have amazing hearing and a good shepherd can work a dog from a quarter of a mile away.

There is so much psychology in sheep herding. Dogs have a natural instinct to chase and round up sheep that goes back to their ancestors the wolves. They are doing what they have done since time immemorial, except that they don't finish by killing and eating the sheep.

Well, I hope they don't, anyway!

The kind of gifted sheep-trial experts that Dad's mate Phil Drabble used to showcase on *One Man and His Dog* all those years ago could nuance their whistles to make their dogs go from a trot to a canter, or drop to the ground. They had the fluency and vocabulary of great linguists.

Even after my intensive sessions with Dick, I never scaled those heights. Today, my herding remains effective but fairly rudimentary and, to be honest, me working with a kelpie is like an average violinist trying to play a Stradivarius.

Dick was not a great fan of the kelpie and persuaded me to buy a collie pup from him that I called Fenn. She was very easy to train and had a lovely nature. It was great advice as Fenn was a master at rounding up the sheep from the fields and then Bundy took over in the pens, making a perfect team.

Yet despite all these courses and my various small changes and innovations, I hadn't returned to Bemborough Farm from abroad intent on revolutionizing the way everything worked. It was more a question of tweaking minor details while I watched and learned from Dad and Uncle John.

I might still have been wet behind the ears and idealistic,

but I also knew you can only learn so much from college and travelling. Dad and John had more than 50 years' experience of running Bemborough Farm between them. They had forgotten more than I had ever known.

The best aspect of being the farm's livestock manager was working so closely with Dad. Between us we took charge of the sheep flock, which was generally about thirteen different breeds and 700 to 800 ewes.

In addition to the rare-breed flocks, we have always had a commercial flock raised for their meat. Some farmers will buy in female breeding sheep and put them with what is called a terminal sire, or meat ram, then replace these ewes when they get old and infertile.

We have never worked that way. Dad preferred – as do I – to avoid buying in ewes, which can bring with them diseases from other flocks, and instead to buy in rams and breed our own replacement ewes. This means that you have to replace the rams every couple of years to avoid them breeding with their own daughters.

Buying good rams was thus of paramount importance to us and Dad and I would go off to market to choose them. These days, dealers will have performance figures of the strength of their rams' genetics, but in those days we just had to put trust in our own eyes and judgement.

I still loved going to market with Dad to buy rams, bulls and boars as much as I had when he was strapping me into my baby car seat before we set off. He shared the same enthusiasm. It always felt fun and exciting, as if we were both two big kids on our way to a sweet shop.

Dad had been suffering with a bad back for years by now, so grabbing sheep was not easy for him. Yet we worked well as a team, with me handling and checking the sheep while he wrote notes in the catalogue to decide which ones to buy.

Nowadays the main rare-breeds show and sale is in Melton Mowbray but back then it was in Stoneleigh. I held many treasured childhood memories of Stoneleigh. One of the side projects of Dad's chairmanship of the Rare Breed Survival Trust was that he had set up an annual rare-breed show and sale that was held there.

This was such a big deal back when we were kids. Dad would select the cows and sheep he was to enter months in advance and exercise meticulous control over their diets to ensure they were in perfect condition. My sisters and I would all pitch in, washing and halter-draining the animals and tarting them up so they looked beautiful.

Mum would do a lot of catering for the show and we would stay in our big caravan up there. It was a four-day holiday, made even better as our stock usually did really well and won lots of rosettes.

This history meant that Dad still knew everybody at the sales, all the auctioneers and fellow farmers. It would be impossible to walk more than three steps without someone greeting Dad warmly and wanting to stop and talk – and Dad always loved to talk.

It was not as if we needed it, but even so these jaunts to market and auctions were great bonding experiences for me and Dad. We would talk openly and freely about everything; including, sometimes, his early years.

There were many things about Dad's childhood and youth that I had never quite understood. Occasionally he would let slip a tantalizing remark, and sometimes I would listen in as he and Uncle Nicky reminisced about their early years. But it never made total sense to me.

I knew that Dad had been an illegitimate baby. This is not a big deal at all nowadays, of course, but things were very different back in the 1930s, when being a bastard, as such children used to be called, carried a huge social stigma.

His father, Leslie, had been married when he fathered Dad. Unfortunately, it was not to his mother.

Dad had always spoken very fondly and proudly of Leslie and a large portrait of him had hung in pride of place in the farmhouse. Yet it was many years before I fully appreciated just what a huge celebrity Leslie Henson had been.

He was a household name who had regularly played the lead in major West End plays as well as hosting shows in theatres such as the London Palladium. In later years he was to co-found the Entertainment National Service Association (ENSA), the organization that took performers overseas to entertain British troops.

Leslie was married to his second wife, an actress named Gladys Henson, when he met Dad's mum, Billie Dell, when they were in the same West End show. The two embarked on a passionate affair and she became pregnant with Dad in 1932.

Back in the thirties, the scandal of an illegitimate child could have potentially ruined Leslie's career. Leslie and Billie agreed to keep the baby a secret, but Leslie would – and always did – provide for them.

So Dad had begun life as Joseph Leslie Collins (Billie's dad's surname) and for the early years of his life was effectively raised by Billie as a single mother. Leslie was still married to Gladys, who had refused to divorce him, and so was only an occasional presence in Billie and Dad's lives.

(Incidentally, it was then that Leslie gained the nickname 'Lally', by which Dad always referred to him. When Dad was learning to talk as a toddler, he couldn't say 'Leslie' and 'Lally' was the best he could manage. It stuck.)

Leslie had set up Billie and Dad in a cottage in Northwood in west London, which was where Dad discovered Park Farm down the road and developed his life-long love of animals and farming. Leslie, apparently, would drop in to see them when he was playing golf nearby.

It was an extraordinary story with confusing twists and turns. Billie had eventually despaired of Lally ever leaving his wife, given up on him and married another man, giving Dad a doting stepfather named Cyril Day.

The tale got ever more dramatic. Cyril Day had joined the RAF and was tragically killed fighting in 1942 when Dad was just ten years old. Apparently Dad had held his mum sobbing in his arms when the postman came with a telegram informing her that he was missing.

This Greek tragedy was to have a happy ending, of sorts. Having finally divorced Gladys, Lally reunited with Billie, marrying her in 1944, and finally became a proper father to Dad. Fittingly, Uncle Nicky was born in 1945 on the day that peace was declared in Europe.

After the Second World War ended, King George VI had

asked to see Leslie Henson. He thanked him for his work entertaining the troops and setting up ENSA and told him that he would love to give him a knighthood if only it were possible.

These were different times, and Leslie's perceived scandalous life – being a divorcee – meant he could never receive a royal honour. However, the king gave Leslie a set of platinum, gold and diamond shirt studs and cufflinks as a personal gift.

One poignant side effect of Dad's confused and confusing early years was that Uncle Nicky was never quite sure that Dad was really his full brother. Dad was 13 years older, and Nicky knew that for years Dad had had a different surname from his own: Collins. So had he also had a different father?

Nicky stewed and wondered but said nothing until Billie died in 1970. After the funeral, Nicky cut to the chase and asked my dad a simple question: 'Are you really my brother?'

'Yes,' Dad replied. 'Yes, Nicky, I am.'

Nicky still describes this as one of the happiest moments of his life and Dad would often shed a tear when he told the story. After Leslie's death, the cufflinks the King had given him passed to Dad and became his most prized possession.

It was a mind-boggling story, and whenever Dad recounted a bit of it, with his natural raconteur's flair, I could only marvel at how different his childhood had been from my own fun, easy early days on Bemborough Farm.

Yet, typically of him, Dad never ever made a big deal of his turbulent past. In fact, he never told the story in full. He would mention bits of it, in passing. Trying to slot it all together was like trying to do a jigsaw with pieces missing.

Because he was always so jocular and easy-going when he talked of Lally and Billie, I suppose I never thought that hard about the profound psychological impact it must all have had on him as a sensitive young boy.

That was only to become clear to me years later.

In any case, extraordinarily close as Dad and I were, we didn't really go in for intense, soul-searching conversations about our lives and our feelings. It just wasn't the way we were. There was always something to take our attention – and 99 per cent of the time it was the farm.

Entrepreneur that he was, Dad had cleverly opened up a new sideline for Bemborough Farm. We were regular providers of animals as bit-part players in top Hollywood and British movies.

Dad had spotted this gap in the market in the early nineties, and as the decade unfolded it became a regular occurrence. In 1993 we provided an Iron Age pig named Sally to play the lead role – sort of – in a film called *The Hour of the Pig*.

This strange movie was based on a real-life story in which a pig was charged with murder in fifteenth-century France. Colin Firth played the gallant lawyer charged with defending the pig, and Sally took quite a shine to him.

Sally would trot around after the handsome Mr Firth on set like a besotted lover, even biting another actor who inadvertently came between them. Yet maybe the regard was mutual: when Sally had her next litter of piglets, Colin Firth posted her a congratulations card.

A couple of years later, we provided various livestock for Mel Gibson's *Braveheart* and I even made a cameo appearance myself. I played a scruffy peasant leading oxen across a field, but if you blinked, you could easily have missed me.

Sadly, my invite to the Oscars that year never arrived.

Better still, we got asked to supply a pig that could sit on command to appear in Walt Disney's *101 Dalmatians*. It took me a week to train a Gloucester Old Spot called Princess to perform this tricky task but it was worth it. A few months later, there was Princess, on the big screen, squatting on Glenn Close as Cruella de Ville.

Yet, in truth, Hollywood glamour impinged very little on my day-to-day life as Dad's livestock manager. Back in the real world, one of my least pleasurable duties was sheep dipping.

Sheep suffer from external parasites such as mites, ticks and blowflies, and government legislation used to insist that all farmers had to dip their sheep twice a year to combat this. This involved submerging the sheep in some pretty hideous organophosphorous chemicals.

Dipping was a truly grisly business. You would have to fill a sheep dip, which is basically a big metal tank in the ground with the water at ground level, with water and these horrid organophosphorous chemicals, which were essentially a form of nerve gas.

It was normally a two-person job. The sheep hated going into the dip (and I couldn't blame them) so you would have to shove them in backwards, to prevent them jumping forwards and out before you could stop them.

I would stand on the side of the dip with a crook, which had a wooden handle with a metal hook on the end of it, and plunge them under the water with it. By law they had to be completely submerged and be in the tank for at least a minute. Very often a man from the Ministry of Agriculture would come to observe and make sure the liquid was the correct concentration and the sheep were spending enough time in it.

The experience would terrify the sheep and so they would be pooing and weeing in the liquid, which thus would get even more filthy and revolting. After the minute had passed we would let them scramble up the ramp at the other end of the dip to safety and stand in the draining pen, where the excess liquid would run out of their fleece, down a slope and back into the dip.

It was a disgusting job in many ways and soon you would be drenched in the organophosphorous solution. Legally you had to wear protective clothing and I would start out in my waterproof trousers and jacket, but as I got hotter and worked up a sweat it was difficult not to shed a layer.

I would be working on a wet, treacherous surface on which it was easy to slip, trying to shove 65kg sheep into the dip. Inevitably, sometimes I would be wrestling with a huge ram, he would suddenly fall into the tank and I would go in with him.

Flailing around in the chemicals, sheep muck and wee was an occupational hazard of dipping. When I was a student at Chatsworth, a shepherd had given me a nudge and shoved me in on purpose, for no reason other than he thought it was hilarious.

One year in the mid-nineties one of the stockmen and I did the dipping at Bemborough and afterwards I got down into the tank to clean it out. Later that afternoon I got a terrible headache, felt really ill, couldn't eat anything and had to go to hospital.

I spent four days in Cheltenham General Hospital and it was a pretty scary time. It was like having meningitis: I had a non-stop splitting headache, my glands all came up on my head and my neck, and all I could do was lie in a dark room and try to sleep.

The doctors couldn't prove a direct link but I had no doubt that it was a reaction to the organophosphorous chemicals. Interestingly, it is no longer government legislation that farmers have to use them on their sheep.

It has never been acknowledged, but I suspect the authorities realized that they were poisoning a lot of farmers and could face legal action. There is even some evidence to suggest that it could lead to Parkinson's and various other diseases.

Nowadays there are alternative methods to protect your sheep from blowfly such as injections or sprays. Some farmers still use organophosphorous chemicals, but there are stringent rules about protective clothing and specific training to gain a certificate of competence.

Even today, if I go to a sheep sale on a warm August day and smell organophosphorous fumes coming off sheep's wool, it gives me a headache, alters my mood and makes me irritable and scratchy straight away. I have to get far away from there as soon as possible.

I filled in the sheep dips at Bemborough many years ago. My experience in hospital was a lesson learned: organophosphorous chemicals are horrible things. Today, I have simply banned them from the farm. They belong in the past.

CHAPTER 9

Old Mates Become Soulmates

As we moved into the second half of the nineties I was still working hard as Dad's livestock manager and learning everything I could about farm management and the business aspect of being a farmer. Every day I discovered that there was a lot more to it than lambing and harvesting: there were forms to fill in, red tape to overcome, budgets to plan.

Dad and John Neave were investing in me in terms of handing down their knowledge and sending me on courses. The idea remained that I would take over the farm in time, and while I never wavered in that desire, I did occasionally worry at my personal situation.

The salary that Bemborough was paying me was enough for my day-to-day needs and for partying in the squat, but didn't allow me to do any long-term planning. I certainly couldn't afford to save anything or do things that a lot of guys in their late twenties do, such as buy property.

Yet if I was having sporadic concerns, there soon came an encouraging development. Two neighbouring farmers with the same landlord as us, the Corpus Christi College estate, decided to retire, and the administrators at the college came to see us.

The landlords were proposing tacking a lot more land on to our farm, but firstly wanted to make sure that it would be in safe hands. 'Are you serious about staying on the farm and eventually succeeding your father as the tenant?' they asked me.

I told them that I was, and they duly gave us the land, which took Bemborough from a 1,200-acre to a 1,600-acre tenancy. This hike in size made it a far better sized holding and considerably increased what we could do with the farm.

A lot of the additional land was along the Windrush Valley, which was lower down the hill than Bemborough and consequently warmer, with less stony, more fertile soil. It also came with extra grain-storage capacity.

All this was quite a psychological turning point for me. I had always intended to stay on the farm, but suddenly having far more land, and the confidence of knowing that the landlords had trust in me, definitely gave me a fresh focus and impetus.

It didn't show itself in any grand gestures. Farming is about hard work, and I kept my head down, carried on working long days and weeks and soaked up as much of Dad and John's wisdom as I could. The livestock continued to occupy the majority of my working day – and nothing gave me more joy than the lambing season.

Even today, with close on half a century of lambing behind me, I have never lost my sense of joy and wonder at helping a fragile, wide-eyed creature to come into the world. I think it would be impossible for anybody with a heart not to be moved by the experience.

I know the whole process inside out now and it still fascinates me. Every year it starts with the ritual of closely watching the flock and waiting for a pregnant ewe to distance herself from the rest of the sheep.

That's a biological hangover from the days when sheep lived in the wild and were vulnerable to attacks from wolves and other predators. The last thing they would want to do before giving birth is to draw attention to themselves.

Once the ewe has withdrawn from the flock and found a secluded corner, there are other warning signs. She will lie down and stand back up, becoming increasingly restless. She will lick her lips in anticipation of licking her newborn lamb and paw the ground.

As soon as she begins having contractions the ewe will lie down. Usually, a sheep sits with her legs tucked under her body, but during lambing she will lie more to one side with the top leg pointing straight out. This puts her into a more comfortable position, widening her hips.

The ewe then does a wonderful thing. She throws her head right back as if surveying the sky like an astronomer: some farmers and vets even call this stargazing. The contractions must be as painful as they are for humans, but the ewe will never make a sound for fear of alerting predators.

At this stage, if the lamb is not presenting correctly, with two front feet and nose coming first, I move in to assist the ewe through the final stages. From the moment they lie down, it takes about 20 minutes for her to give birth.

As soon as the lamb is born, its mother will stand up and begin licking it dry and communicating with it. This is maternal instinct at its purest, and an awe-inspiring thing to see.

Sheep show their offspring a tough love, though. Within seconds of a lamb being born, its mother is pawing it with her foot and urging it to get to its feet. It may give plaintive cries and baas but she urgently encourages it to stand up: again, a reminder of sheep's days of being relentlessly preyed upon.

As soon as the lamb is upright, it instinctively searches for the teats on its mother's udder for its colostrum. This is the first milk that a ewe produces immediately after giving birth and is crucial to her lamb's survival as it is born with no natural immunity at all: it gets it all from the colostrum.

A key part of the shepherding job in the lambing season is ensuring that the lambs have a full belly, as without it they are likely to become ill and die. Occasionally lambs are born too weak to suckle on their own, especially if they are small triplets or quads.

It's the farmer's job to dry these off with towels, get them under a heat lamp and start bottle-feeding as soon as possible, just like Mum used to do in our kitchen by the Aga when I was a boy.

Much like Dad, my showman's instinct comes out when I give lambing demonstrations at the farm park, where I describe the process of the birth as I oversee the ewe. It's fantastic seeing people's faces as they watch, especially those who haven't witnessed a birth before.

They get so caught up in the moment and often spontaneously clap or cheer when the lamb emerges. Of course, occasionally the lamb may be stillborn, which is always difficult, but it is important to explain why this has happened. We try not to hide too much away from the public so they get a true understanding of the harsh realities of farm life.

I also love being in the sheep sheds at night, after the visitors have gone home. With a clear sky full of stars and a nip in the air, there is magic and strange comfort in watching over the heavily pregnant ewes as they rest in the straw, or observing the new mothers quietly nurturing their newborn lambs and murmuring to them.

I have helped hundreds, if not thousands, of sheep to give birth over my many years on the farm. During this same time I have aided no more than maybe half a dozen pigs, but it is an equally amazing and heart-warming spectacle.

Pigs breed all year round and come into season every three weeks. While they are in season, or hogging, as it is known, the boars will mate with them.

If the sow conceives, she will give birth three months, three weeks and three days later. We usually bring them into the stables in the yard to give birth, or farrow. They are perfectly capable of farrowing in the huts in the field, but I like to keep a close eye on them in case anything happens to go wrong.

Pigs give birth with relative ease and will have somewhere between four to a dozen piglets in each litter. The sow will lie in her nest, grunt and 'pop out' a piglet as easily as shelling peas from a pod. Instinctively the piglet makes its way from her mother's back end and touches her leg. The sow lifts its leg and the piglet moves in to suckle.

Sows have 14 teats evenly spaced with seven on either side, to provide plenty of space for all the piglets to feed. When farmers are selecting breeding sows to keep, checking they have the right number of teats is very important.

We let the piglets stay on the sow for six or eight weeks and then they are weaned and taken off the mother. Three days after weaning, when the sow stops feeding her piglets, she comes back into season and the cycle begins again. It means a pig can have two litters per year.

In a commercial system, piglets are weaned at three weeks old and a sow will have 2.2 litters a year. This averages out at 11 piglets a litter, making about 25 piglets a year. Profitable pig farming is a numbers game, so productive animals are key.

Very occasionally a piglet will get stuck during the birth and then it is my job to assist. However, where you can be quite firm manipulating a lamb or a calf into position in the womb, you have to be a lot gentler with a pig. A sow has a very sensitive uterus and you need to know exactly what you are doing.

Although the farm park is all about rare-breed British farm animals, we made an exception in the nineties for a New Zealand bush pig called Kune Kunes. Kune Kune is Māori for fat and round and the pigs are exactly this.

They are not very productive animals (although they do make good sausages) but are incredibly friendly. Where a Tamworth piglet will run away if you approach it, a Kune Kune will be all over you and let you stroke and tickle it. Obviously they were perfect for the farm park.

As I learned my trade and paid my dues at Bemborough, the livestock and the farm park naturally took up the majority of my working hours. However, I also worked closely with John Neave, mindful of the need to continue improving my arable knowledge.

In our part of Gloucestershire, we have drawn a bit of a short straw in terms of the soil known as Cotswold brash. It's very shallow and stony compared with the deep rich soil found in places like the Fens of Suffolk and Lincolnshire.

Cotswold brash has one advantage. The limestone factor of the soil means that it doesn't retain water and is very free draining. When we get very wet weather, or a heavy frost, it dries out very quickly. It has a low fraction of clay so is easy to work, and for this reason some farmers call it 'boys' land'.

However, the major downside is that Cotswold brash has such thin topsoil: only six inches compared to two or three feet for richer soils. If we get an exceptionally dry spring and/or summer it just dries up and we end up with near-drought conditions.

This is obviously dreadful news for spring-sown crops, as if they can't find moisture and nutrients, they will die. Even in relatively good years the yields from our land are often a fair bit lower than you can get from most other soils.

The main crops that we were growing back in the nineties were wheat, barley, beans and linseed. These days we no longer grow beans or linseed, for economic reasons, and have moved towards oilseed rape, with its increasing popularity as a locally grown alternative to olive oil.

The manure that came from our animal sheds during the long winters would be stored in heaps. John Neave and his team would spread this on the fields in the spring as a natural fertilizer. There was never enough to cover the whole farm so we had to add artificial fertilizer as well.

One of the things I had to learn was what kinds of fertilizer to buy, and how much. They tend to be hideously expensive, and it was important not to spread too much of them on the soil for both environmental and financial reasons.

For all that my heart lay with the livestock, arable farming is the bread and butter of any farm and it would certainly be impossible for Bemborough to survive without it. Uncle John was invariably unstinting with his time and advice as he helped me get up to speed with this vital area of agricultural activity.

He would give me a foreman's responsibilities and I helped out by driving tractors and combines during harvest. I had learned about crop husbandry at college and how to deal with our idiosyncratic Cotswold brash. However, putting the lessons from the classroom into practice was a different matter and quite a challenge.

Notwithstanding all this hard work, I was still letting off steam in the squat in the evenings and – particularly – at weekends. There was an ever-changing cast of housemates and lodgers coming and going and (for my sins) my fondness for a good party had not diminished over time.

After leaving Westwood's Grammar School, my ex-girlfriend from the time of my A levels, Charlie Gilbert, had studied photography at Plymouth Art College, before graduating and moving up to London. She was now sharing a flat in Chiswick with her sister, Vicky, and working in TV post-production.

It had been quite a few years by now since Charlie and I had last dated but we had always kept in touch and whenever we had met up we had always got on incredibly well. I suppose, if I am honest, I had always secretly been really keen on her.

You would have to ask Charlie if she always felt the same. Or maybe it's best if you don't!

Her mum was now running a bed-and-breakfast in Stow-on-the-Wold. When a close family friend, Mary, passed away, Charlie came home for the funeral but found her mum had let out all of the rooms, so she phoned me up.

'Adam, I have got nowhere to stay for the weekend,' she told me. 'Can I come and stay with you?'

I was quietly delighted by this request. Charlie came down, she went to Mary's funeral, and although that was obviously a really sad event, we found we had a brilliant weekend. We had always got on well but somehow, this time, there was more to it.

Charlie and I spent the entire weekend together, laughed a lot and talked for hours as we reminisced and caught up on news of old friends. Although neither of us mentioned it, I think we could both sense that our dynamic was changing.

We had always been close, but in the past our relationship had always been about banter, joking and flirting – in a way, quite childish, I suppose. Now we were both adults and not kids, and maybe for the first time we sensed that there could be more to us than being mates.

I had only just split from my last girlfriend and Charlie had a boyfriend in London, so nothing happened between us that weekend that shouldn't have. However, when she called me a few days later and told me that she was now single, I was very pleased to hear it.

We began to spend every weekend together. Charlie would come down to the squat, or I would go up to London and stay in Chiswick. I would even drive up after rugby matches. I *must* have been keen on her!

We booked a holiday off Teletext and spent a week in Egypt. Luxor was beautiful and the tombs in the Valley of the Kings were sensational. We were only in a budget hotel and it was 40 degrees in the shade but we were in love and it was amazing, a really wonderful holiday.

Much like my sisters, Charlie had not embraced the restrictions of country life in her teenage years and she'd been thrilled to escape to Plymouth and then London. Now, more than ten years on, she was feeling differently.

She was ready to move out of the capital, and managed to get another job in post-production in Bristol. We knew by now that we wanted to live together, so she set about preparing to move out of Chiswick.

Charlie had been sharing the flat with her sister, Vicky, and Vicky's boyfriend, one of my old lodgers and rugby-playing mates, Justin Cox. Charlie was happy to sell her share of the flat to Justin and come to live with me at Bemborough.

This meant a few changes in the décor. The squat might have been fine for gangs of partying lads but it wasn't a place that most women would have wanted to live, especially ones that were used to London sophistication.

There was a grotty, stinky old settee that had seen better days even when I'd moved in seven years earlier: *that* had to go! I rolled my sleeves up, did some decorating, bought some new cupboards and furniture, and generally tried to spruce the place up.

When Charlie moved in, she brought her black half-Siamese cat, Percy, with her. Cats are about the one animal I have never really got on with, and I certainly wasn't keen on Percy.

He had a revolting meow and purred like a pneumatic drill. He also had a bad habit of peeing in the house instead of taking advantage of the great outdoors; I suppose he had been brought up in the city, after all. I wasn't Percy's biggest fan but Charlie adored him, so he was there to stay.

Percy aside, it was great having Charlie living with me and I appreciated having a confidante and soulmate on hand to share my hopes and fears. I certainly needed one because, despite my best efforts, Bemborough Farm was starting to get on top of me.

By 1997, Dad and John Neave were both heading towards retirement and keen to offload more and more responsibility on to me. On one level, it was exactly what I had always wanted – to take over the tenancy and to run the farm – but on a day-to-day level I was struggling badly.

I was working ridiculously long hours and was still lacking in crucial management skills. As livestock manager, I was spending my days shearing, crutching and drenching sheep, taking lambs to market and driving tractors: the physical, practical work that I had always done and knew well.

However, I still hadn't totally got my head around the arable side of things. I lacked some technical cropping skills, and it was clear to me that my business attributes weren't yet nearly strong enough.

Too many of the financial aspects of the business were being neglected by me in favour of practical work. It is a mistake that I am sure many farmers are guilty of. Trying to pay the bills and balance the books at night after a hard day on the farm is far from ideal.

In addition, I was getting more and more over my head with the farm park. I was taking on responsibility for buying the stock for the shop, overseeing the café, employing people and managing the cash flow. Apart from watching Mum and Dad do it, I had no real training in that field whatsoever.

I was doing my best but still leaning heavily on Dad and John Neave, and they wouldn't be there forever. No matter how hard I tried to keep up with the various demands of the farm, I was beginning to get seriously stretched and stressed. As I took stock of my situation at Bemborough, I realized that I badly needed help.

And I knew there was only one man that I wanted to turn to.

CHAPTER 10

Taking Over the Farm

After our great adventures in Australia, New Zealand and America, Duncan Andrews's life had gone in quite a different direction from mine.

When we came back from our trip, Duncan had gone to work for the Agricultural Mortgaging Corporation in Hampshire. This is an organization that loans money to farmers to buy farms, and his astute understanding of business meant that he was perfect for the job.

Being Duncan, he had done spectacularly well in the role and after three years his bosses had lined him up for a big promotion due to a reshuffle of department managers. Unfortunately, they had neglected to tell Duncan that they were planning this.

He had been growing bored of the corporate life and so began quietly preparing an exit route. It meant that when his bosses called him into the boardroom to break the good news of his promotion, they were somewhat aghast when their best-laid plans unravelled, as Duncan disclosed that he was leaving to return to farming.

Duncan was in a solid relationship with his girlfriend, Becky, whom he had met at Seale-Hayne. They decided to move back to the Scilly Isles, where Duncan had grown up, and take on a farm tenancy.

While there, they had their first two children, Jake and Sophie, and did a great job turning the farm around. They converted barns into holiday-let cottages, grew vegetables to sell locally and even ran a cut-flower business on the side.

Duncan and I had always kept in touch and met up two or three times per year. After I got together again with Charlie, Duncan phoned up and made me a tempting offer: he would give us a week's free holiday in one of the converted barns if I would shear his six Jacob sheep while I was there.

A week's holiday in exchange for half an hour's work was far too good an offer to refuse. Charlie and I drove to Penzance and got the helicopter over to Bryher. It's a tiny island, only just over a mile long, and the smallest of the inhabited Scilly Isles.

Like all good friends, Duncan and I have always just picked up where we left off every time we meet, even if we haven't seen each other for months. As he and I walked over one of his fields, I came straight out with what was on my mind.

'Look, Duncan, I'm struggling to run everything at home at the moment. Dad and John are retiring soon, and the farm, the farm park, the breeding programme and the arable are too much for me to handle. Do you fancy coming to work with me?'

My timing was good. Duncan did fancy it; he fancied it very much indeed. He felt that he had done everything he could with his farm tenancy and, while he loved the Scillies, Bryher was a tiny, insular society that was very cut off from the mainland.

He suggested that we speak to a fellow former Seale-Hayne student, Paul Simpson, who now worked for Anderson's, a farm business consultancy company. Between us, we hatched an action plan that worked for everybody.

Duncan would come to Bemborough and initially work for me, effectively as the farm manager, alongside Dad and John Neave. Dad and John would sign the tenancy over to me but continue to work with us in a handover period. When Dad and John retired for good, two years down the line, Duncan would buy into the business. He and I would run the farm as equal partners, 50/50, just as Dad and John had always done.

This plan suited me down to the ground. One or two farming mates told me that I was silly to hand over half of my business to Duncan like that – I was the tenant, why didn't I just employ a farm manager beneath me?

I didn't see it that way at all. I didn't want an employee; I wanted a business *partner* in every sense of the word: somebody who would split the responsibility with me and have as much of a vested interest in the farm as I did.

I knew that Bemborough Farm would make profits some years and losses others, and I wanted someone to share both. I also knew Duncan well enough to know that he would be innovative, resourceful and loyal in both circumstances. To me, it was a complete no-brainer.

Signing the papers to take over the tenancy was quite a moving moment. It was what I had worked towards all of my life, but at the same time there was also sadness because it was the end of an era.

Dad and John had run Bemborough for 35 years, they had always been around for me, and taking over from them felt a bit like taking the stabilizers off your bike. I was certainly glad that they would be sticking around for a couple of years to help us out.

In fact, this was a time of life-changing events all around – because Charlie and I had decided to start a family.

Up to that point, I had maybe been a bit too immature to think about having kids. It just wasn't on my radar. When Duncan and Becky had started their family a few years earlier, I was excited for them, but another part of me was thinking: *Are you mad?*

Now, it was different. I had just turned thirty and I felt ready for parenthood. Charlie felt exactly the same. I guess it is one of those things that you shouldn't do until it feels right, and the timing felt exactly right.

Charlie and I decided to have one last memorable child-free holiday and took off to the paradise island of Antigua. This plan did not work out entirely as we'd hoped.

We had kind of envisaged the trip being our honeymoon – without us actually getting married. There was no particular reason why we weren't getting hitched. We just weren't that bothered about it: we were far more focused on having kids.

The beaches in Antigua were beautiful but the company was not so charming. Our fellow travellers seemed to be mainly Brits-abroad lager louts who spent their time getting drunk and shouting loudly by the pool under our window.

The food was mass-produced fodder, the shower was a

breezeblock outhouse with a hosepipe coming out of the wall and our room was horrible. When we complained (I never usually do, I'm far too British) the hotel management moved us into a nicer room, but we could still hear the blokes swearing and fighting by the pool.

Still, at least we could escape to the beach. We could see Montserrat on the horizon, and one day we trained our binoculars on it to discover that the volcano that stands at its heart was erupting.

Charlie's cousin is a volcanologist who happened to be on Montserrat at the time, so we went down to the port and asked if we could hire a boat to go over to see him. The West Indian guy manning the desk gave us a look that spoke volumes.

'Sir and madam, you must be mad,' he told us. 'The volcano is very dangerous! We are sending our boats to evacuate the island.'

That may have been one adventure that didn't quite come off, but the holiday was still entertaining. It also marked the end of one phase of our life and the beginning of another – because very soon after we came back, Charlie was pregnant.

So, I was going to become a dad and take over the running of Bemborough Farm all at the same time. No pressure, then! Both developments were what I wanted more than anything else in the world, but at the same time I couldn't help but feel both excited and somewhat daunted.

And it was all change at Bemborough. Now that I had taken over the farm tenancy, the terms stated that I had to live in the farmhouse, so Mum and Dad would need to move out and live in one of the cottages on the land.

However, Dad's Aunty Nita, who had always adored him, sadly passed away around that time, and in her will she left him a house in Guiting Power. He sold it, and he and Mum then bought a lovely house, ideal for a retired couple, just down the road in Bourton-on-the-Water.

Duncan and Becky had been arranging their own move away from the Scilly Isles, and in October 1997 they and their two kids arrived on the farm. Duncan had already prepared a rigorous business plan of how we could progress things and his steadying hand on the tiller made a difference immediately.

He was a Godsend – exactly as I had known he would be.

It was great to have Duncan by my side because we certainly had a lot to deal with. A lot of people don't understand that farmers have to be a resilient bunch, solving problems from the moment we wake up to the moment we go to bed.

We need pretty broad CVs. Obviously we need to know about animal breeding, biology, physiology, husbandry, diseases and nutrition. Yet from the off, Duncan and I were also involved in budgeting and business planning, as we tried to realize the farm's commercial potential.

There was also the technology and mechanical side of things, as we dealt with high-tech agricultural machinery and its maintenance. Many farmers are incredibly handy at fencing, building, welding and even plumbing, and see it all as part of the job.

Dad was never that good at that side of things and, if I am honest, neither am I. He leaned heavily on John Neave for these practical issues and I quickly started doing the same to Duncan.

There is nothing wrong with that. Dad always said, 'If you can't do something yourself, surround yourself with people who can.' I quickly learned the value of managers who are expert in areas such as animals, crops and admin. In a strong team, everybody does what they are best at.

Initially, I carried on working with Dad on the livestock and the farm park, and Duncan handled the finances, plus ran the arable side with John Neave. Obviously we wanted to do this very sensitively, as the last thing we wanted to do was tread on their toes during this transition period.

We needn't have worried. Duncan and Uncle John got on well and worked really effectively together from the word go, and Dad completely approved of Duncan being drafted in. He knew how close we were and realized that Duncan was a diligent, meticulous bloke: just the business partner I needed.

It was good to know that I had Duncan to take up the slack as I tried to juggle running Bemborough with getting ready to be a dad – especially as it was not to be an easy pregnancy.

Charlie didn't have any exotic cravings but she did develop a love for the smell of both firelighters and petrol, which was a bit strange. More worryingly, she was sporadically troubled by a nasty, fairly insidious rash.

We were going to have a boy. We were convinced of it. When we had the hospital scans we asked the doctors not to tell us the sex, but in our hearts we knew a son was on the way.

We even chose a name for him: Alfie.

Charlie's due date came and went, she was getting bigger and bigger, and eventually the doctors decided to induce the birth. We went into Cheltenham General Hospital on 11 March 1998.

By now I had seen hundreds of animals give birth, of course, but nothing can compare you for seeing your partner do the same thing. Birthing sheep and calves, I was hands-on, but in the hospital I had to be totally reliant on the midwives. I felt helpless and oddly inadequate.

The birth was exhausting and stressful (and probably even worse for Charlie!). Initially a midwife put a heart monitor in the wrong place, so that it was monitoring Charlie's heart rate instead of the baby's.

They gave Charlie an epidural into her spine which somehow went the wrong way and made half of her face numb. Deep in labour, Charlie could not see out of one eye and had to talk – or rather, gasp and moan – out of one side of her mouth.

The midwife didn't seem overly concerned, but I was panicking and imagining being at home with a newborn baby and Charlie temporarily paralysed down one side. At least, I assumed it would be temporary ...

The birth was incredibly fraught and went on and on, and eventually they decided to give Charlie a Caesarean. The baby's heart rate was irregular and they thought the umbilical cord was wrapped around its neck.

A lot of fathers stay behind a screen while they perform this procedure but I was determined to see the whole thing. I will never forget the heart-stopping moment when the midwife lifted the baby up and showed us our newborn ... daughter.

It is a moment like no other. Seeing your child being born is the most amazing feeling, just totally out of this world. You can never understand it until you have done it, no matter how hard you try. And once you have done it, you never forget it.

One thought was running through my head: *I am a father*.

The midwife gave the baby to Charlie, and then she passed her to me and I held our daughter for the first time. *I am a father*.

Well, we are going to have to come up with a new name, I thought to myself. *Alfie is just not going to do*.

Because of the Caesarean, and because they had accidentally nicked Charlie's bladder during the birth, mum and baby had to stay in hospital for a couple of days. After a while, I floated off home on cloud nine to tell my parents the wonderful news.

'It's a girl!'

I was back and forth to the hospital for the next 48 hours until the big moment came to drive my partner and daughter home. Obviously, this would necessitate having a baby seat.

Unfortunately, I would be picking them up in my battered old Toyota Carina, essentially a beaten-up wagon I used to drive around the farm. It was in a bit of a state and I had meant to clean it up before I went to get them but I never quite got around to it.

Still, at least the car seat would be immaculate. Libby had given me her old seat a few weeks earlier, but it was in a bit of a rubbish state. It was covered in dried baby food and bits of half-eaten flapjack and was emitting an odd, musty odour.

I'm not putting my child in that, I had thought, and flung it in a corner of the room. Instead, I went into town and bought a lovely brand-new car seat with a beautiful floral cover and set it proudly in the spare room ready for the big day.

As I tend to do, I had left everything until the last minute before picking Charlie up, and was struggling out of my dirty farming trousers just as I was due to be leaving. I ran into the spare room and picked up the beautiful car seat ...

Hang on. Why is it wet? And what is that horrible smell?

I didn't need to be Hercule Poirot to solve the crime. The culprit was small, furry, black ... and a serial offender. Percy, Charlie's moggy, had at some point crept into the spare room and peed all over the seat.

I swore and ripped the padding off. The plastic seat beneath was swimming in cat wee. There was no time to wash it off and, clearly, no way I could use it. *Bollocks!* I had no choice but to use Libby's manky old car seat.

When new mothers are discharged from hospital with their babies, a midwife generally comes down with them to make sure the child is strapped into the car correctly and is going to be OK on the journey. I'll never forget the look on the nurse's face as she caught sight of my shitty old truck and the stained, moth-eaten car seat.

I could almost read the thought bubble over her head: *This poor child. What hope does she have?*

It was mortifying.

Charlie and I spent hours trying to come up with a name. We eventually settled on Eloise, which we shortened to Ella. Years later, I was to mention in passing that Dad's first-ever

Gloucester cow when I was a boy had been named Ella. My daughter's ears pricked up and she looked at me somewhat suspiciously.

'Hey, was I named after a cow?' she asked me.

'No, of course not!' I assured her. 'As if!'

I'm still not entirely sure that she believes me.

CHAPTER 11

The Countryside Is Closed

T hey say that when you first become a parent, it totally takes over your life. They can say that again.

As for every set of doting but nervous new parents, when Charlie and I brought Ella home from hospital, initially everything revolved around her. Let's face it, a new baby takes over every conversation and dominates everything around them.

We were busy becoming experts in matters that we had never even thought about before. Nappies. Burping. Babygros. Buggies. Strollers. Dummies.

The sleep deprivation was also an absolute killer. Many days I would be stumbling out of the farmhouse and off to the fields or the farm park after a night where Charlie and I had managed a bare four hours' sleep between us. They say that fathers-of-newborns' productivity at work goes down by 25 per cent. That sounds conservative to me!

Mum and Dad were fantastic and Mum helped us out looking after Ella a lot, especially after a few months when Charlie's maternity leave finished and she went back part-time to her post-production job in Bristol. Charlie's family also rallied round brilliantly.

Charlie and her mum had been quite worried before Ella's birth about Charlie's gran, who held very traditional views and so disapproved of us having a baby out of wedlock. I had no time at all for this, especially as Dad, who *had* been born out of wedlock and suffered emotional hardship for it, had no objections whatsoever.

They needn't have worried. As soon as Gardy – our nickname for Charlie's gran – saw Ella she fell head over heels in love with her. She became a regular visitor to the farm just so she could get down on the floor and play with her.

Unfortunately, Ella had arrived into a very loving world but not a terribly financially secure one. As Duncan and I finally took over running Bemborough and Dad and John went off for their very well-earned retirements, the farm was seriously on its uppers.

British farming as a whole was suffering and we had been hit worse than most. The harvests had been disappointing for a couple of years as the weather and the stubborn Cotswold brash combined to thwart us, and for various reasons UK grain prices had gone through the floor. Meat prices were also down and suddenly we seemed to be at the heart of a perfect storm.

Ever since it had first opened, Bemborough had always relied heavily on the income from the farm park if other areas were struggling – but now even that was doing badly as well. From around 110,000 visitors per year at its peak in the 1970s, the Cotswold Farm Park was now attracting barely half that many.

There were plenty of reasons for this. British society had changed a lot since 1971, and the strong pound and the rise of budget airlines meant that a lot of families were now far more likely to head to Greece than Gloucestershire for their vacations.

Public-spending cuts in the 1980s and 1990s meant many schools had less money to spend on trips for their pupils – and, in any case, we were no longer unique. Perhaps to a degree we had become victims of our own success: we were now up against three rival farm parks in the Cotswolds alone.

However, despite these well-founded reasons for the downturn, all of which were out of our hands, I couldn't help feeling that we were also partly culpable for the farm park's current sorry predicament.

After its initial success, I had probably become complacent about the park in the 1990s. We had allowed it to tick over but not really concentrated on it or developed it at a time when rival entertainment options were raising their game.

Frankly, there was a danger we were starting to seem a bit old hat. The basic concept of conserving and displaying rare-breed animals to the public was still a sound one, but in truth the farm park was now lacking somewhat in imagination and razzmatazz.

Duncan and I sat down and looked at our options. Really, we only had two: should we somehow find the money to make the Cotswold Farm Park a far better attraction for visitors and make it financially viable?

Or should we shut it down?

We considered the second option, but not for long. It seemed like such an admission of failure. The farm park had been a beacon and a symbol of Bemborough Farm for getting on for three decades now: did we *really* want to give up all of that at the first sign of adversity?

More importantly, although he would not have objected and would have supported us in whatever we did, I knew that shutting the park would have broken Dad's heart. It had always been far more than a very dear hobby for him: he had thrown his heart and soul into it.

No, the Cotswold Farm Park had been there since I was a boy and the thought of taking over the farm and immediately closing down Dad's life's passion and pride and joy did not sit comfortably with me. It was his legacy and I wanted to enhance it, not destroy it.

So that left us only one way forward – we would have to invest, and invest heavily. As the saying goes, it was time to speculate to accumulate.

Duncan and I hired a tourism consultant to advise us how to pull more people through the doors. Consequently, we built display barns including a petting barn where kids could hold newborn chicks and stroke lambs, and we arranged more demonstrations like shearing and lambing.

We went even further, setting up a tractor school, where our visitors could learn to drive mini farm equipment, and introducing a farm safari: a tractor-and-trailer ride around the outside of the farm park. We also put in new kids' play equipment, including (of all things) an educational bouncy castle that explained where everyday foods come from.

Given the parlous financial state that we were already in, all this was a major leap of faith in the farm park and a serious investment. Duncan and I had already had to borrow heavily from our parents to buy into the business, and here we were taking on further debts to the tune of some £80,000.

Some people might have said this was foolish in the extreme – but, after all, had they not said exactly the same thing when the park had first opened, nearly 30 years earlier?

As we eased into the new millennium, Duncan and I dared to begin to think that the worst might have passed. Crop and meat prices were starting slowly to inch back up and we had high hopes for the farm park when it reopened with all of its new attractions.

Bemborough Farm had had a brutal year in 1999, probably the worst I had ever known, but we were still standing and had clawed our way back a little in 2000. Surely the next year would see us on a better footing still?

Or so we thought.

In February 2001, Charlie and I treated ourselves to a rare weekend away in Devon with Ella. While we were there, my mobile phone rang. It was Libby.

'Have you seen the news?' she asked me.

I hadn't seen it. And when I turned on the TV, I didn't want to.

The government's Department of Farming and Rural Affairs (DEFRA) inspectors had been carrying out a routine check on an abattoir near Brentwood in Essex when they had discovered an outbreak of foot-and-mouth disease. It was the first such instance in Britain for 20 years.

They had diagnosed 28 pigs with the illness, and they and the other 300 animals at the abattoir had been slaughtered on the spot. As Charlie and I sped back to Bemborough Farm, we knew that this was only the start of it.

It meant that the entire summer of 2001 would be an utter nightmare.

Foot-and-mouth is a disease that can affect all cloven-footed animals such as cows, sheep, goats, pigs and deer. Its name reflects the fact that it causes profound and painful blisters and sores on the animals' feet and around their mouths that lead to chronic illness and death.

The worst thing about it is that it is hugely contagious. Foot-and-mouth can be spread not just by direct contact between the animals but via their mucus or faeces or simply on the wind. DEFRA knew there was only one way to combat it and they did it straight away.

They closed the countryside down.

If that sounds overly dramatic, well, it really isn't. DEFRA set up exclusion zones all around the country. The movement of livestock was banned, which effectively meant that farmers could not buy or sell animals. Fox hunting was banned, as in some areas were horse riding, cycling or even rambling.

Next came the slaughters. Within days hundreds more cases of foot-and-mouth had been confirmed in the UK. There was no option but to kill not only all of those animals, but also any who might possibly have come into contact with them. It's the only way to combat the disease.

It's the only way – and it's brutal. Over that summer of 2001, more than 2,000 cases of the disease sprang up across the UK. This was to result in a death toll of more than 10 million animals.

It was a devastating blow for British farming, just about the worst scenario that you could imagine unfolding. And for us, there was a very real danger that it could be a deathblow.

It was up to farmers to report this disease. We kept an extra careful eye on our livestock because we knew that if our animals contracted it, we would have to slaughter every single sheep, goat, cow and pig on Bemborough – including all of the rare breeds.

I arranged that if we did contract foot-and-mouth, Mum and Dad would go up to London to stay with Uncle Nicky for a few days. Seeing his life's work destroyed would have broken Dad's heart.

It would have broken mine, too, but I knew if it ever happened I had no choice but to stay home and manage the situation as best I could, like hundreds of other farmers across the country were already doing.

Thankfully our animals remained healthy, but we couldn't move them, sell them or even display them to the public. We basically had no income stream at all.

So what were we to do?

Many times that spring Duncan and I got our families around the kitchen table for crisis meetings. Whichever way we looked at it, our situation was bleak. We were tenant farmers who lived in rented accommodation on the farm, and right now we had no way to pay our rent, or to pay anything.

Duncan's and my assets were all tied up in animals and agricultural equipment, which were currently useless to us. Normally we would hold a farm sale to raise some cash but even that was not an option. Nobody was allowed on or off our land.

We had banked with the same local bank for years but now that we had our backs to the wall, they refused to support us. We kept explaining our plight and asking for overdraft extensions and they kept coming back and telling us no. Well, thanks a lot!

There was one fallback – or so we thought. Dad had always insured Bemborough against foot-and-mouth. I had thought that it was a waste of money and when I took over I thought about cancelling it: there hadn't been an outbreak in Britain for 20 years, right? But Dad had persuaded me to keep it on.

Duncan and I rang the insurance company to put in a claim for loss of income, because we'd had to shut the gates of the farm park, and no visitors meant no income.

Their initial response was not encouraging. They told us that they could only pay out if we could show them an official letter from DEFRA closing down the farm park.

We then spoke to DEFRA, who told us that they were not officially closing down businesses unless they were within a restricted zone. They were merely *advising* us not to open. We were not within a zone, so they couldn't give us a letter.

This was shaping up to be a classic Catch-22 situation.

The insurance company was point-blank refusing to budge. Duncan and I were growing desperate, so we told them if they would not pay out, we would simply reopen the farm park to the public.

In all likelihood, somebody would bring foot-and-mouth onto the premises, and we would then have to slaughter all of our animals. The insurers would be facing a massive payout to us – not only for loss of income, but also for the value of all our rare breeds that would have to be killed.

It was a last-resort scenario that we were painting, and, if I am honest, I'm not sure we would have gone through with it.

However, if we were calling the insurers' bluff, it didn't work. They just said that reopening while the epidemic was ongoing would be reckless behaviour and would invalidate our insurance, in the same way as reckless driving renders motoring insurance null and void.

They had got us by the short and curlies. And they wonder why nobody likes insurance companies!

Unable to pay our rents, or any bills at all, and with both our landlords and the banks on our backs, Duncan and I were stressed and going mad with worry. Ella was no longer my only reason for sleepless nights, as I lay awake wondering exactly how we were going to extricate ourselves from this mess.

However, if our bank and our insurance company had made themselves absent when the business most needed them, normal people were the exact opposite.

The Bemborough Farm staff were simply unbelievable. Our seasonal staff had contracts with us and could legally have demanded payment even though we were closed; after all, like us, they had families to feed. Instead, every one of them was happy to stand down and wait for us to reopen.

The full-time staff were even more amazing. They knew we were going through a major crisis and there was no guarantee we would survive, but nobody headed for the hills. Most of our employees volunteered to work for nothing as Duncan and I struggled to keep our heads above water.

A lot of local churches and charities rallied around to raise emergency funds for us, and even some regular visitors to the farm park posted us donations to help us pay for essentials like animal feed. Such unexpected, unsolicited kindness was touching and humbling. A neighbouring farmer, Pat Quinn, even gave us 50 bales of silage to help with the expense of feeding our rare-breed cattle.

Yet we couldn't keep Bemborough running on charity and a wing and a prayer. We needed some serious cash to survive – and luckily, just as things looked desperate beyond repair, it arrived.

DEFRA closed down a farm where they had found foot-and-mouth in nearby Teddington. Duncan has always been a man of detail, and going through the small print of our foot-and-mouth insurance policy, he discovered that the company had to pay out if the disease affected even a tiny part of our land.

A large circle on the map defined the restricted area based around the outbreak at Teddington, and the circumference of the circle just clipped the edge of one of our fields. Bingo! The insurers had to pay us £50,000, which meant we could at least pay our outstanding rent.

DEFRA were doing their best to get on top of the crisis but they were not really prepared for it and their reaction was often fairly chaotic. There weren't enough vets to cope with the epidemic on the ground and they began to fly in vets from Europe and even from Australia.

Things got a little better when the government drafted the military into the countryside in May, three months into the crisis. The Ministry of Defence seemed notably more organized than were DEFRA and were extremely robust with the slaughtering and clean-up processes.

Even though Bemborough was not infected, we knew that we couldn't do anything that involved sheep, cows, pigs or goats. Nevertheless, in May Duncan and I took the nervous decision to reopen the farm park with no cloven-footed animals.

We had all the new attractions that we had spent so much money installing the previous winter, and we tried to be inventive. I put on sheepdog demonstrations using ducks, which they drove around a little course and into a pond. It was also OK to display our Exmoor ponies.

Another brainwave came from Kevin, a neighbour of ours. Duncan met him in the village one day and explained our predicament. Kevin was a good businessman, so Duncan was picking his brains to see if he had any income-generating ideas.

Kevin explained, 'I may be shooting myself in the foot here, and I don't know a huge amount about the countryside, but you very kindly let my daughters ride around the farm for free and they absolutely love it. It's beautiful, with the rolling Cotswold Hills, limestone streams and woodlands. I reckon people would drive from miles around and pay for the pleasure of riding their horses across your farm.'

Duncan and I discussed the idea and decided it was certainly worth thinking about. The local hunt already organized a horse fun ride to raise money for charity every year. Maybe we could do something once per month? We decided anything was worth a try and gained permission from the landlords.

Resourceful as ever, Duncan got to work with a hammer and saw and in a few days had rigged up a 12-mile ride with 70 (optional) horse jumps over our land. Maybe because locals were sympathetic to our plight, the first fun ride was a huge success, as well as great fun, and the money certainly helped. We still hold these regular events even today.

The visitors to the farm park slowly trickled back and these bits and bobs of income kept us afloat, just about, until foot-and-mouth was finally under control and DEFRA declared the epidemic to be over that October. Even so, it had been the most desperate summer I had ever experienced on Bemborough Farm and I hope never to have one like it again.

Duncan and I had lost around £100,000 due to the epidemic, which had crippled us financially, but we knew that it could have been far worse. We could easily have gone under, and there were times when we really thought we were going to.

Like Dad and John Neave before us, we had been living hand to mouth, renting our homes and ploughing every penny we made back into the business. Foot-and-mouth had shown us just how precarious that was and how easily disaster could strike.

Both of us had the same thought as we came out of the crisis, bruised and battered: *never again*. When we could afford it, we took a little money out of the business and each bought a small house away from the farm to let out. It means that if Armageddon ever strikes again, at least we and our families will have a roof over our heads.

We also decided to change banks, because we just couldn't forgive or forget the way that our existing bankers had hung us out to dry as they watched their own backs. Thankfully, a good farming friend of mine recommended a local branch of Lloyds, who understand agriculture and long-term strategy. We have banked with them ever since.

It had been a horrendous experience. I truly hope that the authorities have learned from it and would be far better prepared in the case of a similar epidemic, because they were caught wrong-footed in 2001.

Sadly, outbreaks of devastating disease are just something to which farming is very vulnerable. The poultry industry, for example, lives in terror of bird flu. You can take every precaution available, but there are some natural disasters that you just can't do anything about. Ultimately, it is in the lap of the gods.

However, although 2001 had at the time appeared to be our ultimate *annus horribilis*, something else had happened during the year that was to alter my own circumstances, and my day-to-day life, completely beyond recognition.

I had never seriously thought of doing anything to earn my living except being a farmer and running Bemborough Farm. But suddenly, out of the blue, a whole new career was going to come along and blindside me – just like it had my dad, 30 years earlier.

They say that history repeats itself. I was about to become the living proof.

Countryfile, the BBC's farming and rural affairs magazine TV show, had advertised for a new presenter. They asked any viewers who were interested to record and send them a two-minute audition tape.

I often watched *Countryfile* but I hadn't seen their item about the presenter search, and I wouldn't have thought anything of it if I had. However, a girl called Hannah who worked on the farm park saw it, decided to enter the contest and came to see Charlie and me.

Hannah knew that Charlie had a video camera because of her post-production job, and asked if she could borrow it to record her audition tape. If I am honest, the conversation hardly registered with me at all. Charlie handed the video camera over to Hannah and off she went.

That night, after we had put Ella to bed, Charlie and I were sitting having dinner. We were talking about this and that, as usual, when Charlie suddenly took the conversation in a very unexpected direction.

'You know that presenter search for *Countryfile*, Adam?' she asked me. 'You ought to go in for it.'

CHAPTER 12

'Do We Need the Ginger
Farm Boy?'

I may possibly have laughed. Certainly I didn't take Charlie's suggestion seriously. *Apply to host a television programme? I'm a farmer. Why would I want to do that?*

Being on TV had never really occurred to me. It just wasn't in my scheme of things. Show-business genes might have run in our family ever since the great Leslie Henson, but as far as I was concerned, they had stopped when they got to me.

Television wasn't totally alien to me, of course. I had been proud of my dad doing his presenting as a kid, and he had brought the cameras from both *Animal Magic* and *In the Country* to Bemborough to film there. I had also enjoyed watching Uncle Nicky over the years starring in various shows such as *Shine On Harvey Moon*, *Boon* and *Minder*.

Even after Dad had retired from presenting, TV shows had dropped in on us every now and then. *The Really Wild Show* and *Countryfile* had both filmed on the farm. Anneka Rice and *Treasure Hunt* had even come down one year and hidden a clue on one of our oxen.

Yet despite all this, I had never been particularly bothered about television. I had found my occasional first-hand glimpses into how it worked interesting, but that was as far as it went. TV just seemed like something that other people did.

So that was the end of that conversation. Or was it?

Charlie had planted the seed of the idea in my mind, and I suppose over the next few days it began to grow. Charlie kept chipping away at me, telling me that she thought I'd be good at it and I had nothing to lose from going for it. What harm could it do?

She also made the very good point that in the unlikely event that I was successful, the money would be a very useful new supplementary income stream after the horrendous year we had endured on the farm due to foot-and-mouth. We were still seriously skint and could certainly use the money.

That made a lot of sense to me. As a kid, I had seen just how many more people flocked to the Cotswold Farm Park when Dad went on the TV and became nationally known. I asked him what he thought about the *Countryfile* idea, and he was hugely encouraging and said that I should definitely go for it.

Gradually but inexorably, Charlie won me round and I said that I would give it a go. As she said, what harm could it do?

Charlie's TV experience and know-how made her the obvious director for my audition tape so we headed out to the yard with the video camera. I imagined we would probably be there for about an hour.

It took us the entire day.

The main reason for that was that I kept messing it up, because I just wasn't used to talking into a camera. I was also trying to be enthusiastic in communicating my passion for the country, but Charlie told me that it looked like overacting.

The other factor that slowed things down was that I had decided to have animals in my video. I had always noticed that Dad was most comfortable on TV when he had a lamb or a calf to cradle as he talked, so I decided to follow his lead.

I co-opted a huge White Park bull and a goat kid to share my video short. The bull spent a lot of its time slobbering over me as I tried to run through my spiel about my background and my life on Bemborough Farm, then he just got bored and wandered off. I couldn't say that I blamed him.

The baby goat was very sweet – but appeared to be on a mission to sabotage my media career from the outset, and bleated on cue every time I opened my mouth to talk to the camera. As they say, never work with children and animals ...

Eventually, I got the two creatures to fall into line and they stayed quiet and in picture as I did my bit. Charlie was very patient with me, and she and I filmed in different parts of the farm until she had enough rough footage to do something with.

I had no idea how it would turn out but after Charlie had taken it to an editing suite and weaved her post-production magic on it, it came out reasonably well. I was pleasantly surprised that it seemed half-decent: I had expected to be watching it back through my fingers.

We showed it to Duncan and to my dad, who both liked it. Dad's approval meant a lot to me as he was a TV veteran and I knew he wouldn't humour me if it were not good enough. We stuck the tape in the post and I returned to normal everyday farming life and half-forgot about it.

About three weeks later, the farmhouse telephone rang.

'I'm calling from BBC *Countryfile*,' said the voice on the other end. 'We loved your audition tape and would like to invite you on location with us.'

Wow! This was the last thing that I had expected and as we spoke on the phone, part of me quietly wondered if they had made a mistake. Even so, it was an exciting development and I was definitely up for whatever the next stage was.

The producer asked me to go to Lake Vyrnwy in Powys in Wales in two weeks' time. They were to hold a two-day boot-camp-cum-crash-course for the 20 wannabe presenters they had chosen from the audition tapes, after which they would whittle the contestants down to a final shortlist of three.

Before I set out for Wales, I naturally went to see Dad to ask if he had any tips or advice. He said that I should talk to the camera as if it was my friend and I was chatting to a mate. That was what he had always done, and it had certainly worked for him.

The two days in Wales were pretty intensive. The rules of the presenter search said that entrants were not allowed to have any previous journalistic experience, so my 19 fellow hopefuls were a mixed bag of farm workers, gamekeepers, zoo staff and even a jockey.

We were a motley crew and the *Countryfile* producers soon got to work on us, showing us how to write little sections of script and how to do pieces to camera. We did some mock interviews, with the production staff standing in as the rural affairs experts we had to aim our questions at.

They also laid on a few relaxing, team-building activities for us, such as clay pigeon shooting. Throughout the two days they were observing us intently to see who they thought might be a natural and would work well on TV.

For the final exercise, the producers said we had each to film a short item suitable for TV broadcast. They gathered their 20 aspiring broadcasters together and gave each of us a bit of paper with our subject. I had to talk about the hotel that we were staying in, and its food.

Everybody had half an hour in their hotel room to prepare their script. This was a daunting prospect for me, as it was not something I was used to doing and I had never exactly set the world alight in English at school.

Nevertheless I am very competitive and the adrenaline kicked in as I tried to get something decent down on paper. By the time I got a call telling me that a car was waiting to take me down to Lake Vrnywy, I was happy with what I had written.

A director, camera crew and sound operator were waiting by the lakeside. The director took control, taking my script from me and telling me exactly where to walk as I delivered my piece to the camera.

I had to interview somebody who was pretending to be the hotel chef, then read a piece of voiceover and finally do an end piece to the camera. Throughout the exercise, my dad's advice was running through my head.

I was nervous, scared even, but I thought I had done OK. I was used to doing lambing and shearing demonstrations in the farm park while talking to the public through a head mic, which meant I didn't feel too self-conscious, and I guess that must have helped.

We all had one final interview with the *Countryfile* series producer and then that was it: they thanked us for our time and we were on our way. As I drove back to Bemborough, I didn't know exactly how well it had gone but I knew that I had given it my best shot.

A couple more weeks went by and then the programme's producers phoned again. They had selected me for the final shortlist of three aspiring presenters and the choice would now rest with the *Countryfile* viewers.

Luckily, they were not going to broadcast our videos from Wales on the show for a nationwide vote, like some kind of agricultural take on *The X Factor*. Instead, they had sent them to 100 *Countryfile* viewers for them to choose the winner.

One of my rivals was a guy called Michael Keele, whom I'd befriended in Powys. Michael was a farmer's son and a part-time fireman and was a very good-looking, confident chap and an excellent speaker. To me, he seemed like he would be perfect for the programme. We are friends to this day.

To my astonishment, the viewers didn't pick Michael. The next call from *Countryfile* informed me that *I* had won the presenter search contest. Fantastic!

I could not believe it, especially as more than 3,500 people had apparently sent in initial audition tapes. Had I really been chosen from all of those to become John Craven's onscreen sidekick?

Well, maybe not. There was a catch. For the competition prize no longer seemed to be as advertised. In fact, there had been an unexpected complication.

At the same time as the BBC had been holding its *Countryfile* presenter search it had also been broadcasting one of the very first reality-TV shows. *Castaway 2000* had dispatched 36 members of the public to live on the remote Hebridean island of Taransay for a year to attempt to build a community from scratch.

These men, women and children had reared their own cattle, sheep, pigs and chickens on the island, killed their own meat and grown their own vegetables. When the programme was broadcast the following year, it was a ratings success – and one of the participants stood out a mile.

Ben Fogle was a handsome, charming young man from a London acting family and the camera clearly loved him. It soon became obvious to BBC executives that here was a star in the making, but what should they do with him?

Well, there was that presenter's job going on *Countryfile* ...

Some senior BBC execs spoke to the *Countryfile* producers. 'You don't need that ginger farm boy who has won the presenter contest,' they told them. 'This good-looking blond lad from London, Ben Fogle, is a star in the making. Why not use him?'

The *Countryfile* producers had not been left with too much choice in the matter. They thought Ben was great, but it did leave them with the problem of what to do with me. Maybe there was some kind of compromise solution?

They had decided that there was – so when that phone call telling me that I had won came in, the words they used were not quite those I had been expecting.

'Congratulations, Adam!' a woman told me. 'You have won the competition and we can offer you the prize – one day's presenting on *Countryfile* with John Craven!'

Huh? That wasn't what it had said on the tin! *How had that happened?* My mind was whirling. I stayed polite and pleasant on the phone as I tried to demur: 'I had thought it was more of a long-term job than that?'

'Yes, as I say, you will do one day's presenting with John Craven!' repeated the cheery female voice. 'We will be in touch with the details. Bye!'

When I put the phone down, I wasn't too happy. Had I really wasted hours of preparation and two days in Wales chasing what I thought was a full-time job just for *that*?

The BBC had never advertised its presenter search as the chance to make a one-off appearance on the telly and, if they had, I certainly wouldn't have bothered to go for it. I vented to Charlie, who agreed that it was quite unfair. Then I went to tell my dad what had happened.

Dad listened intently and nodded as I told him how unfair I thought it was. Then he delivered his verdict.

'Adam, it's the BBC,' he said with a wry smile. 'If that is what they have decided to do, go along for the day anyway. Have a go at presenting, meet John Craven, have a good day, make the tea and carry the tripod for the cameraman. Who knows what might come of it?'

Dad was right, I realized. There was no point in throwing my toys out of the pram. I decided to suck it up, swallow my pride and take *Countryfile* up on its kind offer. After all, I had not been that bothered about the whole thing in the first place.

I'm so glad that I did, because at that point the BBC did the decent thing and restored the presenter search prize to what it had originally been. I think this was largely down to the series producer at the time, a lovely lady named Sarah Eglin.

Sarah had had to oversee the whole competition rigmarole, viewing thousands of audition tapes, arranging the boot camp in Wales and all the rest of it, while simultaneously producing the regular programme. She had shouldered a huge workload and didn't want it all to have been a waste of time.

Sarah seemed to quite like the look of me and she dug her heels in until the BBC executives relented and said, 'Fine, OK, *Countryfile* can have *two* new presenters.' They would try using both Ben Fogle and me and see how it went.

Now I just had to wait for the details of my first assignment. They came in a phone call from Sarah.

'Adam, can you go to Wales to talk to some farmers who are growing drugs?'

What? Have I heard that right? 'Pardon?'

'We're not talking Class As here, Adam,' she laughed. 'It's a couple of Welsh sheep farmers who have found a unique way to diversify. They have started to grow herbs that can be used in all kinds of natural remedies.'

Phew! That was a relief. It was hard enough having to learn a whole new profession, TV presenting, on the hoof. At least the subject matter for my first story would be agriculture – the thing I felt most confident talking about.

Even so, I could hardly have been more nervous a few days later as I drove to Wales to begin my national TV career. It felt a bit like a first day at school – well, if first days at school were filmed for millions of people to watch them!

The assignment went pretty well but I still found it nerve-wracking. We went to visit one of the farmers, filmed him growing his crop, and I interviewed him about how he'd had the idea and how successful his venture was proving.

It felt like there was a lot to learn and a lot to take in. I had to memorize a script, which I did by pacing around on my own, repeating and repeating it until it seemed to have sunk in. In fact, I still pretty much use that same method today.

I was still nervous talking to camera, I worried about coming across as stiff and wooden, and I stumbled over my words a few times – just like Dad must have done with his stammer, all those years ago. Even so, the director kept telling me it was going well, and it was all wrapped up by teatime.

Had it really gone well? Who knows? As I drove home, I felt a strange mix of relief and quiet elation. It had all been very new and a bit strange but I had enjoyed it and I knew that I wanted to do more, given the opportunity.

When I got home, Charlie suggested we go to see a mate just down the road in Bourton-on-the-Water. When we got there, Duncan and a load of other friends were waiting: Charlie had organized a big surprise congratulations party for me.

It was beginning to sink in for me that this was all quite a big deal.

As it turned out, the *Countryfile* producers liked what I had done on my first shoot in Wales and decided to make a big deal of my arrival on the show. On the week that it was to be broadcast, John Craven would present the whole of the programme from Bemborough Farm.

I had met John once before, briefly, when he had come down

to the farm to interview Dad about something or other for *Countryfile*. He had been absolutely charming and friendly then and I had no reason to believe that he wouldn't be now.

I have never been someone who gets particularly starstruck around celebrities but even so I was pretty nervous meeting John again, this time as his colleague. Like most kids of my age, I had grown up watching him present *John Craven's Newsround* and *Multi-Coloured Swap Shop*. The man is a television legend.

The *Countryfile* producers had planned that I would walk up into the Highlands paddock on Bemborough Farm and find John, who would be delivering a piece to camera. He would turn and greet me and introduce me to the viewers.

I was sure that I would find some way to mess it up, by stepping in a cow pat or stumbling over my words. However, it all went swimmingly and John was just as gracious as I remembered as he officially welcomed me.

So that was it. Now I was part of the *Countryfile* team.

It was a weird experience watching my first report being broadcast, sitting at home with my family. Being as English as I am, I found it quite embarrassing and couldn't help cringing a little, but at the same time I was also quietly proud.

I was even prouder when Dad told me that he loved it and he thought I had done a really good job. I could tell that he was really pleased that I was not just following him into TV but might even be able to make a decent fist of it.

Sarah Eglin gave me a couple more assignments to do as the show pondered how to use Ben and me. She sent me off to March in Cambridgeshire, where there had been reports of huge rats eating freshwater mussels from a local river.

The camera crew and I went down to the river, talked to an ecologist about what was happening and located the mussels in the water. We filmed at night, hoping to catch the rats in action, but they are wily creatures and stayed away.

It was a really interesting trip for me, not least because I had never even known there was such a thing as a freshwater mussel – I had always assumed they lived only in the sea. It's one thing I still love about *Countryfile* even today: how it can educate me as well as the viewers.

My third assignment saw me heading off to report on ponies running wild on Dartmoor. After that, I think the producers thought I had proved my worth, and they told me they would use me, as they would Ben, once or twice a month.

Ben and I got on great from the start. There could very easily have been tension between us as initially at least it seemed as if we were going for the same job, but we just made a joke of it, laughed it off and rubbed along fine.

I didn't really see him that often because we would usually be off doing different shoots. I might bump into him in the Pebble Mill *Countryfile* office in Birmingham every now and then if we were doing voiceover days and we would go for a drink if we got a chance.

Occasionally Ben and I would do double-header presenting and we would make a joke of trying to hog the camera time. He would stand a little in front of me or I'd give him a crafty nudge to put him off. It was harmless and all good fun.

We were joining the close-knit existing *Countryfile* team: John Craven, Miriam O'Reilly, Charlotte Smith and Michaela Strachan. I didn't see that much of the female members initially, except for special broadcasts and Christmas parties, but they were all very warm and welcoming.

Of course, John Craven was the daddy of the show and I was definitely a bit worried about how he might feel about two young blokes coming on the show at the same time. Would he be jealous of Ben and me sharing his spotlight?

I could not have been more wrong. Right from the off, John took me under his wing and was totally supportive. I was incredibly grateful for his encouragement. Was he only helping me because he knew my dad? No: he was the same with everybody. It was obvious he is just a really top bloke.

In my early days, John gave me countless tips and nuggets of advice. For example, initially when I was sent scripts the day before doing an outside broadcast I would pore over them at home for hours, trying to memorize them.

John told me not to bother. Virtually every time, the script would change on the day of filming, either because a date or a fact was wrong, or more often because a director or a producer simply changed their mind.

If I had memorized the piece the night before, it would be embedded in my brain and I'd find it hard to make subtle changes. It made far more sense to skim the script for general content the night before, then learn the specifics on the spot during the shoot.

However, I admired John from the off not just because he is a helpful, avuncular mentor. He is also a proper, investigative, old-school journalist.

When the BBC had moved him from editing *Newsround* – *John Craven's Newsround* as was – to hosting *Countryfile* in 1989, there was a lot that was wrong with British farming. John had not hesitated to shine a bright, pitiless light upon it – to the profession's great benefit.

Because of the nature of Dad's farming and the emphasis he put upon preserving rare breeds, I wasn't really aware as I was growing up of the iniquities of intensive farming. However, in many ways farming in the UK in the 1980s and 1990s was pretty brutal compared with today.

Some of the big, intensive farms had thousands of battery hens living in miserable conditions, and pigs in tethers with chains around their necks. BSE was rife at times, and some of our methods of applying pesticides and fertilizers and disposing of waste were damaging the environment, too.

In addition, more-than-generous European Commission and UK government regulations gave farmers subsidies for the number of ewes that they had or the amount of food that they produced. The payments were well-intentioned but the system was easily abused.

Thus you would get farmers buying and selling ewe quota from each other like stocks and shares to ensure they picked up the maximum subsidy payments. On the crops front, it led to the infamous EU food mountain of tabloid notoriety. It was no real surprise that farmers didn't have a great reputation with the British public for many years.

John had gone into *Countryfile* and started reporting on all of these issues. I suppose in a way he was a whistleblower. It had not made him popular with a lot of farmers – but it was not his job to be popular.

John had not reported these controversial stories because

he had an agenda or any kind of axe to grind. He had just done it because they had to be reported. Throughout his career he has had a rare journalistic integrity that he maintains to this day.

In my early days on *Countryfile* there was probably only one person whose approbation I craved more than John's – and that was Dad. Happily, and characteristically, he did not stint in giving it.

Dad quickly became my biggest fan on *Countryfile*. It was a rare week that he did not ring me after a show had aired or, next time I saw him, make a point of telling me how good he thought I had been that week.

He gave me tips but mostly he gave me praise. In the way that he had done ever since I was a small boy, he educated me, but mostly he encouraged me in what I loved and what was important to me.

In later years, as I learned even more about Dad's own very troubled childhood and the often absent Lally, I reflected upon how his loving fathering of me was pretty much the polar opposite of what he had received as a child.

Still, the full enormity of that story was yet to unfold for me. For now, I just knew that my being on *Countryfile* made Dad very happy – and for me, that was all the more reason to do it, and to do it well.

As he knew, and as I knew, I still had a lot to learn.

CHAPTER 13

Practising My Autograph

O nce I was firmly part of the *Countryfile* team, the jobs kept coming. If I had fondly imagined that I would be the show's 'tame farmer', much as Dad had been on the BBC for so many years, I soon realized that I would have to think again.

In my first few months I covered plenty of farming stories, but *Countryfile* is a magazine programme that reports on many, many aspects of British rural life. As its wide-eyed, wet-behind-the-ears roving reporter, I was dispatched to all sorts of wild, weird and wonderful events.

I'd always expected my new TV job to require me to discuss the logistics of lambing, breeding and crop rotation. I didn't know I'd also have to talk about ... toe wrestling.

Countryfile dispatched me to Derbyshire – to be exact, to a pub called the Ye Olde Royal Oak in Wetton. Since 1970 it had been holding the World Toe Wrestling Championship, an event that had been inaugurated by a local lad named George Burgess.

The idea behind the event was that two competitors lay down barefoot on a platform (or, as they preferred to call it, a toedium), linked big toes and tried to force the other person's foot down like in arm wrestling (oddly, Sky Sports had yet to bid for the world rights to this extravaganza).

I had gamely agreed to give it a go, so after interviewing the organizers I lowered myself onto the toedium and locked toes with a young local chap. I twisted my foot, his leg went down, and I was the winner. *Ha! There was nothing to this lark!*

Or so I thought.

Before leaving for Derbyshire, I had carefully cut my toenails and made sure my feet were nice and clean for their big TV debut. I was quickly to realize that not every contestant had been so considerate.

In the next round, my opponent was a huge bearded bloke with a Mohican, covered in tattoos and sporting a waistcoat made from stitched-together bar towels. When he sat down and took his socks off, the whiff from his feet nearly knocked me over.

His toes looked pretty unsavoury and I was sure there was some athlete's foot going on. I was a bit unnerved by the sight of his tootsies and he rapidly made mincemeat of me. At the end, as he pulled his foot away, his jagged nail cut the inside of my big toe. *Ouch.*

The toe wrestling set the benchmark for some pretty wacky early *Countryfile* assignments. I was back in Derbyshire not long afterwards for the World Hen Racing Championship.

This event took place in the car park of the Barley Mow Inn in Bonsall, near Matlock. I might have had no idea how to prepare for toe wrestling but I fancied my chances on this one and I got to work training my chickens.

A *Countryfile* camera crew came down to Bemborough and filmed me putting two of my hens, renamed Charlotte and Michaela in honour of my fellow presenters, through their paces. They would have to run down a short course and be first past the post to bring home the prize.

The trick was to treat 'em mean, keep 'em keen, so I didn't feed Charlotte or Michaela for a couple of hours before my practice run on the farm. I then stood 30 feet away from them and shook a tin of corn. They were so keen for the food they came pounding across the yard like a pair of feathered Usain Bolts.

It was pretty impressive and I set off for Bonsall wallowing in the near-certainty of glorious victory with this pair of spring-heeled, clucking athletes batting for me. What could possibly go wrong?

They didn't win. The other chicken trainers must have kept their hens hungrier than mine, or had some more exciting treats to encourage them to run down the track!

I can't rule out the possibility that as the *Countryfile* newbie, I was initially getting one or two short-straw assignments that maybe the more established presenters might not have fancied. This was definitely the case when the producers entered me into the Maldon Mud Race.

This saw contestants having to run, walk and crawl around a demanding course on the feet-deep, energy-sapping mud flats around Maldon in Essex. When I realized how filthy and mucky I was going to get, I started getting mental flashbacks to falling into the sheep dip.

The *Countryfile* production team turned up at the farm to see me train, playing the theme from *Rocky* as they filmed me doing press-ups and sit-ups in the yard and out in the fields. I felt pretty daft, and was quickly learning that television can take you a long way outside of your comfort zone.

It was great fun, although I was hacked off when I twisted my ankle training a few days before the race, meaning that I couldn't finish the course. Even so, all those years of hurling myself around rugby pitches stood me in good stead and I did OK.

Not all of the jobs were quite so preposterous. Another of my early reports involved me grilling a minister, Elliot Morley MP, about his government's official handling of the recent cataclysmic foot-and-mouth crisis.

I knew that farmers had plenty of questions they would like put to Mr Morley, such as why there had not been enough trained vets ready to cope with the epidemic, and I tried to extricate answers to these crucial questions. Yet politicians are very good at ignoring the question they have been asked and answering a completely different one instead.

I did OK with Elliot Morley, I thought, even though he did manage to sidestep quite a few of my lines of enquiry. But I think a few months down the line, I would have held him to account rather better.

Really, I was learning how to interview on *Countryfile* as I went along. I had the advantage that I like talking to people and most times I am genuinely interested in what they have to say. Yet I quickly learned that I needed to ask open-ended questions, so the interviewee can't just say 'Yes' or 'No'.

Even doing only one or two stories a month for *Countryfile*, my new job was proving time-consuming. Generally I would travel to the location on a Sunday night, film on Monday and Tuesday and get back late on a Tuesday night. Wednesdays were generally spent in the BBC Pebble Mill studio in Birmingham doing voiceovers.

It made me realize that it would be virtually impossible to do the job had I not been self-employed. I was only able to take on the shoots because Duncan could run the farm while I was away and we had such a good team of people in place.

I did miss it while I was away, though, and in any case there was a very good reason for me to want to be on the farm as much as possible just at that time – because Charlie was pregnant again.

After the trauma that Charlie had been through with Ella's birth we had decided to leave having another child a little while, but we had always known that we wanted to have more than one. Ella was now four and happily romping around the farm and it definitely felt like time to try again.

We had been so delighted to have a girl the first time around and it really wasn't important to us if our second was a boy or a girl. We would have been happy with either. Like any dad, my top priority was for Charlie and the baby to be safe and healthy following the birth.

Once again we asked the nurses doing the pre-natal scans not to tell us the baby's sex. Everything seemed easier the second time around, and Charlie's pregnancy was a lot less difficult.

We were obviously nervous on 28 May 2002 as we returned to Cheltenham General, but this time the elective Caesarean birth went like a dream instead of a nightmare. The surgeon was brilliant and in no time the nurse was handing Charlie our second child.

'Congratulations,' she told us. 'It's a healthy baby boy.'

We were both over the moon. I found it totally overwhelming and shed a tear. Having lived for years with my three sisters, I also had a private smile at the thought that I would not be sharing my home with three females again!

My son's very welcome arrival also meant that we could finally use the name Alfie – the one that we had had to shelve the first time around.

Before long I was back filming for *Countryfile*. My assignments continued to veer from the sublime to the ridiculous. Sometimes, I wasn't sure which was which. For a winter special, I was sent up to Scotland to take part in husky mushing.

The locals organized annual husky races where the big dogs pulled sledges behind them. When there was no snow, they improvised and instead of sledges they got the dogs to pull giant prams.

Once the dogs were moving, the competitors would run and jump onto the sledge and command them by voice. There were 'Go left!' and 'Go right!' commands, just like sheep herding. Game as ever, I had a go at it, and it was great fun.

I did enjoy making the zany reports that seemed to be my lot in the early days of my *Countryfile* career. However, I got a far deeper, more profound thrill when a few of the jobs brought me in close contact with the wonder and majesty of nature.

We went up to the Inner Hebrides to report on the basking shark trade that used to take place on an island just off Mull. There was once a thriving local industry hunting the sharks for meat and selling the blubber for use in soap, oils and cooking.

A local conservation group researching the numbers of whales and porpoises offered to take the crew and me out on the boat to try to get some footage of the basking sharks. We didn't see any basking sharks – but we did see something even more spectacular.

The sea was flat and calm that day, and as we bobbed in the water, the conservationists complained that they had been going out for a fortnight and still hadn't seen anything. That was about to change.

Suddenly, in the near distance, we saw shoals of dolphins, a few porpoises and these amazing minke whales. I had never seen a whale in the wild before and here they were, swimming freely and coming up to within 50 yards of our vessel.

I sat in the bow of the boat, the crew started filming and I did an improvised piece to camera about being so close to these gorgeous creatures. My adrenaline was flowing and I didn't try to hide the fact: 'My heart is pounding here!' I told the *Countryfile* viewers.

Later, I was doing the voiceover to accompany the report and the producer, a lady named Teresa Bogan, complimented me on my work: 'Adam, that was a lovely piece to camera. Was your heart *really* pounding as you did it?'

I wholeheartedly assured her that it was. Even before I had applied to *Countryfile*, a friend in Gloucestershire had once asked me, 'What would be your dream job if you weren't a farmer?' With a slightly embarrassed laugh, I had told him that I wanted to be David Attenborough.

I have always thought that I would love to do what he does. He is such an amazing man. Well, sitting in that boat off the

Isle of Mull with the minke whales surfacing to blow in shot behind me, I guess I was having my own little Sir David Attenborough moment. It felt as if I was living the dream.

In fact, *Countryfile* was often making me feel that way. As well as traversing the length and breadth of Britain to cover rural and country stories, I was even venturing further afield on a few international assignments.

The producers asked me to cover a festival in Switzerland based around the locals bringing their sheep in from the mountains for the winter. It fell at a time when Charlie and I had booked our summer holiday in Italy, so I left her, Ella and Alfie on the beach for the last couple of days of our break and jetted to Switzerland.

During the festival, local shepherds went up into the hills to fetch their distinctive black-nosed sheep that had been grazing up in the mountains all summer long. There were thousands of them and they were all herded back down to their holdings in a celebratory procession.

It was a glorious late summer's day and the villagers were all dressed up in their traditional Heidi-like costumes. Once the black-nosed sheep were all safely down, the locals cut loose with a massive banquet, complete with yodelling. It was a fantastic day.

While we were in Switzerland, we also filmed with what is known as the Swiss fighting cow. This evocative phrase may conjure up images of bloodthirsty cattle charging around the mountains, but in actuality the animals are nothing like that.

The name derives from a festival when the cows fight with each other to determine the dominant cow that will lead the herd up the mountain. No harm comes to them as when they fight their horns are wrapped in bandages, and as soon as one cow overpowers another they are separated by the handlers.

When I first came across these beautiful dark mahogany creatures, they wandered over to me with their bells gently ringing around their necks and let me scratch their heads. They were not what I had expected at all.

We also made a third film about Swiss mountain goats, which look similar to the Bagot goats we have at home, with their black heads and necks and white bodies. The billies have impressively long, sweeping horns.

Their herders are super-fit, as they have to walk up the steep mountains to check the herds frequently. Grazing the goats there is hugely important locally, as they keep the grass short and spiky. It means that when the snow comes it sticks to the grass spikes rather than slipping downhill and causing avalanches.

On another occasion, I went to southern Russia to film a report on an English farmer who had bought some land out there. He had shipped out state-of-the-art agricultural machinery to farm the deep, rich soil and was using Russian workers to operate them.

We learned that there is a huge unfulfilled potential for arable farming in Russia and Eastern Europe. It was fascinating stuff and in fact *Countryfile* went on to win an award for best BBC foreign report for the story we filed. I was incredibly proud of that.

Even more amazingly, I got to return to Australia for the first time since Duncan and I had been roustabouting and driving the Ford Falcon XB through the desert more than a decade earlier.

We went there in search of Hereford cattle. These magnificent, versatile white-faced beasts had first been exported to Australia in 1826, in the days when that journey meant a turbulent sea voyage of many months rather than buying a ticket on Qantas.

Countryfile had got hold of the herd records of the very first Herefords that had been shipped out to Tasmania and traced direct descendants of that herd over here in Cambridgeshire. The next task was to go to Australia to see if we could do the same thing there.

It was an unbelievable trip. We did manage to find the first herd's direct descendants, and we went up in a helicopter over the outback to film from above as the local farm workers, who are called jackaroos, rounded the cows up on horseback.

Being out on the horses, the dust flying up as we rounded up the cattle, was like heaven for me. When I was six years old, riding (or more often falling off) Domino, I had dreamed of being some kind of farming cowboy.

Now, here I was: living the dream again.

The jackaroos had real work to do. They had to round up the herds of cattle, brand them, tag them and castrate the male calves, not to mention get them through a handling system. I joined in, and loved it so much that I carried on working with them long after the *Countryfile* cameras had stopped rolling.

One Christmas, we filmed a *Countryfile* special in Italy. It was fun because usually I would be reporting alone, but this time John Craven, Charlotte Smith and some other presenters all flew out with me. We had a great time covering a big food festival and we just felt like a close-knit, happy team.

Around this time I also branched off into doing some radio work. The *Countryfile* executive producer, Andrew Thorman, was also responsible for the Radio 4 programmes *Farming Today* and *On Your Farm* and asked me whether I might be interested in covering some farming stories for them.

Well, why not? I quite liked the idea of gaining a new string to my bow, so I did a few reports for them. It didn't take me long to realize that radio is a very different discipline from TV.

Put simply, it is easier in some ways and harder in others. You can certainly work a lot quicker. On TV you spend hours or even days getting cutaways and incidental pictures: a shot of a sheep going through a gate, or walking up a hill. They can be slow to set up and film and hugely time-consuming. To put it in context, filming an eight-minute TV report will usually take two days; you can make a 20-minute radio item in four or five hours.

On radio, all you have to do is tell the story. I suppose it is a purer form of broadcasting in some ways. The other side of this is that whereas TV viewers can see for themselves where you are and what is going on, on the radio you have to describe everything. I had to learn to paint word pictures: luckily, it seemed to come fairly naturally.

I enjoyed the radio work, but one downside was that it did not pay as well as TV, nor as much as working on the farm, for that matter. It made it a little less of a priority for me, fun though it was, and gradually my Radio 4 work fell away as I concentrated on other things.

Of course, even while I was getting more and more involved in the media world, I remained first and foremost a farmer. My day job was still Bemborough Farm. Even so, I couldn't help but notice that me beaming out of the nation's television screens on Sunday lunchtimes had changed a couple of things at home.

One was very positive. A lot more people were coming to the farm park. Obviously I couldn't plug the Cotswold Farm Park on TV because it would be product placement but viewers were perfectly capable of putting two and two together and working it out for themselves, and our visitor numbers were up considerably.

The second consequence of being on TV threw me a little, and I wasn't sure what to make of it. People had begun to treat me differently.

As my weeks and months on *Countryfile* went by, I slowly became aware of people staring at me while I was out and about. They would do a double take if they spotted me in the street, or blurt out 'Hello!' as if they knew me.

I suppose it reminded me of how people used to react to my dad when he was doing *In the Country* in the 1970s and got asked for autographs at the farm park. The first time I got asked for mine, though, was fairly inauspicious.

I was minding my own business in Cheltenham one morning when a woman came up to me. 'You're Adam Henson off *Countryfile*, aren't you?' she asked me, excitedly. 'Can you sign this, please?'

'Yes, of course!' I told her, and took the pen and paper she was holding out. As I wrote my name, I heard a chuckle a few feet away. I looked up to see a mate of mine laughing at me. The woman was his wife, whom I had not met before, and they were winding me up.

That was funny, but soon people were genuinely asking me for my autograph, either at the farm park or while I was out and about. It was nice, and quite flattering, and I was keen to oblige them, but I wasn't quite sure how to do it.

I didn't really have a proper autograph. I had my normal old signature that I used on my chequebook but, to me, it looked a bit rubbish, and I couldn't imagine anybody wanting it. So I sat at the kitchen table one day and made up my autograph.

If I'm honest, I still think it looks a bit rubbish.

You sometimes read about rock stars who long to be famous and who practise signing their names even before they pick up a guitar. Really, I am the complete opposite.

I had never craved being famous as a kid, even when I saw people like my dad, Uncle Nicky and Aunty Una Stubbs on TV. I just never had that gene. Even when I had idly thought of being an actor in my teens it was because I liked acting, not because I wanted to be famous.

So this new attention took some getting used to. It helped that 99 per cent of the time people were really nice. They felt as if they knew me because they saw me on TV every week, so they would come up to me and talk to me like a friend.

Usually, they just wanted to say hello or make some small talk. They might tell me they loved the show, or my dogs, or ask me how such-and-such a bull was doing. Because it was so good-natured it rarely felt intrusive.

Some people would be very complimentary and it was very humbling to talk to them. Other farmers would tell me they enjoyed seeing somebody on TV who actually knew about agriculture and was giving them a bit of a voice.

Occasionally I would be wandering down a street and some bloke would shout from a passing car: 'Oi, *Countryfile*!' or 'Where's yer sheep?' or something like that. I'd yell back something equally inane and everybody would be happy.

My dad had a good angle on it all. He told me it was simply part and parcel of being on TV. 'People talk to you because they enjoy or respect what you do,' he advised. 'You need to look after that respect and always make time for them.'

It was no hardship or effort for me to do that. I enjoyed it, and I still do. Most of the time, anyway – very occasionally somebody might come up and buttonhole me while I am in a hurry, or if I'm trying to do something with my kids, but thankfully those instances are few and far between.

Yet at the same time, coping with low-level celebrity such as mine has taught me that I would never want to be properly, full-on famous like a David Beckham or a Jamie Oliver. Not to be able to walk down the street like a normal person would be too much for me.

Thankfully, I don't think that is too much of a danger!

Another interesting side effect of going on *Countryfile* was that people began to assume that I was loaded. They read in the papers about the salaries that top stars such as Jeremy Clarkson or Jonathan Ross get paid and assumed that all BBC presenters got the same treatment.

Nothing could be further from the truth. I didn't have an

agent when I first went on *Countryfile* and had never even thought of getting one, so for my first four or five years as a freelance roving reporter I was on the BBC's set daily rate, which is adequate but certainly not lavish.

Countryfile is a friendly show and the directors and camera crew that I work with have virtually always been supportive and helpful. In my early days they would coach and coax me through broadcasts and be very patient with my mistakes.

A director might tell me to relax or slow down if I was stumbling over my words, or tell me not to worry if I cocked something up. They knew that everybody has to learn as they go along and they wanted me to do well. Ultimately, television is a team sport.

However, not everybody is as understanding and as my time on the show continued, I found myself working with one particular female director who would get angry if I made mistakes – and didn't try to hide her impatience.

This woman would yell at me in front of the camera crew or make me do interviews over and over again when I thought the first or second attempt had been fine. I knew that I had a lot to learn but this did not seem like the way to do it.

It wasn't great for my confidence either. I would have a long drive home from a shoot on a Tuesday night with her lectures playing on my mind. *I don't need this*, I would think. *I'm not a television presenter, after all. I'm a farmer.*

At the time this was happening I had been away from home with *Countryfile* a lot. Duncan was getting quite stretched on the farm and I was feeling guilty about leaving Charlie on her own with Ella and Alfie for long stretches. Two particularly tricky shoots brought me close to breaking point.

Was I really cut out for all this? Was it worth it?

Yet, apart from that particular hassle, I was still enjoying doing *Countryfile* and a huge part of me was loath to give it up. I talked to Charlie and my dad, mulled it over, and then decided to have a word with John Craven.

John was great. He listened to me, went to see the director and asked her to calm down a little and not be quite so hard on the presenters. I think she understood and was fine after that, although she and I didn't work together again. I was hugely relieved because I was having way too much fun on *Countryfile* to jack it all in so soon.

So, everything was looking rosy. *Countryfile* was fun, Bemborough Farm was ticking over nicely, and Ella and Alfie were growing up happy and well. At such times as that, you really should enjoy just how lucky you are, because things can turn dark just when you least expect them to.

Little did I know it, but we were about to be hit by a devastating family tragedy.

CHAPTER 14

A Beautiful Boy

S ome siblings don't stay terribly close as they grow older. After they hit their late teens and leave home they naturally drift apart, most likely only seeing each other at Christmas and other major family occasions.

My sisters and I have never been like that. We are more like great friends who just happen to be related. We have always known that we are there for each other, and we've helped one another out of various scrapes over the years.

My eldest sister, Libby, moved for a while to the US, where she was executive director of the American Minor Breeds Conservancy – their equivalent to our RBST. She has worked on Bemborough Farm too at various times, running the farm park and helping Dad to coordinate the lambing exhibition.

Libby has also overseen many breeding programmes on the farm park and been a consultant to the UN on conserving endangered livestock and poultry. Nowadays she lives with her family in Devon, runs a company providing pedigree software to livestock breed societies, and sits on the government committee on farm-animal genetic resources.

Lolo still lives close to Bemborough and these days is the managing director of The Forest People's Programme. Her team of nearly 50 people specializes in supporting the rights of people who live in tropical forests and depend upon them for their livelihoods.

Lolo still has a strong connection to the land and raises beef cattle on her smallholding down the road from me. Indeed, she always says she is never happier than when feeding her herd on a crisp Cotswolds morning with buzzards mewing in the blue sky above.

Becca was working as a stage manager in London in 1986 when she married Nick Wilson, who worked – and still does – for his dad's business. She was the first of us siblings to get married, and still claims that I cried when she told me the news! I'm very close to Nick, who is near to being the brother that I never had.

In the late 1980s, Becca and Nick moved back to Nick's native North-East, where Becca's jobs included ten years at the BBC, including being a floor manager on *Byker Grove*, starring the young Ant and Dec. In 1994, she and Nick had a daughter, Emily.

Two years later a little boy, Ben, followed. Like Emily, Ben was a fantastic kid. He was a lovely blond-haired lad who always seemed to be happy. He was a joy to be around whenever we visited them in the North-East or they came down to stay on the farm.

Ben was only two years older than Ella and the two of them got on really well. When he visited Bemborough they would play together on the farm and make dens in the woods, just like Ben's mum and Ella's dad had done 30 years earlier.

One school holiday in 2001, Becca, Nick, Emily and Ben came to stay for a few days. Ben, then aged five, had just got over what they thought was a virus but was still pretty poorly while he was here. He was sick when he tried to eat dinner in the farm park café.

He had been ill quite a lot in the preceding months, so when Becca and Nick got home they took him to see a specialist who gave him some scans. They showed that Ben hadn't had a virus. He had a brain tumour – and he needed an immediate operation.

It was such a huge shock. One day he was a happy little boy, going off to school and playing with his toy trains. Then, from nowhere, he was in hospital with a shaven head, and a huge scar where they had operated, and tubes sticking out of him everywhere.

Poor Ben stayed in hospital for ten months. He had a series of operations and they gave him courses of chemotherapy and radiotherapy. It was an experience that no happy-go-lucky five-year-old should ever have to go through. He suffered infections and complications, including meningitis, which damaged his brain.

Becca and Nick were by his bedside every single day. As a dad myself, I can still only imagine how agonizing it must have been for them to watch him suffer. Ben didn't understand everything that was happening to him, of course, but he went along with everything that he was asked to do.

Then something terrible happened. Ben was given a drug which after several weeks sent him into a coma. The doctors managed to revive him, but when he came round a terrible side effect soon became apparent. Ben had gone blind.

A few months after that, Ben went into remission and the

doctors thought they had beaten the cancer. When he came home, as well as being blind he couldn't walk very well, because the operation on his brain had affected his mobility. He just used to shuffle around the floor.

It was heartbreaking to see, but Ben was incredibly brave. He simply got on with his life as well as he could – he adapted so well that you would have thought he had been blind his whole life. I don't think I ever heard him complain once.

Charlie and I, and Becca and Nick, took our kids on a couple of family holidays together. One year we went skiing; another time, we went to Portugal. It was humbling to see how patient Becca and Nick were with Ben, and he and Ella hung out a lot and grew really close.

After four years, in February 2005, Ben's tumour came back. This time the growth was right in the middle of his brain and the specialists told Becca and Nick that it was impossible for them to operate. All that they could do was make Ben's life as easy and pain-free as possible until he died.

He may not have been in physical pain for those last few months but the emotional suffering was horrendous for Becca, Nick, Emily and all of the family. As Ben deteriorated still further, early in 2006, I went up to the North-East for a couple of days to try to help out.

It was obvious that Ben was entering his last few days. When I phoned home, Duncan said, 'I can look after things here, so stay as long as you need to.' It was over a week before, with a heavy heart, I started home knowing that in all likelihood I would never see Ben again.

He died a few days later. He was just ten years old, and in his short life he'd had to endure more pain, discomfort and suffering than most people go through in a full lifetime. That he did so while remaining plucky and cheery was truly little short of miraculous.

Ben was such a special, amazing little boy and when he died the whole family was devastated. Yet the way that he'd coped with everything was humbling and inspirational. In a way, he made us all better people who appreciated life so much more.

Becca and Nick will never stop thinking about Ben – none of us will – and they wanted something positive to come out of the whole horrible experience. When Ben went blind, Becca and Nick realized that there was a lack of facilities and support for families with blind or partially sighted children. They set up a charity, Useful Vision, to support families in the North-East with children suffering from this disability.

Useful Vision organizes activities, events and workshops to help vision-impaired children and their families across the North-East. I was delighted and honoured when Becca and Nick asked me to be the charity's patron and will always do anything I can to help such a worthy cause.

Nick is an avid runner and has taken part in many events over the years to raise money for Useful Vision. One year he persuaded Charlie and me, my sister Lolo and her daughter, Kate, to take part in a half-marathon along with him.

I felt that it was a great opportunity for us all to raise funds for the charity but I hadn't really taken on the idea of running 13 miles – something I had never done before. On the day I was incredibly impressed that the organizers had got so many runners into position so efficiently.

The atmosphere and camaraderie between the participants and supporters was something that I had never experienced before. We all had a job to keep up with speedy Nick but we made reasonable times. Crossing the finishing line was so emotional, considering the reason that we were doing it.

We also occasionally hold charity events at Bemborough Farm for the same cause. Having seen Ben struggle to cope with blindness, it feels great to help other kids in the same plight to understand that they are not alone in their world of darkness.

I would say that Useful Vision helps to keep Ben's memory alive, but that is not true – we never forget about him. There is hardly a day goes by that I don't think at least once about Ben Wilson.

He was a boy in a million.

CHAPTER 15

Hit By Disease

In 2007, *Countryfile* dispatched me to Belgium to report on a revolting disease named bluetongue which was wreaking havoc on the sheep and cattle population of Belgium and Germany.

Bluetongue is a horrible non-contagious virus that is spread by midges in the late summer and early autumn. It begins by causing ulcers and blisters around the animals' mouths and feet and they go on to suffer swollen heads, lameness and internal bleeding before the disease kills them.

The midges will feed on an infected creature and then go on to a clean animal, infecting it in the process. In many ways, the virus spreads a little like malaria.

Bluetongue had been a problem in mainland Europe for the last decade, killing close on 2 million animals, but the Channel had always protected British farms from its malign influence. However, UK scientists were concerned that the wind could blow the midges across to Britain, where they could survive and even flourish in our now slightly warmer climate.

I headed off to Belgium and we filmed some very deformed and sick cows and sheep stricken by bluetongue. I also interviewed some of the farmers and my heart went out to them, seeing them brought to their knees by this cruel virus.

It was a traumatic report to film – but I never in my wildest dreams imagined that it would turn out to be a journalistic scoop. Just a week after I returned, the first-ever case of bluetongue on British soil emerged at a farm in Ipswich in Suffolk.

Journalists who had never heard of the disease before then naturally turned to *Countryfile* for a crash course. My report from Belgium was to turn up on various news programmes, including the BBC's *News at Ten* and *Sky News*.

Thankfully this outbreak of bluetongue was fairly quickly contained due to the speedy development of a vaccine. However, as a farmer I know exactly what it is like to live in constant fear of one particular animal disease.

It's a fear that hangs over us like a permanent black cloud – and that cloud was about to break on Bemborough Farm.

Mycobacterium bovis, or bovine tuberculosis, is a chronic and highly infectious lung disease that is better known to the layman as TB. By law, every British cattle farm has to be tested within certain time periods – dependent on the number of outbreaks in an area – to check whether any of its cattle are infected.

In the eastern counties of Britain and much of the North, testing can be as infrequent as once every four years. However, in our own area, which is unfortunately a TB hotspot, it can be every six months.

As I said, we have never had a dairy herd on Bemborough Farm. However, we do have what is known as a suckler herd of various breeds including, over the years, Longhorn, Gloucester and White Park, to name but a few. They are all breeds that

Were it not for Dad and his work with the RBST, many species of British domestic rare breeds would be long gone.

Cotswold Farm Park. Then and now.

Our longhorn oxen,
Philip and Edward.

Gloucester cattle enjoying
a day in the sun.

Hebridean and Manx loaghtan –
Watch those horns!

Cotswold Sheep and their golden fleece.

Learning the Bowen shearing method in Australia.

Long hours on the combine.

Alfie helping with the lambing.

Making a plan at market.

Filming with Neil Heseltine
in Malham.

The early *Adam's Farm* team. *Left to right*: Sam Bailey, Dan Davis and me.

Countryfile moves to prime time. *Left to right*: James Wong, Katie Knapman, me, Julia Bradbury, Matt Baker and John Craven.

Filming *Lambing Live* with Kate Humble.

Flying high filming *Secret Britain.*

Filming with minke whales (courtesy Gordon Ross).

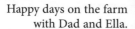

Happy days on the farm with Dad and Ella.

Posing for the perfect cover shot with Alfie.

Great North Run supporting Useful Vision: *Left to right*: James Collett, Charlie, me, Becca, Nick, Kate Bridges.

Opening the 2015 Salmon Season on the River Teith with Duncan, 2nd February 2015.

Graduation Day at Reaseheath College, October 2012.

With Dad after he was awarded his MBE. A proud day for the family. *Left to right*: Lolo, me, Dad, Mum, Becca and Libby.

The next generation of Hensons: Alfie with ferret Scratchy, Charlie with Beatrice, Ella with Romeo, me, visla Boo and collie Peg.

How we will always remember Dad – with his animals at the Cotswold Farm Park.

Dad was very involved in helping to preserve many years ago.

A suckler herd is when the cows suckle their own calves and they are reared naturally on their mothers. This is different from a dairy herd, where the calf is taken away from the cow and reared on milk that it drinks from a bucket, so that the cow can be milked to produce the daily pinta.

With all of our rare breeds and the great reputation that Dad had built up amongst other enthusiasts, we had no trouble selling surplus stock to other breeders. The castrated males, or steers, are raised for beef and sold through specialist butchers. All of the breeds are on display in the Cotswold Farm Park, to explain their place in history.

Our local vet, Gill Allen, arrived on the farm in July 2007 for our compulsory TB test. The procedure for this test is a fascinating one, and never fails to tie my stomach in knots every time I have to endure it. It is the same for every farmer.

Gill injected every member of my herds with two shots of a TB inoculum in the neck. She would return three days later to see if any lumps had formed where she'd injected them. If they had, and the bottom lump was bigger than the top, then that animal had TB.

That three-day waiting period is always near-unbearable. In previous years I had always got lucky, but in 2007 my luck ran out. When Gill returned, she had to tell me that one cow was definitely a reactor. The farm had TB.

As soon as a farm is diagnosed with TB, it is effectively shut down. You are no longer allowed to sell breeding animals to other people, although you can still send cattle reared for beef for slaughter.

Our rare breeds can't compete on a commercial basis as beef, but they excel in flavour and can command a slight premium. Eating rare breeds may sound misguided but if more people can be persuaded to eat them, more farmers will breed them and the less rare they will become.

At the end of the day rare-breed conservation is about finding a use for the animals and giving them commercial outlets, from meat production to conservation grazing and specialist markets.

The most profitable market is selling breeding stock, which commands a far higher price than beef. A Longhorn breeder might pay £1,500 for a high-quality heifer, whereas sending them to the abattoir we would only make about two-thirds as much.

The TB verdict was thus disastrous for Bemborough, as we no longer had an outlet for our valuable females. Our breeding-stock programme had been going really well, but the TB closed it down overnight. It put the farm, and the breeds, in a very difficult place.

It was an incredibly hard time, made even harder for us by a further very sad event – the death of John Neave.

John had been a mainstay of Bemborough Farm alongside Dad ever since 1962. He had retired at the same time as Dad but sadly had not been as able to enjoy his twilight years.

John had contracted Parkinson's disease, which was especially horrible for him as one of his favourite hobbies in retirement was model-making. It must have been so frustrating for him as his condition resulted in uncontrollable shakes, but with his calm patience he had soldiered on and both Dad and I still saw him regularly.

John had had to go into hospital for an operation on his knee but developed a blood clot and died. His passing was devastating for Dad but also deeply upsetting to me: he had always been like a second father to me. He was a good man, and a farmer to his soul.

Meanwhile, we laboured on under the restrictions of the dreaded TB shutdown. They can only be lifted if you pass two consecutive tests, held 60 days apart, so I had no choice but to sit and stew until Gill came back two months later.

TB tests are incredibly pressured in more ways than one. Not only is the farmer waiting to see if the animals he cares for and looks after will be taken away, but the animals themselves hate the testing process, which can leave them very stressed.

On Bemborough, it would take three of us working flat out all day to bring the cattle in for testing. We would have to round them up in the fields and herd them over to the cattle handling pens. Every animal is itching to make a break for it and you need your wits about you.

You then have to encourage the beasts into a small metal pen known as a cattle crush to restrict their movements and let the vet get at them. The animals don't like being pushed, contained or injected, and they can be very reluctant and agitated.

It's difficult on every level. The bulls hate being near to each other, and bellow aggressively. The cows also find the whole business horribly stressful and it is not at all good for them if they are heavily pregnant.

It's therefore quite an undertaking to get your entire herd ready for the first stage of a TB test, and then do it all again three days later for the second part of the process. Yet there is no choice, so we did it all again when Gill returned 60 days after the positive test that had closed us down.

There is nothing else in farming that stresses me out as much as TB testing time. It is totally unbearable watching the vet move along your herd measuring the lumps in your animals' necks with their little calipers. Absolutely everything is at stake, yet you are powerless to do anything about it.

It makes it even worse that it's impossible to predict which animals will be stricken. With most cattle diseases, such as pneumonia, you can spot the symptoms if you know what you are looking for. With tuberculosis, there are hardly any clues at all.

When Gill came round for her repeat visit, the news was no better. There was a lot of shaking of her head as she wielded her calipers, and this time she sadly confirmed that quite a few animals were infected and would have to be dispatched straight to the slaughterhouse.

This nightmare was to be a situation that would get a lot worse before it was to get better. One low point came just before Christmas 2007. An all-clear would have been the best Christmas present that I could imagine, but Gill looked as upset as I felt when she broke the news that I had no less than 12 reactors.

In some ways, she probably was. Vets train for years and go into their noble profession in order to save animals' lives, not to condemn them to death. Gill was later to confide in me that that black Christmas was possibly the worst day of her career.

They say the darkest hour comes just before the dawn. Well, that certainly wasn't true in my case – because, after that black day, we stayed stricken by TB for another 18 months.

Every 60 days Gill would trek out to Bemborough Farm and every 60 days the result would be the same. Sometimes we had a few more cases, sometimes a few less, but we seemed nowhere near being clear of the debilitating disease.

Trying to manage any kind of breeding programme under the restrictions imposed by TB is like trying to work with both hands tied behind your back. It was impossible and it was completely crippling that side of our business.

I longed to get things back to normal and for the heartache to end, but throughout the whole of 2008 it was Groundhog Day every time Gill pulled out her calipers. It was so lucky that we had the income from *Countryfile*, the Cotswold Farm Park and Duncan's arable operation to keep us going.

My TB shutdown continued all the way through that bleak 2008; another black Christmas came and went. It was February of the following year before Gill could meticulously inspect my entire herd and announce at the end of the day that they were finally all clean.

It was a relief – or, rather, half a relief. The rules are that a farm must pass two consecutive TB tests before it can begin trading breeding animals again. When Gill returned for the follow-up tests in April 2009, I was so nervous that the whole day was like an out-of-body experience.

At the time I had 76 cows and five breeding bulls for her to look at, and as my rookie sheepdog Millie helped my stockmen and me to herd them along to the cattle crush, I felt tense and pessimistic. My mood wasn't helped when two White Parks bolted and came within inches of trampling poor Millie underfoot.

I was particularly worried about two of the Gloucester cows, which had been looking emaciated for weeks. Nothing I had tried to beef them up had worked. I feared the worst, and I could hardly believe it when Gill gave them the thumbs-up.

To add to the pressure, I had invited the *Countryfile* cameras down to the farm for the testing and so was attempting to give a running commentary on events as they unfolded. It was one of the hardest reports I have ever had to film for the show.

By lunchtime Gill had cleared half of my herd and I tried to deliver a piece to camera. There are times for everyone when it is all a bit too much, and this was one of them for me. My TV job requires me to have professional detachment, and at that second I had none.

The noise of the bellowing bulls and of the cows calling for their calves in the yard around me suddenly seemed deafening, the stress of seeing these animals' lives on the line yet again was intolerable, and as I tried to express my feelings to the camera, words failed me and I had to shake my head and walk away.

It was a picture that spoke a thousand words. Seeing how overwhelmed by emotion I was, the *Countryfile* producers left that clip in the final broadcast. It made for compelling human-interest TV – but I certainly wasn't enjoying being the human interest!

When the testing recommenced in the afternoon, things still seemed to be going well. My entire herd of shaggy-coated, rust-coloured Highland cattle sailed through the test, as did a sweet little White Park calf that I had had an irrational bad feeling about.

Yet after so many negative tests over the last two years, I could not shake off my feeling of deep, doom-laden pessimism. *Surely something will go wrong soon.* My worst fears looked confirmed when Gill began shaking her head at a White Park in the crush in front of her.

'There is some thickening,' she warned, caressing its neck. I could see two distinct lumps, and if I were a religious man, I would have been praying as she applied her calipers to measure them.

'Fifteen millimetres on the top,' she told me, which made me wince and gasp. I knew the *Countryfile* cameras were on me, but at that minute I simply didn't care. The bottom lump looked bigger than that to me.

Time stood still as Gill slowly measured the second lump.

'Thirteen on the bottom,' she proclaimed, happily. 'This one passes.'

Phew! And, despite the negative expectations that I found impossible to shake off, the rest of the afternoon's testing passed without any more scares – until, that is, the last animal, a two-year-old bull, trundled into the crush. I held my breath as Gill wielded her trusty calipers one last time. Then she turned towards me and the *Countryfile* cameras.

'Adam, I'm delighted to say that you have a clear test,' she informed me.

At last! My ordeal was over! All the frustrations and tensions that had been bottled up in me for the best part of two years came pouring out as I grinned, howled and punched the air like a footballer celebrating a goal. *Yes!*

Any professional decorum went out of the window, and the *Countryfile* camera crew knew they were getting some great shots as I grabbed Gill in a bear hug and lifted her clean off the ground. Well, I didn't care if I looked silly. I had been waiting for this sweet, sweet moment for far too long.

Just for a few seconds, I wasn't Adam Henson, TV presenter. I was Adam Henson, farmer, who was incredibly relieved to get a huge chunk of his livelihood back. I could not have felt happier.

It is fair to say that I would not have been quite so elated if I had known that my respite from TB would last less than a year.

CHAPTER 16

All Change on *Countryfile*

A ll this time, *Countryfile* was going from strength to strength. A show about rural affairs, which some people might have dismissed as being quite niche, was regularly attracting a remarkable 2.5 million viewers in its traditional Sunday lunchtime slot.

Without being too immodest, its success never surprised me. I thought *Countryfile* was a great show long before I became involved with it. I loved – and I still do – the way that every weekend it beams the countryside into millions of people's front rooms, and explains to them what goes on there.

I think country people like the programme because it is a rare voice for them, and hopefully that voice sounds reliably authentic. For city-dwellers, I hope that the show gives them some valuable insights and helps them to understand a world that might otherwise be a bit of a mystery to them.

I believe that *Countryfile* both celebrates the countryside and tries to explain the many issues and problems that it faces. I like the fact that it is a magazine programme, in bite-size chunks: if there is an item that a viewer doesn't like, he or she knows there will be something else along in five minutes' time.

In 2007 the show celebrated its 20th anniversary. With it came the launch of a spin-off magazine, which marked our birthday with a hilarious photo shoot of John Craven, Miriam O'Reilly, Michaela Strachan, Charlotte Smith, Juliet Morris and me mucking out pigs, chasing chickens and milking cows dressed in tuxedos and ball gowns (the presenters, not the animals).

The magazine even asked me to write a monthly column about life on the farm. I was honoured to accept, while also secretly wondering exactly what my long-suffering English teachers in Cheltenham would have made of this unexpected development.

There was also another, rather more profound consequence of our continued ratings success. Late in 2008, the BBC told us that *Countryfile* was to move from its usual lunchtime slot to be broadcast on Sunday evenings – peak viewing time.

Wow! This was quite a major promotion for the show – yet I wondered if I would still be around to enjoy it. Because, to tie in with the move, the programme was also going to be given a major revamp and shake-up, including new presenters.

I hated the idea of being yanked off the show at this point. I was still loving doing *Countryfile*, filming the investigations and reports still felt fresh and exciting to me, and the income was coming in very handy when the farm was poleaxed by things like the TB shutdown.

At the same time, I had been on the show for eight years now and I supposed I could understand it if the bosses decided the viewers might be bored of me and want somebody new and more fresh-faced.

They say familiarity breeds contempt: was this the end for the competition-winning ginger farm boy?

I thought it probably was. As I glumly confided in Charlie, Mum and Dad, I thought I was most likely a goner.

We all carried on filming as normal during the run-up to the big re-launch and the switch to prime-time. Like everybody on the show I was desperate to learn my fate, and there was no shortage of tantalizing whispers behind the scenes.

I took John Craven, who by now I saw as a good friend as well as a mentor, to one side to ask him if he knew anything. Yet John has always been immaculately professional, and whether he knew what was going on or not, he was keeping schtum. Which left me on tenterhooks.

Slowly, the backstage gossip hardened into fact. I heard that Juliet Morris had been told she would not be required in the new time slot. Juliet had joined the show after me and I had not worked that closely with her, but I felt sorry for her – as well as wondering if I would be next.

Miriam O'Reilly being let go was a real surprise. She was one of *Countryfile*'s main presenters, as well as being a farmer's daughter and working on the radio too. I always had a high regard for Miriam's presenting skills and got on well with her, so was amazed to see her go.

It also made me fear even more for my own fate. I figured if the executives were willing to cast *Miriam O'Reilly* adrift, then nobody was safe.

Eventually, Andrew Thorman, who was the editor of the BBC's rural affairs department at the time, called me in for my fateful meeting.

'There are going to be a lot of changes on the programme, Adam,' he began, 'and a lot of new faces.'

Uh-oh. Here it comes.

'But we want you to stay. We would like you to present a new segment of the show each week from Bemborough Farm. We will call it "Adam's Farm".'

I was nodding eagerly even before Andrew had started outlining what this new role would entail. My first reaction was that it sounded a great idea, though primarily I was just relieved still to be part of the team. I knew it could so easily have gone the other way.

The new format of the programme now became clear. John Craven had been *Countryfile*'s lead presenter and lynchpin for years but remained at heart an old-school journalist and so was going to work on more investigative reports.

This left a vacancy for the main host, which two new people were going to fill. Matt Baker was a smart and enthusiastic young guy who had grown up on a smallholding in the North-East, and who had previously been working on *Blue Peter*.

Julia Bradbury was a very capable TV presenter who had presented a host of BBC and ITV shows from *GMTV* to *Watchdog*, as well as a cooking series called *Kill It, Cook It, Eat It*. She was clearly a true all-rounder who could turn her hand to just about anything.

After so many years of *Countryfile* having a settled cast, it was certainly all change. In with Matt and Julia also came James Wong and Katie Knapman. The idea was obviously to give the show an infusion of youth, and even glamour.

Another addition was Tom Heap. Tom is the same age as me, and came in to present some of the heavyweight investigative issues when John Craven wasn't available. He thus has to play it very straight and serious onscreen, but I quickly learned that he is a lot of fun when the cameras stop rolling.

Naturally, with so many new arrivals there also had to be further casualties. Michaela Strachan was about to move to South Africa with her husband so was fairly sanguine about being let go, but Charlotte Smith was probably a little more disappointed.

Despite this, Charlotte didn't make a fuss and, being a very skilled broadcaster, was able to find plenty more work within the BBC. Nowadays, she co-hosts Radio 4's *Farming Today*, as well as making occasional appearances back on *Countryfile*.

Ben Fogle was miffed to be let go and I was sorry to see him leave. Since those edgy early days when we had effectively been rivals for the same *Countryfile* job, we had got on great and had become firm friends. I knew it could just as easily be me getting the chop, were it not for my unique selling point of being an actual farmer.

Well, you can't keep a good man down. Ben is such a great performer that he has since hosted a head-spinning array of travel and adventure shows from glamour spots all around the globe. He also currently presents ITV's *Countrywise*, their rival show to *Countryfile*.

Of course, *Countryfile*'s radical reshuffle did not pass entirely without protest. A few months after she was ousted, Miriam O'Reilly sued the BBC for ageism, victimization and sexual discrimination.

Miriam's case was essentially that the Beeb had dropped her simply because she was an older woman. Her lawyers pointed to the fact that the casualties of the show's relaunch were all women in their forties or fifties: Miriam, Charlotte, Juliet and Michaela.

It was true that it didn't look good from that angle, and the subsequent employment tribunal gathered a lot of media attention. Miriam argued that it was sexist and unfair that the show had ditched four middle-aged women to bring in younger presenters like Matt and Julia while keeping John Craven, who was then sixty-eight.

Miriam clearly had a case because the tribunal found in her favour on the ageism and victimization charges – although not on the sexism accusation – and the BBC apologized, saying it 'clearly did not get it right in this case'. In the wake of this finding, Miriam was to become a high-profile campaigner against ageism in the media and elsewhere.

I have always liked Miriam but I wasn't sure what I thought of the court case, so I stayed well out of it. At the end of the day, everyone moved on, and Miriam was later to work for the BBC on other programmes.

Aside from all that, having breathed a massive sigh of relief that I was still part of the *Countryfile* presenting team, I began to digest just what my new 'Adam's Farm' segment of the show would mean for me. I could not help feeling that it was fantastic news.

In my eight years on *Countryfile* I had travelled the length and breadth of the country umpteen times, as well as going as far afield as Russia and Australia. I have always loved travelling the world, but at times it could get to be a bit of a slog.

The show regularly took me away from my family for two days at a time and I had spent many bored, aimless evenings in far-flung Premier Inns and Travelodges. Once or twice I had begun to wonder if it was still worth it.

One recent week, *Countryfile* had sent me on a mission to locate the most remote bothy, or basic shelter, in Britain. The camera crew and I had journeyed to one of the most inaccessible corners of the Lake District.

It was an interesting story but it could hardly have been harder to get to and the rain had chucked it down non-stop the entire time that we were there, as it tends to in the Lakes. I was soaked to the skin, then, after we finished filming on the Tuesday, I had a miserable four-and-a-half-hour drive back to Bemborough.

That's the thing with *Countryfile*: by definition, you're nearly always outdoors and up against the weather.

By contrast, my commuting on the 'Adam's Farm' strand would be way more straightforward. I would be able to get up at a civilized time, have breakfast with Charlie and the kids, and then step outside the back door and begin work.

Having spent so many years slogging up and down the M4 and the M1, this new regime was a relief. I could even do an hour or so's farming work before the camera crew turned up to film my *Countryfile* report. After a few hours' TV work, rather than facing a mega-drive home from Carlisle, I just had to wander back inside the farmhouse door.

It also meant that I could become much more proactive in selecting the stories that I covered, which was a nice change. Rather than being randomly dispatched to toe-wrestling or chicken racing in Derbyshire, I could give real-time insights into the day-to-day life of a farmer.

If there was a major event going on, such as a harvest, the cameras could follow it week by week. If I was going off to buy a new bull, *Countryfile* came with me. I would be able to help out with work on the farm and explain it to the viewers as I went, killing two birds with one stone.

Yes, 'Adam's Farm' was a very happy development from my point of view. It's just a pity that one of the first big stories it had to cover was the return of TB to Bemborough.

It had been less than a year since Gill Allan had given us our priceless all-clear but in the meantime the situation in the Cotswolds had worsened severely and many of my farming neighbours were now shut down by the disease.

Just a couple of days before Gill was due back on Bemborough, I went to see a friend and a local dairy farmer, Stretch. Stretch had been closed down by TB for two years and had had to send hundreds of cattle to slaughter. To make matters worse, he had just learned that more than 20 of his cows had been newly infected, half of them in calf.

Things were looking bleak locally, and why on earth should I think that I would be exempted? *Countryfile* had come down to film the testing again for 'Adam's Farm', and the night before Gill's inspection I was far from optimistic.

The dreaded next morning was overcast as Gill arrived to check if any of my herd had reacted to the TB inoculum that she'd given them three days earlier. There was an early scare when she discovered lumps on one of my Dexter steers but, to my surprise, it was fine.

That day I had a job to at least partly distract me from the horrible business going on with Gill's calipers. I was wearing a backpack of chemicals, and as the cattle left the crush after Gill had checked them, I was spraying them from it to treat them for worms and parasites.

There is a withdrawal period on the medicines, meaning you have to wait a certain number of days once an animal has been treated before it can enter into the food chain. I had to wait until each animal was given the all-clear before it was treated.

Unfortunately, one cow would not now be getting its wormer dose. As Gill felt the neck of a pregnant Gloucester before her in the crush, her face grew as dark as my mood.

'Eighteen on the bottom and only ten on the top,' she sighed as she withdrew her calipers. 'I'm afraid she is a reactor, Adam.'

So there we were. My worst fears realized. The farm would be closed by TB for at least another six months and a mother and her unborn calf would be heading for slaughter, with who knows how many more to join them?

I felt like crying, or kicking something, but the TV camera had its red light on and I had my job to do. I told *Countryfile*'s viewers that TB was back on Bemborough and so I would not be giving the poor Gloucester her worming treatment.

'What's the point?' I asked, turning away from the camera to try to hide my feelings. 'She is going to have her throat cut.'

The comment looked brutal on TV but I thought that it was necessary and justified. *Countryfile* may be Sunday-evening family TV, but it is its job to reflect all facets of country life and farming – and it can often be a brutal business.

A terrible day was to get far, far worse. A young White Park heifer was an obvious reactor. It would be dispatched to the abattoir, as would a Belgian Blue calf and, the cruellest of the blows, a valuable shaggy Belted Galloway.

That made four different animals from four different herds from four different parts of the farm. This time around, Bemborough was riddled with TB.

Losing animals like this goes against the grain of being a farmer. It's just not the reason why we do this job. I know we send animals for slaughter all the time, but when they have been raised for beef or lamb, that is the natural order of things.

This was different, and horrible. Sending a breeding bull or a pregnant cow or one that has her young calf suckling on her is a different matter, and is horrible. It just feels plain wrong.

I felt devastated and hollow inside at this latest setback and poor Dad was even worse. He had come down for the day to watch the testing and as he saw one animal after another fall foul of Gill's calipers, he was inconsolable.

Partly he was upset because he knew that I was and he hated to see me unhappy. Yet mostly it was his pure countryman's instinct kicking in, and sorrow at the unfairness of it all.

As I said, *it just feels wrong.*

Dad was always an emotional man – when I was a kid, I can remember him crying at sad films on TV – and situations of genuine tragedy such as this really affected him. He tried to do a short comment piece for the *Countryfile* cameras but had to cut it short as his eyes filled with tears.

He let them flow in the farm office shortly afterwards and I felt like crying along with him. This new TB outbreak would mean far too many more months of problems, restrictions and financial hardship for the livestock business.

As Duncan and I chewed over the consequences that evening it felt like a never-ending battle that we just could not win. Not for the first time I was wondering why we bothered.

It was to be another 18 months before Bemborough was clear of TB again. The final inspection was as fraught and as nerve-wracking as ever, not helped by the very first cow to be tested, a pregnant Belted Galloway, panicking in the crush, crashing out of the cage and escaping.

Still, once our nerves were calmed, Gill's testing went as well as could have been hoped. A lot of farms in the vicinity had been declared clear recently, and it was a huge relief when Bemborough joined them.

For the moment, at least.

And that's the point. With frequent tests, farmers can never fully escape the threat of bovine TB, which looms around every corner. There was no way we were going to get rid of all our valuable rare-breed cattle at Bemborough. I love livestock, as did Dad, and it is a huge part of why I became a farmer.

Yet our two TB shutdowns made Duncan and me realize just how vulnerable and exposed that side of the business was. After we got the second all-clear, we thought carefully about our future plans.

It was with heavy hearts that we decided to sell all of the Longhorns. Dad and I were very sorry to see them go, as they had been part of the farm, and Dad's life, for many years.

Like many rare breeds, the Longhorn just couldn't compete with more productive, continental breeds and had slipped by the wayside nationwide. Thirty years ago the Longhorn was a very rare breed and Dad had collected a few of them to help with their plight and breed them on Cotswold Farm Park.

He was so passionate that he became chairman of the Longhorn Breed Society, and Libby the breed secretary. Along with an incredibly enthusiastic group of breeders, they helped the Longhorns go from strength to strength – so much so that they are no longer classified as a rare breed. Dad agreed that the breed was now in safe hands, with good numbers nationally, so our work was done.

For our other cattle breeds, we decided to reduce the numbers in each herd slightly, while keeping the breeding numbers high enough to support rare-breed conservation and showcase them at the Cotswold Farm Park.

Thankfully we have now been clear of TB for more than two years, and have even brought in another struggling rare breed, the Irish Moiled. Dad was delighted when these lovely brown-and-white polled (naturally hornless) cattle arrived, and I was proud to show them to him.

It sometimes felt like these were the moments that we were closest – and I know for sure that he found comfort in the fact that Duncan and I were continuing his legacy.

CHAPTER 17

'Which Camera Am I On?'

Farming can be a hard-headed business at times but at others it is hugely sentimental. Working so closely with animals, it is no surprise that you get emotionally attached to many of them – and none more so than the sheepdogs.

We have had some wonderful dogs on Bemborough over the years. I loved my Border Collie sheepdog, Fenn, that I bought from Dick Roper, and Fenn's daughter Maude was my top dog and worked side by side with me in the fields for more than ten years.

Maude had a puppy, Pearl, who unfortunately was run over when she was very little and so has never really been a great sheepdog. Yet Ella has always adored her and so we have kept her on as essentially a family pet that does a bit of part-time herding every now and then.

Then there are the kelpies. Bundy, the very first kelpie that I introduced to Bemborough after my jaunt to Oz, gave us so many years of sterling service – and her daughter, Ronnie, did even better.

Ronnie had a fairly tumultuous introduction to the world. She was one of the 12 puppies that Bundy had in her third litter, and in fact was one of the yellow ones that I was so concerned about that I rang a mate in Oz to check that they were OK.

She wasn't just OK – that sleek little yellow kelpie grew to be one of the most reliable, fast-thinking and efficient sheep-dogs that I ever had. She was an integral part of our family life – no, of our family – for more than a decade and Alfie, in particular, loved her to bits.

I am not ashamed to say that we all shed a tear, me included, when Ronnie passed away, as I also had for Fenn, Maude and Bundy. When all those beloved dogs died, we marked their passing with a ritual that has become a Bemborough Farm tradition.

Buttington Clump is a bunch of beech trees at the highest point of the farm, around 900 feet above sea level. You can see it from 20 miles away: as kids, we would always know that a journey home was nearly over when we could see the clump from the car.

Well, whenever a dog that is dear to us dies on the farm, we bury it at Buttington Clump. In some ways, it's a weird place to choose: it's stony even by Cotswold brash standards and there are tree roots everywhere. It is a hell of a job to dig a hole.

Even so, we lay all of our loyal sheepdogs to rest there, and it has become a very special place in our own family lore. Dad always said that that was where he wanted his ashes to be spread – in among all of his dogs.

Along with the farm, the farm park and my *Countryfile* work, Duncan and I were still running the sideline business of occa-sionally renting our animals out to television shows and movies. We were about to have one of our more unusual rental requests.

Young British Artist and controversialist Damien Hirst had bought a country house in Gloucestershire after he made his fortune, and his people now got in touch with us. They wanted to borrow a black ram for a photo shoot at Sotheby's in London.

One of Hirst's latest works was typical for the artist, in that he had cut a black ram in half and placed it into a glass tank, pickled in formaldehyde. A magazine wanted to do an arty photo shoot with the artwork, a living black ram and a naked female model.

Our livestock manager, Mike Caunter, took a Hebridean ram up to London for the shoot. It was lucky that he went with it, because only his farming knowledge and instincts prevented an utter disaster.

Much like bulls, rams are extremely hostile and aggressive towards each other, and as soon as our ram caught sight of Damien's masterpiece in its display case, it wanted to batter it. It fixed the pickled carcass with a glare and lowered its head.

Spotting the telltale signs, Mike sprinted across the gallery, past the surprised photographer and even more shocked naked model, and managed to grab our ram just before it charged. They pack a serious punch and it would easily have smashed the glass of the tank.

Had it done so, it is pretty safe to say that we would have been facing a hefty insurance bill – especially as the pickled ram was later to sell for millions of pounds. Mike certainly earned his money that day.

I have to say, good luck to Damien Hirst, but the appeal of cows or sharks cut in half and preserved in formaldehyde rather passes me by. I'm not a philistine, and I enjoy some modern art such as Banksy, but a lot of it leaves me cold.

I remember once going to the Guggenheim in New York and looking at an exhibit that was just four pebbles lying on the ground. There was an explanatory note saying that the work 'captured the sea moving across the earth'.

All around me, Americans were reading the sign and saying 'Wow!' but I couldn't help thinking, *No, it doesn't! It's just four pebbles on the ground!*

After all the upheaval of the *Countryfile* reboot, the shift to prime-time broadcasting was proving to be a huge success. The programme was regularly getting twice as many viewers as it had at lunchtimes, and some weeks as many as 7 million.

The new team had also bedded in really nicely. Matt Baker is a larger-than-life character and took to the show brilliantly. Matt was great with Ella and Alfie when he came to film on the farm and is a real perfectionist, working hard with the production team to get things right.

Ellie Harrison had also joined the presenter line-up and is exactly as she comes across onscreen. Bright, bubbly and extremely hard-working, she is a lot of fun to be around and always lifts the team's spirits.

By now, of course, I had nearly a decade of *Countryfile* under my belt and could easily have started thinking that I was an experienced veteran who knew all there was to know about making nature TV. How wrong I would have been, because I was about to enter a whole new confusing, terrifying world.

Live television.

Good grief! If I had thought joining *Countryfile* was hard, this was something else again.

It had all started when a BBC producer, Lisa Ausden, phoned me from London. Lisa had been watching some footage of me lambing a ewe on *Countryfile*, and it seemed that she had liked what she had seen.

'We are looking at filming a week-long series called *Lambing Live*,' she told me. 'We would do a one-hour show each night, live from a lambing. Do you think that could work?'

I wasn't sure, and I said so. I love sheep – I have 14 different breeds on Bemborough Farm – and I can talk about them 'til, well, the sheep come home. But I am a farmer. Would normal people really care enough to watch live lambing every night for a week?

Also, I wasn't sure exactly what Lisa wanted from me. Was she hoping to film the series here? Was she thinking I could present it? Or was she just after some friendly advice?

She was giving few clues away, although the next time she rang she said that a sheep farmer out in Monmouthshire had agreed to host the show, so clearly she wasn't looking to use Bemborough. Even so, her calls were becoming very regular.

Her producers were asking me detailed, technical questions about the biology, practicalities and timescale of lambing, and I was spending a lot of time on the blower. Eventually, I bit the bullet and asked her directly.

'Lisa, I'm giving you a lot of free advice here,' I told her. 'Am I possibly presenting this show?'

'Well, it is between you and Kate Humble,' she admitted.

Ah. *Well, that's that, then*, I thought. Kate is a fantastic live broadcaster who already had many series of *Springwatch* under her belt. Why would the BBC ever choose me over her? They were clearly just pumping me for free info.

Disappointed, I told Lisa that I would carry on helping her production team out on the phone, but we would need to negotiate a consultancy fee for my advice. She went away to have a think.

Two days later, she phoned back: 'Adam, I would really like you to be part of this show. Would you co-present it with Kate?'

Obviously, I said yes like a shot. What a fantastic thing to be asked to do!

And then I took a very deep breath. *Just what am I letting myself in for?*

I was about to find out.

Lisa packed me off to *The One Show*'s studio in White City for a crash-course rehearsal in live television. Suddenly I was sitting on the famous couch, holding a fake sheep and listening to the director talk in my earpiece as cameras zoomed around me.

'Tell us about the sheep, Adam ...'

'Link to VT in fifteen seconds, Adam ...'

'Switch to camera four and begin the next interview, Adam ...'

It was confusing, incredibly difficult, and overwhelming. When I was first starting out, I had found it hard even to talk to a camera. Now, I had to do so whilst working out which camera I was on, thinking on my feet non-stop and, hardest of all, coping with the continual voice in my ear issuing its instructions.

'Ask him this, Adam ... Actually, no, ask him *this* ...'

It was horribly hard to concentrate on what the interviewee was saying to me while also taking orders from the director.

'Wind up this interview in fifteen seconds and link to the pre-record on camera six, Adam ...'

Aargh! Where am I, and what is my name?!

In that one very intensive practice session on *The One Show* sofa, my already healthy respect for presenters like Kate Humble and Matt Baker, who make live TV look easy, went through the roof.

Attempting to follow the director's instructions, stare into the right camera and keep the show moving, I felt as if I were trying to juggle eggs on a unicycle. I drove home petrified at the prospect of doing so, live, in front of millions of people.

Can I really do this?

A week later, I was on Great Tre-rhew Farm in Llanvetherine near Abergavenny in the Brecon Beacons. The Beaven family had run the farm for three generations and the current farmer, Jim Beaven, had 550 sheep.

The Beavens were lovely people and were extremely welcoming, despite the huge intrusion from the BBC. I had no idea how big a team was needed for a live show of this size, with broadcasting trucks, catering vehicles, wires and lights everywhere and 60 people behind the scenes.

As a farmer, it was lovely to be on another farm to see how they did things – but this was more than just a farm tour. Far more.

For the first two days' shows, Kate Humble had introduced the episode live. Then we had shown recorded footage of Kate working with Jim as he prepared for the lambing, and some short items that I had filmed about the more general aspects of sheep farming. Now, it was time for me to introduce the show as we went fully live.

It should not have been too taxing. Standing next to Kate in the lambing barn, all I had to do as the camera came to me was to smile and say, 'Welcome back to *Lambing Live*, here at the Beavens' farm in Wales!'

It should have been easy. But it wasn't. Standing in the barn, the director was counting me down in my ear: 'Sixty seconds to go, Adam ...'

I was waiting for the camera, hung from a giant crane jib, to burst through the huge barn doors, swing in and focus in on my face. *This is it. There's no escape now.*

I was absolutely bricking it.

'Forty-five seconds to go, Adam ...'

I was trying to run through the words in my head, but they were all jumbling together. 'Welcome to *Live Lambing* ...' *No, no!* 'Welcome to the lambs of Beavens' farm ...'

Oh, this was hopeless! I couldn't even think the line straight, let alone say it!

'Thirty seconds to live ...'

I could hear the camera crane outside and I froze. I felt like a complete rabbit in headlights. I am sure I was almost hyperventilating. Kate Humble, the live-TV veteran standing next to me, could sense my panic.

A lot of presenters would have lost their rag with me or just barked, 'OK, you clearly can't do the line, I'll take it!' Kate is made of kinder stuff. As the countdown continued ('Twenty seconds!') she smiled and looked into my eyes.

'Right, Adam, what is it you have to say?' she asked me as she gave my tense shoulders a helpful rub. 'Just take a time-out. Look at me. Now tell me the line.'

'Fifteen seconds to camera ...'

'Welcome to *Lambing Live*, here at the Beavens' farm in Wales,' I said.

Was that right? Was it in the right order?

'That's it, easy, you've got it!' she encouraged. 'Now just do it when we go live.'

The crane pulled in through the barn doors, the BBC camera swinging in on its jib.

'Five, four, three, two, one ... cue Adam!'

The red light came on.

'Welcome to *Lambing Live*, here at the Beavens' farm in Wales!'

Somehow, it came out exactly right. We were up and running.

The first show seemed to pass both in slow motion and a speedy blur. I was trying to ignore the voice in my head telling me: *There. Are. Millions. Of. People. Watching. You!* and instead focus on the more helpful voice: the director.

I think that anybody's first live TV broadcast would be terrifying, but it helped that at least I was in an environment that I loved. This was my home. I was at ease with the sheep and the lambing: after all, I had been doing it my whole life.

There were no lambs born on the first two live shows and a few members of the public even emailed in complaining but by the third night they were popping out all over the shed. I almost forgot about the cameras and went into autopilot: it was just like doing a lambing demonstration on the farm park, albeit on a much grander scale.

I got a couple of things wrong, and once or twice I began to deliver a link to the wrong camera, but there were no real howlers or bloopers. I got more relaxed as the week went on and somehow by the end I had not only survived it, but even mostly enjoyed it.

The show worked really well. We videoed some ewes giving birth during the night and also followed the little stories that arise in every lambing. We showed lambs that were rejected by their mums but adopted by other ewes – often ones who had only had one lamb rather than the usual twins.

To our delight, the experiment was a big success. The viewers seemed to love the show, and a few farmers even got in touch to tell us they were leaving their own lambing sheds each evening in order to watch *Lambing Live*. It was hard to think of a bigger vote of confidence than that.

One happy consequence of *Lambing Live* is that Kate Humble and I have become friends. After our first broadcast, she fell in love with a weak little black lamb that she'd helped to deliver.

Unfortunately it wasn't strong enough to stay with its mum, so became a pet lamb and was given the name Humble. At the end of the series, Jim Beaven gave Humble to Kate, who asked me to look after her at Bemborough. Humble was to stay with us for years.

Kate already had a few pigs and some chickens at her home but with her husband, Ludo, she has now bought a small county-council farm where she has a mix of animals, some of which I have sold her. They run courses on everything from hedge-laying to – yes, you've guessed it – lambing.

We've done two more series of *Lambing Live*, in Cumbria and Scotland, and I hope there are many more to come. I was more nervous tackling live TV than probably anything else I have ever done – but I am so glad that I did it.

The most wonderful part of all three series has been getting to know the amazing farming families that we have had the privilege to spend time with. Each of them has had a real connection with the land, a love of animals and a bond with each other.

In that respect, they were very like my own family. It's the country way of living – and for those of us who are living it, it is a very special gift. There again, sometimes even the most seemingly straightforward family lives can hide profound secrets ...

CHAPTER 18

A Life in a Letter

Mum and Dad were happily enjoying their retirement just down the road in Bourton-on-the-Water. After almost four decades of running Bemborough Farm and raising a family, they loved finally having time to kick back and spoil the grandkids.

Naturally, Dad couldn't stay away from the farm and the farm park. They were in his blood, and he remained an invaluable source of help and support for me. If I found I had a problem with the livestock or in my TV career, he was always the first person that I turned to.

He was also still involved in various rare-breed and farming associations, nature trusts and country shows. His reputation in the agricultural world remained extremely high, although in the minds of many his success had never been truly celebrated and deserved more recognition.

In 2010 Tony Fisher, a friend who had always had a close association with the farm and admired Dad's work, decided to nominate him to be the recipient of a UK honour.

The way the honours system works is that the proposer sends in a detailed recommendation about the nominee's life and work to the Cabinet Office, together with supporting letters from public figures and people of note where appropriate.

Dad was not short of advocates. Supporters who wrote in support of Tony's recommendation of him included two members of the House of Lords, Lord Apsley and Lord Barber of Tewkesbury, who were both keen supporters of rare breeds.

In fact, Dad had helped return Gloucester cattle to the Bathurst Estate for Lord Apsley. He and I had also taken a pair of Longhorn oxen to Lord Apsley's wedding, to pull him and his bride by ox cart as they left for their honeymoon. It had been a memorable day for them – and for us, too.

The poet Pam Ayres, who lives locally and is a long-standing family friend, also lent her voice to the proposal, as did the Dowager Duchess of Devonshire, the Mitford sister who had given me work experience on her Chatsworth estate in my youth. Despite all this, the application was not successful.

Dad had no idea about this application, of course, and I don't know what he would have made of it if he had. He had never been motivated by personal gain in his tireless work to conserve rare breeds, nor was his TV work founded on a desire for fame and recognition. It had always been about the animals, and it always would be.

I still loved hanging out with Dad on the farm every week, and discussing anything and everything. In 2010 one of the big films was *The King's Speech* starring Colin Firth, who had kindly written that congratulatory note to our sow, Sally, all those years ago.

Dad and I happened to see a clip on TV of Firth stuttering and stammering as King George VI, and in a totally matter-of-fact fashion, Dad told me, 'That was me, when I was a boy. Lally always used to shout at me for it.'

How awful that must have been for poor Dad. My heart went out to him.

In fact, Dad's backstory had always both intrigued and – more to the point – confused my sisters and me. He would tell us snippets, but we never quite understood the exact timeline or the chronology.

It felt like dipping in and out of a tremendous film or a book where you were fascinated by the main characters but had missed – or been confused by – some of the storyline or plot developments. The whole thing seemed so compelling and yet so complicated and one day, trying to work out some detail or other of the tale, I told him, 'You know, Dad, you ought to write all of this down!'

Being Dad, he did. He said nothing but he went away, and a few days later he produced a long, handwritten letter that he gave separately to my three sisters and me.

So here it was, down in black and white – everything that he had gone through in his life. It was the most extraordinary document and suddenly, as I read it, everything fell into place. Here was the making of Joe Henson:

My mother was born on January 6th 1910 as Harriet Martha Collins. Her mother was Rebecca Ruth Collins nee Klaxtein and her father Edward Collins.

They lived in a flat in the East End of London and her mother – whose stage name was Queenie Dell – was on the Halls. She did the sand dance and used to demonstrate it to me as a child.

Edward joined the army and was sent to France in the First World War, where he was gassed. After the war they had a second daughter, Grace. Edward was a billiard table maker but never recovered from the gas on his lungs.

Queenie was still on the Halls so Mum had to look after Grace while they were out. She kept her quiet by pretending to be the coalman, who Grace was afraid of. Edward died in about 1934.

On leaving school Mum wanted to become a milliner, but Gran said, 'A good-looking girl like you could earn a lot more on the stage.' She took her to see an agent, who said, 'Harriet Collins is no name for the stage!'

There was a show on in town called Billie Kelly and that was the name Mum wanted. The agent said, 'You can't have the same name. Why not take your mother's stage name and call yourself Billie Dell?' That is what she did, and she was known as Billie or just Bill for the rest of her life.

Because she was so good-looking she had stage jobs as a showgirl. Very little costume but not allowed to move. Lots of ostrich feathers! She always loved dancing, and was a natural for the chorus line. While in the chorus she met her lifelong friend, Celia Glyn.

Cele, as she was known, got a job in the chorus for Jack Hulbert, who was taking a show to America. She persuaded Jack to include Mum in the chorus, but as she was underage (15), Cele had to agree to be her chaperone. Mum always said it was the blind leading the blind!

The trip to America was an amazing experience. In Chicago she witnessed a fistfight and could not get over the noise of fist on face. She was persuaded to drink hooch, as it was Prohibition, which temporarily made her blind.

This gave her a taste for alcohol, which she returned to in times of need for the rest of her life. She was never a regular drinker, but if she had one drink she was on it for a week. When I was a child I used to dread this happening.

On her return she had no trouble getting stage work and fell in with a group of young actors led by the very handsome Edward Scott-Gatty. The group included Dave Hutcheson, Robert Newton, Frank Lawton, Cyril Campion and Bill Kendall.

Edward owned a Mercedes-Benz tourer that he had been given in 1928 by Earl Cowley, who had purchased it in 1913. Earl Cowley was also an actor with the stage name of Arthur Wellesley as he was related to the Duke of Wellington.

Edward Scott-Gatty would take Mum driving in his Merc and she fell madly in love with him. Because he could not afford to run it all the time he rode a motorbike. The gang would go to the Isle of Man for the T.T. races. The bike had a fixed front suspension and one day in March 1931 on a rough road surface it broke and he went over the handlebars and was killed.

Mum was devastated as they had talked of marriage, but the aristocratic family did not approve of the Cockney chorus girl. Mum attended the funeral at the church at Old Welwyn but his family ignored her. Edward had a signet ring, which Mum badly wanted, but his mother would not hear of it going out of the family.

The family later erected a magnificent stained-glass window in Old Welwyn parish church in memory of Edward, showing Edward in the act of removing an actor's mask. Years later, when I still did not know my true parentage, Mum took me to see the window and let me believe that he was my father. She never actually said so.

His family, surrounded by the old gang, buried his beloved Merc in the grounds of Lullingstone Castle in Eynsford, Kent, where, as far as I know, it remains to this day.

For many years up to the Second World War Mum and some of Edward's friends made an annual pilgrimage to the church and cemetery at Old Welwyn with Dr Arthur Morris, the honorary doctor of the Green Room Club and a great mate.

At the time of Edward's death, Mum was in a West End show with Leslie Henson as the star. He was at the peak of his career as an actor and comedian. He admired Mum and he caught her on the rebound. He showed her the high life, but was married to Gladys Henson, also an actress.

Then Mum became pregnant by Leslie and did not know what to do, as if it came out it would ruin his career. Cele said she should have it terminated and told her to go to Arthur Morris for advice.

Arthur was a lovely caring Welshman and asked her if she really wanted to get rid of the baby. She burst into tears and said that was the last thing she wanted to do. He said he would talk to Leslie.

Leslie and Mum agreed to keep the baby and I was born

in a London hospital on 16 October 1932. They agreed that I would be called Joseph Leslie: Joseph after his father, Joseph Lincoln, and Leslie after him.

When the registrar came round the ward to register the baby, he asked, 'Name of father?' Mum panicked, as they had not discussed this, so she blurted out 'Edward Collins', her father's name. So I started life as Joseph Leslie Collins.

To start with, we lived in a small flat which Leslie rented in London. His close family wanted to have me adopted, which Mum fought tooth and nail. They never told his mother of my existence, which years later his sister Nita said was terribly sad as she felt that she would have loved me.

Leslie visited us regularly, but while I was learning to talk I could not say 'Leslie' but called him 'Lally', which stuck for the rest of his life. My favourite toy was a small model farm.

Lally was a keen golfer and played for the stage golfing society. His favourite course was Moor Park near Northwood in Middlesex. My two godfathers, Arthur Morris and an old army friend, Den Critchley Salmonson, suggested that Lally bought a small house and put it in my name for my future.

He chose to buy one near Moor Park for convenience and called it Little House. It was in Green Lane, Northwood. Gladys refused to give him a divorce and he did not want the adverse publicity.

Lally and his golfing friends, many of them the same old gang, would visit Little House regularly on their way to or from Moor Park. They knew that Billie would give them a *good meal. She was always a good cook and a wonderful loving mother to me.*

Just up the road was a lovely farm called Park Farm where the cows were hand-milked. The milk was delivered to our door by pony and float, the hens laid their eggs under the ricks in the rickyard and the pigs were fed on locally collected swill. All the fieldwork was done by carthorses as they only had one old tractor, which did the ploughing.

Mum used to take me up to the farm every fine day and I used to help collect the eggs. That decided me that I wanted to be a farmer. Some chance! When I left school, Mr Nichols at Park Farm gave me my first job.

After a few years, Mum decided that she was becoming a landlady for Lally and his golfing friends and he would never divorce Gladys. She could not sell the house as it was in my name so she decided to let it out and to rent a house in Bournemouth. This decision to escape was a brave move and was only possible as Lally gave her an allowance on the understanding that he could visit me on a fairly regular basis.

My godmother, Aunty Cele, used to visit us regularly. She had married a rich man on the stock exchange, Nick Prinsep. She persuaded Mum that we should have a dog to protect us, and for me, and she bought a lovely Great Dane called John.

John and I became firm friends. On nice days in the summer Mum would take John and me to Branksome Chine beach for a swim in the sea.

Edward had taught Mum to drive. There were no driving tests in those days and Lally had lent Mum his pale fawn Chrysler. The local residents said that this glamorous actress who had moved down from London had a car and a dog to match her blonde hair! Actually Mum dyed her hair and eyebrows, which seemed to convince people it was natural.

Gran, Mum's mother, had remarried a lovely man several years her junior called Bill Geeves, who became known to me as Grampy Bill. He was a stoker on the LNER railway lines. He told me that he always had two shovels, one for the coal and one clean shiny one to fry his bacon and eggs on the fire. At one time he was stoker on the Flying Scotsman.

Edward Scott-Gatty had paid for Mum to have riding lessons in London and they used to ride together on Rotten Row in Hyde Park before his death. Mum loved riding and was keen to take it up again so while I was at school she started going to a riding stables in Christchurch.

There she met the next love of her life: Cyril Day. He was unmarried and was manager of Woolworth in Christchurch. He was also a very good dancer as, of course, was Mum. A neighbour used to babysit me for Mum to go dancing with Cyril. She was happier than I had ever seen her in my whole life.

Cyril was a lovely man and I learned to love him too. They used to go to the Barn Club in Christchurch and the manager had a bull terrier bitch with a litter of pups. Cyril bought a dog pup, which he called Barney. I thought the world of Barney, too.

Lally still used to come down to stay and one night I heard he and Mum having a terrible row. They were screaming at each other. It was a few days later, after he had returned to London, that I found out why.

Cyril had proposed to Mum and she had accepted. I did not understand why Lally should object, but now I know that he would not divorce Gladys and Mum wanted her own life with the man she loved. I did not go to the wedding (in those days it would not have done) but I do know that Grampy Bill gave her away.

Suddenly war was declared and the world went mad. I was seven years old and found it hard to understand. Men were cheering, 'We'll beat those Jerries by Christmas!' Little did they know. Suddenly the beaches were fenced off with barbed wire and that was the end of swimming.

Cyril joined the RAF and went off for training. Mum could not be called up because she was caring for me. Aunty Cele came to stay and told Mum that I should have a pair of rabbits to teach me about sex, as I had no father living with me.

Mum was criticised for keeping a big dog during rationing. Some said, 'Look at that poor skinny dog – she can't possibly get enough meat for it.' Others said, 'Look at that great big fat dog – it must be eating enough meat for two children.' Unable to bear the criticism, we took poor John back to the kennels he had come from. I was heartbroken.

To cheer me up, Grampy Bill arrived with my rabbits on the train: Loppy and Queenie. Queenie was very prolific and Grampy taught me to make rabbit hutches out of tea chests.

As the war went on Cyril passed his exams as a navigator. He joined the crew of a Blenheim bomber based on an air base near Christchurch. He kept his dog, Barney, with him.

One day he brought his whole crew home to us for the day. Mum had been saving up her ration cards to give them a slap-up lunch. To me, he appeared much older than the others, who looked like boys. In fact they called him 'Pop'.

We were sitting on the front lawn resting after lunch while Mum cleared the table indoors. Suddenly, one of the boys said to Cyril: 'Is he really your son?' Cyril grinned at me and said, 'Yes, of course he is!' That was the proudest moment of my life so far.

The Germans started bombing Poole Harbour just up the road. They moved ack-ack guns onto the beach, which disturbed me more than the bombs. Mum put mattresses in the cupboard under the stairs and when the sirens went off she would grab me out of bed and carry me down to our shelter. Hitting my head on the door as she carried me in is the thing I remember most.

One night there was a terrible explosion and in the morning we found that a German plane, trying to avoid the houses and reach the sea, had crashed into a house on the cliff just up the road. That brave pilot may have saved my life. The crew bailed out into the sea where the locals were dragging them in.

As food rationing took hold, I am sure Mum fed me most of her rations. We started a system of barter in the area. On his visits from London, Grampy Bill taught me how to kill *and prepare my rabbits for eating, and we had a big apple tree in the back garden. We swopped oven-ready rabbits and apples for other people's eggs and home-grown vegetables. I don't remember ever going hungry.*

One day, which I will never forget, the postman called with a telegram for Mum. Cyril was reported missing. Mum collapsed in tears and I held her in my arms, telling her that he was only missing. She seemed to know that she would never see him again.

She went to the base and collected all his belongings, including his brindle bull terrier, Barney, who became mine. Barney was a fighter and he had one ear up and one ear down.

Years later I went to Runnymede with my wife Gill to the RAF Memorial. There I found Cyril's name among the missing. It was a very moving moment.

I would take Barney for walks in the Chime while collecting bracken for rabbit bedding. I had to hold him on a lead if I saw another dog, as he was a terrible fighter. One day he had a fight with an Alsatian dog and a Policeman called on us that night. Barney saw a man in a uniform and made a huge fuss of him. He said, 'He's a lovely friendly dog. You need him to protect you. Keep him under control in future and I will say no more.'

One day I took Barney on the ferry from Sandbanks to Shell Bay. We slipped down on to the beach and ran along it for a while. I then cut up through rough ground to the road. Barney kept turning and barking and I followed him to the road. Once there, I turned and saw a notice: 'KEEP

OUT. HEAVILY MINED.' I had been following him without knowing.

Life seemed to settle down and we had given up getting any news about Cyril. Lally continued making spasmodic visits to see us when he was not abroad entertaining the troops with ENSA, which he did a lot.

One day when he was staying he wanted to come for a walk with Barney and me. Barney suddenly attacked another dog and got hold of him and would not let go even though Lally was hitting him with a stick. We finally got them apart and when we got home, Lally told Mum that she had to get rid of him.

Lally was doing a show locally for the Fleet Air Arm and they agreed to have Barney. When I used to take him to the beach he would run straight through the barbed wire, catching his skin as he went to chase seagulls. The soldiers on guard called him 'Ironsides'.

His new owner was a seaplane pilot and we heard later that Barney used to swim after him till he took off. The men called him 'Flannel'.

Towards the end of the war I was suddenly sent to a boarding school, which was evacuated to a rat-ridden vicarage in Puddlestone near Leominster in Herefordshire. I did not understand the need until I was told that Lally and Mum had got married and I had to be got out of sight of the press as Lally was a famous actor.

When I went home for the holiday, home was Chislehurst in Kent and not Bournemouth. Mum had taken all my rabbits

with her: bless her. There was a big garden with some rough
ground and Grampy Bill soon got me some chickens. It was
called Lake House and Lally bought me some ducks for the
lake. After two terms, I was taken out of the boarding school
in Hereford and sent to a posh local day school.

When Mum had married Cyril they had my name changed
from Collins to Day. At my second school in Bournemouth
I was Joe Day. Now they changed my name to Henson so
that at the new school I was Joe Henson.

Lally then told me one day that he was my real father. He
even got his solicitor to have my birth certificate changed so
he was [listed as] my father and not Edward Collins.

Our house was in Doodlebug Alley and we used to hear
the flying bombs flying over. In fact they often used to cut
out over us before gliding on to London.

Mum then became pregnant and the first thing they did
was show the little baby boy to me. He was born on the day
the war in Europe came to an end. They called him Nicholas
Victor Leslie: Nicholas after his godfather, Auntie Cele's
husband Nick Prinsep, who was an officer in the RAF,
Victor for VE Day, and Leslie after his dad, like me.

When Mum brought the baby home, I said to them, 'Can
I call him Nicky?' I had a mother, a father and a brother.
We were a real family at last.

What a life! They were all facts that I had known – or most
of them, anyway – but previously they had been a jumble, a
confusing blur of stories. Suddenly, seeing it all laid out like this

made me realize just what devastatingly unsettled early years Dad had endured.

It was the complete opposite to the secure, idyllic childhood he and Mum had given us kids on Bemborough Farm. Was that the point, maybe? That he was giving us kids what he had never had?

I tried to think myself into his shoes, when he was a boy and a teenager. The constant moving from place to place, the absentee father, the uncertainty as to who his father actually was, the death of his beloved stepdad.

It made me wonder: *how would I have even begun to cope with it? Would I have been able to?*

Dad always spoke lovingly and glowingly of his mother and father. There is no doubt they both loved him: even when he was forced by circumstance to be absent, Leslie had always provided for Dad as a boy. How hard it must have been for him, also, to be separated from his son.

Dad seemed a little hesitant, or even nervous, when he gave us kids this letter. I think he wanted to get it all off his chest, yet maybe he was also wary of finally spilling all of his secrets – and of what we would make of them.

Was it possible that a tiny part of him was still ashamed of his past?

I sincerely hope not, because it had the absolute opposite effect on me. It made me love and admire Dad even more, if possible, and marvel that somebody who had undergone such a hugely difficult childhood could have become such a warm, loving, strong and openly emotional family man.

It also made me wonder, slightly, if his turbulent boyhood was what had made him form such a devout and instinctive bond with the animals of Park Farm. To me, it all suddenly made sense.

You know where you are with animals. They never let you down.

More than anything, it made me happy that Dad's epic tale had at least had a happy ending and Leslie and Billie had, at last, been able to be together and raise him and Nicky in a proper family unit. The pain that preceded that must have made it all the sweeter.

Mum, Dad and I naturally talked after Dad unveiled his letter and they told me a little more. As ever, from our chats it was evident just how much Dad had loved Leslie and Billie, and also just what a dramatic, quasi-Shakespearean love story theirs had been.

Dad told me that when Billie had died at Bemborough Farm, when I was just four, she had lain on her deathbed and cried out: 'Lally, come back to me!' As he told me this he burst into tears – as did Mum, sitting beside him, who had nursed Billie right at the end.

Wow. It was quite a story – and in fact, a few months later Dad, Uncle Nicky and I went to see some London publishers who were interested in turning the Greek melodrama of Dad's life into a book. It would certainly have been a page-turner!

In the end, nothing came of those meetings – but I hope that, in some way, this book now fills that gap. I hope that it can show people that there was so, so much more to Joe Henson than a genial, well-loved farmer.

After his initial wariness, Dad appeared relaxed and very happy to have told his children his amazing life story – and the plotline of his life was about to have another dramatic development. He was about to be honoured.

Undeterred by the previous year's setback, Tony Fisher had co-opted Dudley Russell, a family friend and the husband of Pam Ayres, and the two of them had reapplied to the Cabinet Office to have Dad's work with rare breeds recognized. This time, there was a far more positive response. Dad was to be awarded an MBE for his services to conservation.

It was such wonderful news and, in a strange way, such a relief, because I was so desperate for Dad's lifelong work to be recognized in this way. Dad was never one to brag, but I could see he was incredibly touched by the news.

As we waited for Dad's big day, he and I had a very special trip as we retraced the steps of one of the great adventures of my youth.

Countryfile sent me up to North Ronaldsay in the Orkneys to check on the wellbeing of the indigenous sheep there that Dad had done so much to preserve. Nearly 40 years after our original trip, when I was just eight, Dad came with me as we retraced our great adventure.

It was a truly amazing few days. Considering I was so young on our first visit, I remembered the island vividly. A few of the crofters that we had met in 1974, such as the Muir family, still worked there so we were able to go to see them and reminisce.

On our first trip, Dad had shot some cine film of our visit that he had kept ever since. We gave it to *Countryfile*, and their editors were able to splice this grainy old footage of the young me walking into a cottage, aged eight, with shots of me doing the same thing fully grown. It was very effective.

Countryfile also filmed Dad and me walking down the beach and chatting as seals swam in the sea behind us. Even after all these years he was still a real old TV pro, so it didn't take them long to get what they wanted.

In the evenings we went for meals and spent some quality time together, talking about how North Ronaldsay had changed and yet in some ways was still the same as when we were first there.

There again, that was also true of the two of us. Dad and I had both grown, and changed – and yet our relationship was still as close and intense as ever it was.

It was a magical trip, just as the first one had been, and I think we both felt sad to bid farewell to the Orkneys once more. Yet we had a great incentive to head home – it was time for Dad to receive his MBE.

The ceremony was held at Windsor Castle in October 2011. Dad was only allowed to take three guests to the presentation so just Mum, Lolo and I went inside with him, but the whole Henson family made the trip to Windsor en masse.

Dad was normally a cheery, upbeat soul but I am not sure I ever saw him happier than here, being honoured for his life's work and passion. Naturally, he wore his most prized possession: the gold-and-platinum cufflinks given to his own father by King George VI.

In a stateroom at Windsor Castle, Princess Anne presented Dad with his MBE, which was fitting. Her interest in farming meant that she and Dad had spoken before: in fact, he had even sold her a few White Park cattle over the years.

Probably part of me felt that it was a shame that it was not the Queen herself dishing out the honour, but Dad was delighted that it was Princess Anne. He felt that the fact he knew her, slightly, and that she was a huge advocate of farming made it highly appropriate.

After the ceremony, we all went for a family meal in a pub near the castle. It was an incredibly joyous occasion, and I made a little speech telling Dad how proud we all were of him being awarded the MBE, and how much he deserved it.

Dad sat in the middle of us, as smiley and twinkly-eyed as ever, waving away my compliments self-deprecatingly and just loving being at the heart of his family. He could not have been more contented – and nor could any of us.

It was a special day that none of us will ever forget.

CHAPTER 19

Going to London to
See the Queen

F arming has changed so much in the time that Duncan and
I have been running Bemborough, and I'm glad to say
that nearly all of it has been for the better. In particular, it's
heartening how much greener everything is now than it was
back in less enlightened times.

Thirty years ago, when Duncan and I were at Seale-Hayne,
there was a course called 'Rural Resources and Their
Management' that taught caring for the environment and
looking after wildlife. Well, we were far too busy studying
practical farming to bother with all that: we called those students 'roomies' and saw them as hippies. Our own course
didn't cover farming for wildlife at all.

If I were there now, I would take far more interest in rural
resources because environmental concerns underpin a lot of
what we do. Our agronomists, who recommend which wheat
and barley seeds to grow, and which sprays or fertilizers to
use, nowadays also advise us on conservation.

Thankfully, today's farmers are far more aware of their
responsibilities towards the environment. As well as conserving rare breeds on Bemborough Farm for the past 25 years,

we have been doing a huge amount to protect and enhance the farm's biodiversity.

For example, we plant areas around the outside of our arable fields with specific seed plants like millet, sunflower and rye for the farmland birds to enjoy over the winter. Once these crops have been depleted, we continue to feed the birds, spreading about three tons of seed on the farm tracks. It is a large-scale version of what people do at home on their bird tables.

We also have specific areas known as pollen and nectar mixes to encourage bees and butterflies. In late spring and early summer they are full of insects and a riot of colour. As well as being beneficial to the environment, farmers need insects both for pollination and to feed on other insects that can be damaging to the crops.

We manage a lot of our grassland by conservation grazing, whereby we only graze at certain times of the year and leave areas for wildflower meadows to flourish and set seed. Our livestock manager, Mike, works to strict guidelines grazing the right amount of animals at specific times of year to keep the grass, or sward, at the right height for whatever the conservation aim is, be it burrowing bees or cowslips.

This is where rare breeds come into their own, as many are great at conservation grazing. Traditional British breeds are robust and can make the most of poor-quality pasture.

Our little Irish Moiled cows, for example, can prosper in rough, marshy grazing land where big modern Charolais cattle would struggle because there just wouldn't be enough food for them and they would churn up wet ground due to their weight and size. Breeds like Exmoor ponies or little Soay sheep, which have little use commercially, are also excellent for this purpose.

Of course, we need to make up for the arable income that we forego when we get involved in such schemes, and DEFRA very admirably pays out grants to incentivize farmers to get involved. We are now in a Higher Level Stewardship scheme and very happy to be doing this good work.

We are lucky enough to have a designated Site of Special Scientific Interest (SSSI) on the farm due to a rare plant called the Cotswold Pennycress, which has a tiny white flower that comes into bud early in the spring. Also in this area is the Duke of Burgundy Fritillary, a rare butterfly that lays its eggs on the underside of the leaves of a cowslip situated in a certain amount of shade.

It's all quite a contrast to the 1960s, 1970s and even beyond when the government paid farmers like Dad to rip out hedges and clear woodland to make fields bigger and more productive. Nobody knew any better then, but that style of farming went too far, and no one considered the harmful effect on wildlife. I'm proud that on Bemborough we have done a lot of work to re-establish hedges and maintain the dry stonewalls.

I am also pleased that many farmers today are taking note of the organic principles and have realized that managing the soil is crucial. To reduce our reliance on artificial fertilizers, we now farm on a rotational basis, using cover crops such as black oats and vetches. The root systems and organic matter encourage microbial activity and worms to ensure a healthy soil, thus providing natural nutrients for the following crop.

We are always looking for new ways to develop the farm. A

few years ago we formed a very useful and productive joint venture with an immediate-neighbour farmer and friend, Hamish Campbell.

We have around 1,000 acres of arable land and Hamish has 1,200. Equipment costs can be horrendous: a new tractor can be in the region of £120,000 while a top-of-the-range combine harvester can set you back as much as £250,000.

Hamish pointed out that we were both about to spend vast sums on new machines and suggested that, instead of doing that, we pooled our resources and bought some top-quality equipment together. We could share the machines and even do some outside contracting with them.

So we set up a limited liability partnership, went halves on all of the expensive machines, and now split all of the profit made from them 50/50. It's been very successful and has allowed Bemborough to employ a bespoke arable manager, Martin Parkinson, and skilled machine operators to work closely with Duncan.

New innovations are happening all the time. In 2012 I was delighted to set up a licensing agreement with Butcombe Brewery. We grow a winter barley called Maris Otter which is great for brewing real ale, so we decided to create Adam Henson's Rare Breed, a distinctive golden ale.

Seeing my face grinning from a bottle for the first time was weird, but with the team at Butcombe we are continuing to develop the Rare Breed brand, which is now sold in around 70 local pubs as well as in stores nationwide. I like a beer so obviously I make it my duty to drink as much as I can, so I can make back my few pennies a bottle!

Of course, in addition to trying constantly to improve and develop Bemborough, media activities also take up a large part of my time. My profile on *Countryfile* means that I get asked to take part in all sorts of unexpected activities.

A few of them rather leap out at me – such as the letter that my trusted PA and office manager, Paula, opened in the late summer of 2012:

The Prime Minister requests the pleasure of the company of Adam Henson at a Farming Lunch at 10 Downing Street on Wednesday 19th September 2012 (12.30 p.m.–2 p.m.).

Crikey! I hadn't seen that one coming! Still, it sounded like it would be an interesting experience and I had no reason to turn it down, so a few weeks later I nervously presented myself at that world-famous black door.

As it happened, I was with a couple of familiar faces. John Craven was there, having previously interviewed David Cameron for *Countryfile*, as was Matt Baker, representing young farmers. Also in attendance were Peter Kendall of the NFU and representatives of the pig, poultry and dairy industries.

The Prime Minister arrived exactly on time, having just chaired a military meeting and with one on education to follow. Yet if I expected him to coast his way through a discussion in which he had no great interest, I was to be very mistaken.

Mr Cameron said that he had called the meeting because he wanted to learn what the government could do to help British agriculture. He added that he had specialist advisers but he was also keen to talk to the agricultural industry directly to find out what was what.

When not in London, the Prime Minister lives quite near to us in Chipping Norton, and he certainly knew his stuff. Our discussion over lunch was fairly wide-ranging and he listened closely as we spoke, taking lots of notes.

He asked how we thought the government could encourage young people to take up farming, and we also talked about how to better facilitate trade and collaboration between different areas of farming. It felt a very useful discussion.

There are always battles going on between farmers and big retailers, so I piped up to remind the Prime Minister how powerful supermarkets are, and asked him whether such power made them capable of influencing government decisions. I don't think that it was his favourite question that he was asked during the meeting.

Mr Cameron was quite sharp with me, saying, 'Absolutely not – we are in control of the situation.' He put me back in my box slightly, but I didn't mind that – at least he seemed to know and care what he was talking about, which has not always been the case with politicians I have encountered.

When I first joined *Countryfile* I was very much a farmer who was dabbling in a bit of TV presenting. By contrast, I have to admit nowadays there are occasionally times that I can feel like a TV presenter who manages to do a bit of farming.

I am never entirely sure how I feel about that, because my first love is the land and it always will be. Nevertheless, I am always grateful and interested when the BBC comes to me with suggestions for possible new programmes.

In 2013 they asked me if I would like to co-present a series with food writer Nigel Slater called *Nigel and Adam's Farm Kitchen*. The idea was that we would explore how food gets from farm to fork by sowing, growing, rearing and cooking Britain's favourite foods on a working Cotswold farm.

It sounded a fascinating idea, and it was. A great thing from my point of view was that it was filmed on a farm down the road in Moreton-in-Marsh, which meant that I could fit it around my work on Bemborough and shooting my usual *Countryfile* slots.

The filming for the new show ran from spring until harvest time and I grew strange crops such as rice, durum wheat (to make pasta), and weird and wonderful mushrooms. I also reared different breeds of pigs and cows as we attempted to show viewers exactly where the food on their plates comes from.

I enjoyed doing it. I'm not a great cook and I can be perfectly happy munching on a bacon butty from a roadside café. However, at the same time I love eating good food and the idea of explaining about local fare and how we produce it via traditional farming methods appealed.

So I introduced Nigel Slater to the alien world of farming and he showed me the equally alien practices of cooking. Before we met I was slightly wary of him, as he had a reputation for being very particular about his work and a little pedantic at times.

Well, if that is the case, I didn't see that side of him at all and he was great to work with. Nigel seemed a lovely, genuine guy who was every bit as in love with cooking as I am with farming.

Before we started filming, I was advised that Nigel would be unlikely to want to jump in the sty with the pigs or to cradle a chicken while he talked to the camera. I decided that the best way to test this out was via some direct action.

When we came to film a piece about pigs and pork to camera I simply told him, 'Come on, we're getting into the pen with the pigs now!' then picked up a pig and handed it to him. Nigel's initial look of surprise, or possibly horror, quickly gave way to a tentative smile.

'Oh, actually, this is quite nice, isn't it?' he admitted. He was cool with everything he was asked to do on the farm, we got on really well, and I hope the series showed a few people how food gets to their supermarket shelves or market stalls.

We also discussed the value of food and the amount of energy and effort that farmers put into producing it. Nigel was keen to showcase the value of eating as a family, where good food goes hand in hand with conversation and a chance to take time out of our hectic lives.

Another project the following year saw me team up with one of my *Countryfile* co-presenters, Ellie Harrison, for the second series of *Secret Britain*. The two of us headed off to explore hidden corners of the countryside and of the UK in general, following leads suggested by *Countryfile* viewers.

The filming was hard work with long days, but the places we visited were fascinating and we had a lot of fun making it. One of the first episodes sent us to the Brecon Beacons to look at an almost completely unknown water world at the heart of this South Wales beauty spot.

There, we met a lady whose mother had grown up in an

incredibly remote spot that today is totally forested over. Her grandparents had raised sheep and milked cows by hand, and she took us through the woods to the ruins of the house where the family had once lived and where her mother had grown up.

As a girl, her mum had had to walk five miles to school every day through deep forest. We retraced the walk, through a beautiful gorge and along a path that, amazingly, passed right beneath a waterfall. Only keen walkers knew that path was there – well, until we broadcast it to millions of viewers on the BBC, anyway!

We also visited Yorkshire, where we went up in a glider. The passenger sits in front of the pilot, which meant that we got some absolutely breathtaking views, especially when the pilot took it upon himself to do a loop-the-loop. Flying in silence, like a buzzard being lifted up in the thermals, was an amazing experience.

I loved it, although Ellie was less keen. I found out why later: before we went up, she had seen a newspaper article in the mess room about a pilot on the same gliding strip who had hit another glider in the air, parachuted out and come down in a farmer's field, just missing landing in the blades of a combine harvester!

On a trip to Scotland, I visited a cattle ranch in the Highlands and even climbed up the 'secret side' of Ben Nevis. I am not the most confident climber in the world and beforehand, to be honest, I was more than a little nervous.

My guide and I made our way along ledges with a drop of hundreds of feet and I was very grateful to be roped to him. The views were spectacular – although unfortunately, when we reached the summit, it was shrouded in mist.

There's a strange thing about going on the television. It doesn't really change you and you are still the same person, but it means that you get offered the chance to do things that you never thought you would do in a million years.

If I had imagined that meeting the Prime Minister was the biggest honour that would come my way due to being on *Countryfile*, I had to think again when I received an excited phone call from Paula, my PA, early in 2015.

Buckingham Palace had phoned her asking if I would like to have lunch with Her Majesty the Queen. I think Paula must have made the Master of the Household smile when she advised him that she would contact me and get back to him, as she didn't feel it appropriate to accept on my behalf.

Of course an invitation from the Queen is not something you turn down and this was a very big deal for me. I am not a political animal at all but I am definitely a royalist and I felt hugely proud to be invited to Buckingham Palace.

This sense of pride increased when the official invitation to dine with Her Majesty and the Duke of Edinburgh on 19 May 2015 fell onto the doormat at Bemborough. It was to be a spring luncheon for eight invited guests and a very exclusive affair.

We've always had a daft family joke. Whenever my kids have asked me where I am going, if I am heading up to London I tell them, 'I'm going to London to see the Queen.' Well, on that particular May morning it was absolutely true.

After my taxi pulled into the gates of Buckingham Palace past the guards, the Queen's equerry briefed the other guests and me on the etiquette of the occasion.

He explained that we should call the Queen 'Your Majesty' the first time that we spoke to her, and then 'Ma'am' after that (said so that it rhymes with 'jam'). I also got to sneak a look at the seating plan – which was when I learned that I would be sitting right next to the Queen. What an honour!

As the guests all milled around an anteroom nervily eating nibbles and sipping Champagne, I had a stroke of luck. One of the waiting staff sidled up and introduced himself: 'It's lovely to meet you, sir,' he said. 'I'm a big fan of *Countryfile*.'

A-ha! This was good news! My memory of my silver-service *faux pas* next to the Duchess of Devonshire at Chatsworth House 30 years earlier still hadn't fully faded, and I didn't want a repeat.

'Look, I'm not very good at this sort of thing,' I confided in him. 'If I get anything wrong, just put me right, will you?'

He assured me that he would. I had an ally.

The Queen and Prince Philip came through and we were all introduced to them, and then took our places at the table. I was sitting to the Queen's left, with the curator from Kew Gardens to the other side of me.

The curator was really interesting, but I couldn't help but notice that the Queen had not addressed one word to me or even looked at me, and instead spent the entire first course deep in conversation with the person on the other side of her.

Hang on! Why isn't she talking to me? What have I done wrong?

I suddenly feared that I might spend the entire meal sitting next to the Queen and not say a word to her, so after about 15 minutes I took the plunge and asked her a question. I did know that I was supposed to wait for her to talk to me, but I just couldn't stop myself.

I learned later that it was actually even more of a breach of etiquette. The convention at such meals is that the Queen speaks to the person on her right for the entire first course, then turns and talks to the neighbour on her left during the next course.

Thankfully, the Queen didn't seem to mind me blundering in. She listened attentively as I asked my question.

'Your Majesty, with such a busy life, and having to attend so many events, what is your true love and passion in life? Is it art, or architecture, or politics?'

Her answer possibly revealed why I had been invited to such a venerable gathering, and seated next to her.

'Well, Adam, it is really animals, the same as you,' she told me. 'I love my horses and my dogs and my farm animals.'

At first I thought, *I wonder if she is just saying that to put me at my ease?* Yet it quickly became clear that she meant it. I had previously bought a bull for Bemborough Farm from Dochy Ormiston, her stockman at the Balmoral Estate.

Countryfile had filmed me buying the Highland bull, named Archie, and taking it back home, and Her Majesty had clearly been among our viewers.

'So, how is Archie?' she asked, and seemed genuinely pleased when I said he was doing well on the farm.

If I am honest, for the first few minutes there was a voice in my head that was screaming: *Oh my word, I'm talking to the Queen!* It was so loud that I thought she might hear it. Yet it soon passed and our conversation flowed naturally.

The Queen knew all about my dad, and also about his father, Leslie, and how he had founded ENSA. She was engaging and enjoyable to talk to, and made me feel very welcome.

Of course, I relaxed so much that I committed my inevitable silver-service *faux pas*. By the time the dessert came around I was chatting to the curator from Kew Gardens again and hadn't noticed how the Queen had taken her dessert.

My comradely waiter was holding out a tray with some fruit and a bowl of water on it. I noticed that the Queen had a few grapes and strawberries on her plate so I reached out to take the same from him.

'Ah, the finger bowl, sir!' the waiter whispered to me. 'You need to wash your fingers first.'

Honestly, I don't think I will ever get the hang of this silver-service lark! My accomplice quietly talked me through the niceties of using a silver fork to spear some pineapple, then we all retired to the drawing room for coffee.

I talked to Prince Philip for half an hour over coffee. Like the Queen, he was very well informed on agricultural matters so we chatted about farming tenancies and milking dairy cows. It was so natural that I could have been talking to anybody.

I had a very broad grin on my face as I walked out of the gates past the hordes of tourists and hailed a taxi on the Mall. It had been a remarkable experience, a real treat, and definitely one of the highlights of my life so far.

I try not to show off and tell too many people about it – but sometimes I just can't help myself.

I suppose adventures such as meeting the Queen served to emphasize to me just how good life was around this point.

Bemborough and the farm park were thriving, *Countryfile* and my various other TV projects were going well, and I had no real reason not to count my blessings on a daily basis.

They say life is a rollercoaster. How true that is. Just when everything looked fine, I was about to experience tragedy and sadness beyond anything that I had ever felt before.

CHAPTER 20

'I've Packed My Bags and I'm Ready to Go'

D ad was invariably in rude health. He had never smoked and hardly drank, and his face usually boasted the ruddy glow of a farmer who was lucky enough to spend the vast majority of his working life outdoors in the glorious Cotswolds.

Nevertheless, like everybody, as he headed into his early eighties he inevitably had a few health scares. He suffered a small heart attack, followed a little while later by a minor stroke. He came through both of them but they naturally left him a little diminished.

Even so, he was the very opposite of a hypochondriac. Like so many men of his generation, he would never complain or moan about any health problems. He would keep them to himself and not, as he would see it, 'bother anyone'. He was very old-fashioned in that way.

Which was why it was such a surprise to me when, early in 2015, he took me to one side and told me that he thought he didn't have very long left.

'I think my days are nearly up,' he said.

Naturally, I told him not to be so ridiculous. I wasn't done with him yet, I said. He had to pull himself together and be there for me and the family, like he always had.

Of course, he laughed and agreed with me – typical Dad – and the conversation moved on. The moment passed.

Yet a few weeks after that he was getting very breathless and having trouble breathing generally. We fixed him an appointment with his doctor and I worried that the doc might say that he had pneumonia and would need to go to hospital.

It was far worse than that. The doctor examined Dad and sent him straight to hospital to have scans. When the results came back, they showed that not only did he have cancer in his lungs but it had also spread to his liver and kidneys.

It would have been virtually impossible to cure it and Dad didn't give them the chance to try. As soon as he heard the news, he declared that he did not want any chemotherapy or radiotherapy treatment. This was the end, as far as he was concerned.

Dad knew, as we all did, that having chemotherapy would mean weeks upon weeks of debilitating treatment. He might get another year of life – if he was lucky – but it would be a year of going to hell and back. He knew that it just wasn't worth it.

By now he was eighty-two years old. He had had an amazingly rich life and as he put it to me in his characteristically cheery and positive manner, 'I've packed my bags and I'm ready to go.' He was content with everything he had achieved and was ready to move on.

I thought fleetingly of trying to talk him into treatment but I didn't because, ultimately, I knew Dad was right. I hope that this doesn't sound weird, but as a farmer you learn to be very pragmatic about life and death.

Over the years, Dad and I had put countless sick animals out of their misery because we didn't want them to suffer any more. Nobody in the family wanted to see Dad suffering in his final days, even if we got six more months out of him.

Yet it was the hardest conversation that I have ever had in my life, and that I ever will. *This was Dad*, the man that I had adored and looked up to for my entire life, and who had taught me everything that I knew. Could he really be about to go away?

Once Dad had decided not to have any treatment, we all set about making his last few weeks as comfortable and as pain-free as possible. We moved a hospital bed into his home and a district nurse began to visit him every day.

Mum cared for him as devotedly as she had done for nearly 60 years and the rest of the family called in all the time. It was fairly unpredictable how we would find him. Some days he was very sleepy and would drop off after 10 minutes.

Yet at at other times we would find him as upbeat and cheery as ever, eyes smiling as he greeted us. He would climb out of his sick bed and into a high chair and would be animated as we talked over all that we had done together.

It was heartbreaking, and special, and life-affirming all at once. I feel so incredibly lucky that I always had such a close and loving relationship with Dad, that he was always my hero, but I also knew that it was going to make it incredibly hard to say goodbye properly.

Yet we did it. In those precious final visits, I managed to find the words. I told him that I loved him, and had looked up to him all through my life, and I thanked him for all that he had done for me and shown me, about farming and about life.

I assured him that I would look after Mum, and Bemborough Farm, and that I would continue to conserve the rare breeds that he was so passionate about and to carry on his legacy. I knew how much those things meant to him and I hoped my words were bringing him comfort. I think they did.

Particularly, I told him how much I admired the fact he had been such a great father to my sisters and me despite having had such a crazy childhood himself. Leslie had loved him, but he had rarely been around to teach Dad how to be a man. He had worked it out all by himself, and done so brilliantly.

Dad listened, and smiled, and told me that he loved me, and how proud he was of everything he had watched me do. They were incredibly poignant and intense conversations and often I would be blinking away tears as I headed to my car.

Yet I am so pleased that we had those chats and I will never forget them. When many parents die, their children are left thinking, *I wish I had told them that I love them,* or *I never said how I felt*. At least I will never feel that.

It's so strange, but in many ways we had led the same life. Dad was very much his own man, and so am I, yet both of us had fallen in love with Bemborough Farm and made it our *raison d'être*. In a way, it had come to define us.

Then, extraordinarily, both of us had fallen quite randomly into television and media side-careers. Well, had it all been a coincidence? Or was I always subconsciously following in Dad's footsteps?

The truth is that I don't know – but I am so happy that things have worked out the way they have.

Because Bemborough Farm is set on top of a hill, we have always had spectacular sunrises and sunsets. On cold nights the fog will rise up from the valleys like a thick blanket and from the hilltop it is magical to look down and see the trees coming out of the mist.

I visited Dad in his hospital bed early one morning and told him how I had just seen the mist coming up from the valley in a field we always called Taylor's. He gave me one of his best smiles and said how much he loved those moments.

During one of those last, emotional meetings, Dad handed me something very special – the golden cufflinks that King George VI had given to his own father, and that Leslie had passed on to him. They had always been Dad's most prized possession. Now, suddenly, they were mine.

Dad was a religious man and one of his best friends, Andrew Bowden, is a vicar. Years ago, Dad had encouraged him to get into rare breeds. As Dad weakened, Andrew came down to the house and anointed him with holy water, and he became very calm after that.

The end came very soon afterwards, on a Monday morning at the start of October. I was at a meeting with a solicitor and got a call from the family saying that Dad had asked for me and wanted me to go to see him.

I drove over and joined Mum, Libby, Lolo and Becca at his bedside. Each of us talked to him quietly, said what we wanted to say, and told him, 'Goodbye.' It was moving and very hard to get through.

I don't know if Dad could hear what we were saying to him. I hope that he could, because I think it would have helped him to pass away in the peace he deserved. He certainly seemed content as he slipped away.

We had been waiting for weeks for Dad to leave us, dreading the moment – yet now that he had gone, it seemed so stark, so sudden. It seemed impossible to believe.

Was that it? Had Dad really gone?

There was a two-week gap before the funeral and it was a strange, dazed time. I felt numb or like some kind of zombie, as if I had somehow grown hollow. Mostly, I drifted through the days on autopilot, barely able to think.

Some days I was OK and could talk to people almost as usual. Other mornings I would wake up and it would hit me like a hammer blow: *Dad is gone*. I would be walking across a field, or driving my truck, and I would just burst into tears.

It was incredibly tough. I suppose I always knew that losing a parent would be hard, but I had never expected to feel pain like this. I felt empty and wrung out.

The national newspapers ran their obituaries of Dad, and *Countryfile* put a tribute together. The series producer, Jo Brame, asked me if I wanted to be involved but I knew that I would be a wreck. 'No,' I told her. 'I trust you to get it right.'

She absolutely did. The six-minute film was a lovely tribute to Dad's life, tracing his career from Cirencester Agricultural College to taking over Bemborough Farm, forming his passion for rare breeds and founding the Cotswold Farm Park.

It dug out old footage from *Animal Magic*, *Barnyard Safari*, *Great Alliance* and *In the Country*, and showed him strolling around Bemborough in the 1970s with Angela Rippon, who asked him why he had become a farmer. His reply was simplicity itself: 'I've never wanted to do anything else!'

It was great that Dad's old friend and colleague John Craven did the voiceover as they captured Dad talking to me on one of my first *Countryfile* appearances, weeping on TV over one of the Bemborough Farm TB outbreaks, making our return trip to the Orkneys, and getting his MBE from Princess Anne.

After the tribute aired, I got hundreds of cards and letters from the show's viewers, passing on their condolences and saying what a pioneer Dad had been. It was terrific to know he was so appreciated – yet none of it could bring him back.

Dad's funeral began at Cheltenham crematorium. I knew it would be hard to get through, and it was. I had ordered a woollen coffin for him, and before the service I cut some wool from my best Cotswold sheep and placed it in his hand.

It's a Cotswold tradition. Dad, with his love of spinning a good yarn, had once told me all about it.

'Shepherds are always buried with Cotswold wool,' he'd said, 'so when they meet St Peter at the Pearly Gates he'll know they are shepherds, which was why they hadn't been able to get to church on Sundays.'

After the cremation there was a service and a celebration of Dad's life at the parish church in Cirencester. It was the same church where he had first caught sight of Mum at that fateful wedding, 59 years earlier.

The church can hold 700 or 800 people and I had been a bit worried about booking somewhere so big, but it was a good job that we did. The place was rammed.

Everywhere I looked, there were friends from all areas of Dad's life: fellow farmers; former employees; colleagues from rare-breed societies; producers from *Countryfile*. They had come from all over the country to pay their respects. He would have been blown away to see it.

It was an incredibly moving day. Our old family friend Pam Ayres came along and gave a lovely reading. She had even composed one of her inimitable verses for Dad:

Goodbye to someone precious
Goodbye to darling Joe
We were blessed to have his friendship
(Even if he couldn't sew!)
He upheld a great tradition
As his father did before
He made everybody love him
And he left us wanting more.

The line about sewing referred to a misunderstanding from a few years earlier. Pam had phoned the house to talk to Dad, and thought Mum had told her that he was out 'at a sewing meeting'.

'I assumed that among his many other talents, Joe did some kind of needlework like the old fishermen who knitted Guernsey sweaters in the Channel Isles,' Pam later admitted. When she next saw Dad and asked him about it, he looked amazed, then burst out laughing. He had been at a meeting about Soay sheep.

Pam wasn't the only speaker. Libby's son, Ewan, bravely spoke on behalf of the grandkids, and Uncle Nicky also stood up for Dad. As you might expect given his profession, Nicky is a fabulous speaker. Yet this was no acting job – this was real emotion. He had taken the loss of his elder brother very hard and at the funeral he articulated so well what everybody was feeling.

Dad's oldest friend, a lovely man called Norman Cudderford, shared his memories of being at school with Dad and John Neave. Then he read special tributes to Dad from Libby and from me.

I knew that I wanted to write something for Dad's funeral, but I also knew there was no chance I would be able to read it myself. I was far too emotional and would never have got through it: I would have been weeping buckets. Libby felt the same.

So Norman read them out for us. Libby wrote a wonderful address, talking about Dad's wartime experiences and his pre-Bemborough career and making the congregation laugh by describing him meeting Mum – 'a redhead in a green dress' – in that very church.

Libby described Dad's big gamble in founding the Cotswold Farm Park, his TV career and, most of all, his endless and insatiable kindness. 'An eternal optimist, Joe always saw the best in people,' she wrote. 'His enthusiasm and joy in life was infectious. A conversation with him always involved laughter and invariably made you feel better.'

My own contribution was short, simple and straightforward. It was a heartfelt goodbye that I simply entitled 'My Dad':

What a remarkable man. You couldn't help but love and respect him. He was kind, fun, loving ... and a bit of a softy. It was Mum that was the enforcer and kept us clean, fed and organized, with plenty of love too.

Dad was an intelligent man and well-read. He had a wonderful way with words, a lovely voice and was a brilliant storyteller. Whether the punchline made you laugh or cry, the timing was impeccable; something he must have inherited from his famous dad.

We know he loved us and was very proud of us and of his grandchildren, because he told us.

Then there is his rock, the woman who stood by his side through thick and thin, sharing so many adventures. Mum helped shape the amazing man he was. He loved you very much, Mum.

He was a great mentor and role model and he touched and influenced so many lives in a positive way. It has been a privilege and an honour to have him as our dad. He leaves a massive hole in our lives but a wonderful legacy, and we still have each other to share all those stories and memories.

I hope he's looking down on us all, reflecting on his life using one of his little phrases: 'Job's a good 'un!'

We love you, Dad.

At the packed reception after the service, a lot of people came up to me, commiserated with my loss and then told me 'Well done' for my tribute. It was nice of them and I thanked them, but I couldn't help privately feeling that my words had not been enough.

How could they be? I was trying to praise the man who had taught me everything I knew, who had loved, protected and guided me, and who had instilled in me the passion for the land and for farming that has shaped my life.

I had been saying thank you and goodbye not just to a

father but to a mentor, a hero... and a best friend. So it is really no surprise that I had struggled to find the words to express the depth of what I was feeling.

Those words do not exist.

Like Farmer, Like Son

T he calendar can sometimes be cruel. Just over two months after we said goodbye to Dad, we had to face our first family Christmas without him.

Dad had always been the laughing, joking heart of our family at Christmas and his absence was going to be keenly felt, especially with the holiday falling so soon after his death. However Becca and Nick had an idea at least partly to alleviate the mourning.

They invited everybody up to the North-East for a few days. It was generous and thoughtful of them. They figured that a change of scenery might help everybody, especially Mum, rather than us all sitting around Bemborough Farm, where every corner carried a memory of Dad.

Even so, I have to confess that I felt rather apprehensive as I drove up with Charlie and the kids. Christmas tends to focus you on where you are at – how could we expect to enjoy it with Dad's loss still so recent and so raw?

Well, in the end, it went extremely well. The grandkids encouraged us to play games and mucked in with the cooking and tidying up. We went for long walks despite the rain and called in at a local pub for a couple of mulled wines to warm up before heading back to the house.

It was a lovely, solid family feeling and Mum coped really well. It was never going to be the merriest Christmas we had ever had but together we made it a memorable one.

Libby gave me a very special Christmas present. Mum had once made her a skirt from Cotswold fleece that had been made into cloth at the Cotswold Woollen Weavers in the Filkins, west Oxfordshire.

Libby had worn the skirt when she was presented to Prince Charles at the Stratfield Fayre at Stratfield Saye, home of the Duke of Wellington. At the time, the Duke was trying to persuade the Prince of Wales to become the patron of the RBST.

Now, Libby had had the skirt transformed into a waistcoat for me. I knew that Dad would have loved this story, which made it quite an emotional moment for me – which was fine, as it was never going to be a Christmas without a few tears. I had one moment when I took myself off to a quiet corner of the house to let it all out. My gorgeous Ella sensed what was wrong, came to find me and gave me a comforting hug.

The post-Christmas goodbyes were tough, especially for Mum, but despite the emotions we had all coped really well. It helped that Nick and Becca had been such amazing hosts.

Sometimes, life throws a few significant landmarks at you in quick succession. Two weeks after Christmas, I celebrated my fiftieth birthday.

In the circumstances I thought I would keep it pretty low-key and Charlie agreed. She said that she would just book for the two of us, Ella and Alfie to have a quiet family meal.

I assumed we'd go to a smart hotel up the road but as we were driving towards it, Charlie turned the car left. 'I thought we would just go to the Halfway,' she said, which is our friendly local pub.

'Oh, OK!' I said, while quietly thinking, *Huh! We ate in there three nights ago! We could have done something a bit more special – it IS my fiftieth!*

Then we walked into the bar and the whole place yelled, 'SURPRISE!'

Charlie had arranged a big bash without telling me. As I took in the roomful of people, I knew everybody: guys off the farm, local rugby-club mates, college buddies, *Countryfile* people. There were close on 100 great friends there.

Charlie knew that if she had asked me if I wanted a big party I would have said no, because of Dad, but she also knew that it was exactly what I needed. She was right. It was a great night.

Fifty is the kind of age where you reflect and take stock of your life, so naturally I have been thinking over things a bit lately. On the whole, I think I'm in a pretty good place.

I was driving along not very long ago pondering on what I have done in my life so far, and what I am pleased with – and there is not too much that I would want to change.

I've experienced and achieved so many amazing things and am extremely lucky to have such an incredible family with a beautiful partner and two brilliant children. I have certainly packed a lot into my years to date.

I'm still loving being on *Countryfile* and the programme continues to educate and surprise me. It is known as quite a heart-warming show, and quite rightly, but sometimes it can also be heart-rending.

Every year we invite nominations for our Farming Hero of the Year. Last year it was a lovely lady named Joan Bomford from Evesham, who started farming in the 1930s and was still going at eighty-two, despite having just lost her husband.

It was a deserved victory, but equally moving to me was the story of a lad in Scotland, sixteen-year-old Cameron Hendry, whose father had dropped dead from a heart attack on Christmas Day. Distraught with grief, he had nevertheless rolled up his sleeves and taken on all of his late father's work.

'I lost my dad and I was determined not to lose the farm as well,' he told me. I felt slightly like our cameras were intruding on his private grief, but my heart went out to this admirable young man in so many ways.

Well, I couldn't help but think, *at least I had my dad until I was nearly fifty.*

As well as filming on Bemborough for *Countryfile* I've recently started travelling for the show once again. It's fine because I still love going around the country hearing farmers' stories, even if it means I'm away from home a bit more than I'd like.

The show certainly still has its lighter moments. Just a few weeks ago I was dispatched to Stratford-on-Avon to film a special item to mark the 400th anniversary of the death of William Shakespeare.

Shakespeare's father, John, had been a glove-maker by trade, using sheepskin from Cotswold sheep and selling off the spare clippings. In Elizabethan times the wool trade was like the oil trade was at its peak, and it made Shakespeare senior very wealthy. William also got involved in the business, and in fact to start off with, it financed his illustrious writing career.

So the *Countryfile* producers had the idea that I should walk a herd of sheep down Sheep Street in the centre of Stratford-on-Avon. I liked the idea, and was quite excited that I would be the first person to do this for hundreds of years.

I've walked sheep through towns like Stow-on-the-Wold before so I was fairly confident as I set off. Initially it went very well, and I interviewed the local mayor as I herded a dozen Cotswold sheep I had borrowed from a neighbour along Sheep Street.

There were around a thousand people watching us go but Cotswold sheep are fairly docile and they were remarkably well behaved. They didn't seem fazed by the crowd and it all seemed to be going swimmingly.

That all changed when we reached the end of Sheep Street and hit a big, open grassy area. The sheep sensed freedom and made a bolt for it, haring off across the park in front of the Royal Shakespeare Company Theatre.

I ran after them, a few local lads helped me out, and after a few lively minutes we had them all rounded up and safely in their pen. It made for good TV but it was over in no time. The national press went to town and made a meal of it, of course, but it was all a bit of a storm in a teacup – albeit quite an amusing one!

Yet I have to admit that the best part of going away on a job for *Countryfile* is the coming home. Wherever I go in the UK, every time I come back to the Cotswolds it reminds me what a beautiful place I live in, and how lucky we are.

I will never tire of the rolling Cotswold hills: the patchwork, undulating fields with the mix of colours from the various crops, and the gentleness of the landscapes, so unlike the harsh nature of moors and mountains. To my eyes, even the oolitic limestone of our dry stonewalls always looks more warm and welcoming than the other, darker stones such as granite and slate that you get in other parts of the UK.

I adore the mix of farmland and deciduous woodlands breaking up the Cotswold villages and small towns such as Upper and Lower Slaughter, Chipping Campden and Stow-on-the-Wold. They are locales that are steeped in history, especially that of the wool trade and Cotswold sheep.

Some people are restless and always want to be moving on, and good luck to them, but I am grateful that, at fifty, I am still as in love with the place where I was born as ever I was. For me, the old adage rings true: there is no place like home.

More than anything, of course, home means Bemborough Farm.

I've learnt from hard experience over the years how quickly things can change, but right now, as I write, the farm is doing well. It is now four times the size of the farm that Dad took over in 1962. That is a testament to the hard work that he and John Neave always put in, and that Duncan and I have tried to equal since taking over.

Farming always faces fresh challenges, and right now we are facing issues as varied as global warming and the political uncertainty of whether we are leaving the European Union, and how that would affect our trade.

Well, we will deal with these problems as best we can, as and when they arise – because that is what farmers do.

The farm park is also thriving. Nowadays it employs 13 full-time staff and 80 seasonal workers and welcomes between 110,000 and 120,000 visitors per year: more than 2,000 per week. It's a far cry from the dark days around the millennium when Duncan and I feared that we might have to close it down.

Now we have a skilled management team running the park – and the days of me trying to organize the café menu are long behind us, thank goodness! My role has changed from being totally hands-on to trusting our managers.

I don't have as much time to spend there as I used to, or as I would like to, but whenever I get a chance I will still pop down and meet our visitors. I might even do a lambing demonstration, for old times' sake.

Yes, Bemborough Farm is in good shape right now – but what does the future hold for it?

For many years, I quietly hoped that Ella or Alfie would fall in love with farming and want to inherit the tenancy from me, the same as I did from Dad.

Ella and Alfie both love growing up on the farm and as young kids they raced around playing with the animals just like I did. Yet they have never been quite so transfixed and in thrall to the agricultural life as I was.

Probably this is partly down to circumstances. When I was a boy, it was a lot less technological and more hands-on. Today, with the training required to operate the high-precision machines, it is not easy for youngsters to help out.

Dad was always there, always farming, always showing me something new and educating me. He was like a one-man university of agriculture and I was a devoted scholar.

It's been different for Ella and Alfie. My *Countryfile* and other media duties have meant I have had to be away and delegate far more. On any day I might be giving a talk to a Women's Institute, or doing an evening theatre show, or opening a fete.

As my children have grown up, I have been far less hands-on as a farmer than Dad ever was. Sometimes I wish it hadn't been that way, but there you go. It's brought me a lot of great opportunities and I'm not complaining.

In any case, the kids have their own interests. Ella is big into the theatre and is about to go to university. Alfie adores the great outdoors and zooming around the farm on his Polaris buggy, but he is only just fourteen – who knows what he will want to do for a career?

All that Charlie and I can do is to support the both of them in whatever they choose to do. If they decide one day to come back to the farm and they are suitably qualified, I am sure we can find them a job and I would be delighted to be working alongside them. With the diversity of our business from farming to tourism there are plenty of opportunities.

Thanks to the solid foundation created by my dad and John, Duncan and I continue to grow and develop the farm, taking it from strength to strength. Along with our team, we hope to continue running a successful business for many years to come.

I enjoy *Countryfile* and would love to carry on working in the media, but when that inevitably comes to an end, I will go back to my proper job as a farmer and live off the land, just as Dad did all those years ago.

I miss Dad terribly, and think about him every day. I often have things I wish I could ask him, or new animals I want to show him. He remains my benchmark and my beacon, and I feel his presence. In fact, I would be incredibly proud if even one person who knew Dad well were ever to look at me, smile in recognition, and quietly think:

'Like farmer, like son.'

Acknowledgements

I would like to thank a number of people who have helped me write the story of *Like Farmer, Like Son*.

I am incredibly grateful to my mother, my sisters Libby, Lolo and Becca, my brother-in-law Nick and Uncle Nicky for allowing me to share our personal family stories and photographs. Without their blessing, this book could not have been written.

My wonderful partner Charlie and our children Ella and Alfie who have offered encouragement and advice throughout this process – Ella even thought up the title of the book!

My dedicated business partner and friend Duncan Andrews who I rely on enormously and trust completely to run our business when I'm away filming or writing books.

The amazing team that help run the Cotswold Farm Park and Bemborough Farm; thank you to each of you for your hard work helping to make the business what it is.

Thanks must go to the close friends and colleagues that Dad and I have had over the years; our lives have been enriched by them all and we have always appreciated the support of the farming community and its wide network.

I am very grateful to Yvonne Jacob and the team at BBC Books who commissioned this story and to Ian Gittins, who with incredible patience put my words on to paper. Special thanks must go to my PA, Paula Duffield, who spent hours alongside me helping to fine tune the book.

It is the BBC and incredible *Countryfile* team that have allowed me to convey my passion for farming and the country-side. There are too many people to mention individually, but you know who you are and I am grateful for your trust and kindness when working with me.

Finally, I would like to say a heartfelt thank you to my dad who was working with me on this book when he died. Sadly, he didn't have a chance to see the end product, but I very much hope he would have approved. He is hugely missed.

Index

(AH in subentries refers to Adam Henson, GH to Gillian Henson, JH to Joe Henson)